9.60

Inge

Inge

A GIRL'S JOURNEY
THROUGH NAZI EUROPE

Inge Joseph Bleier
&
David E. Gumpert

William B. Eerdmans Publishing Company

Grand Rapids, Michigan / Cambridge, U.K.

$10.00

To Rösli Näf, Maurice Dubois, Margrit Tännler, Anne Marie Im Hof-Piguet,

and all the other Swiss Red Cross officials who risked their lives

to save the children of Château la Hille.

© 2004 Wm. B. Eerdmans Publishing Co.
All rights reserved

Wm. B. Eerdmans Publishing Co.
255 Jefferson Ave. S.E., Grand Rapids, Michigan 49503 /
P.O. Box 163, Cambridge CB3 9PU U.K.

Printed in the United States of America

08 07 06 05 04   7 6 5 4 3 2 1

Library of Congress Cataloging-in-Publication Data

Bleier, Inge J.
Inge: a girl's journey through Nazi Europe /
Inge Joseph Bleier & David E. Gumpert.
p.   cm.
ISBN 0-8028-2686-5 (pbk.: alk. paper)
1. Bleier, Inge J. — Childhood and youth. 2. Jewish children —
Germany — Darmstadt — Biography. 3. Jewish teenagers —
Europe — Biography. 4. Holocaust, Jewish (1939-1945) — Europe —
Personal narratives. 5. Darmstadt (Germany) — Biography.
I. Title.   II. Gumpert, David E.   III. Title.
DS135.G5B55   2004
940.53'18'092 — dc22
[B]
2004040940

www.eerdmans.com

Contents

Preface

I T IS OFTEN SAID that we gain a fresh perspective on life by observing children. *Inge* is a view of the Holocaust from a child's perspective.

As the Holocaust descended on Europe during the late 1930s and early 1940s, many thousands of Jewish children were separated from their parents and left to fend for themselves. They wandered among such countries as Belgium, Holland, Denmark, France, Spain, and Switzerland — sometimes under adult supervision and sometimes not, but always trying to avoid capture by the Nazis or being turned over to the Nazis.

Many of these children, of course, were caught and sent to concentration camps where they were killed. Others did manage to elude the ever-more-intensive Nazi dragnet.

Dramatic stories involving children who managed to hide out or who were hidden by heroic Christians in Nazi-occupied Europe have been published over the years. What has received less attention, however, is how children dealt with the seemingly endless family, religious, political, and other dilemmas raised by their situations. How much assistance should they expect from well-off relatives? Should they continue to practice their religion? Should they actively resist adults who abused them? Should they share their limited food rations with others who had even less? What should they ask of non-Jews in a position to help? Should they go meekly to death or stand up to Nazi captors?

Beyond these external dilemmas were the internal ones — coping not only with anxiety about possible capture by the Nazis, but also with feelings of abandonment, loneliness, rejection, and anger. In many cases, the children directed these feelings toward the parents who sent them away in desperate efforts to save their lives.

Inge is the story of one Jewish child, Inge Joseph, left behind in Europe, and of her attempt to deal with the agonizing decisions and feelings that confronted her and many of her friends. It is jointly authored because Inge Joseph Bleier died before she was able to complete the story of her adolescence spent wandering Nazi Europe. It was left to me, her nephew, to fill in and complete the story she had begun. Based on some ten years of research and analysis, this book is a reconstruction of her nearly unbelievable story of love and loss as a teenager and of the suffering it caused her. It is based on a sixty-six-page manuscript discovered after her death, along with her letters, the recollections of her friends and relatives, the memoirs of people who were with her, and my relationship with her. In assembling all this material, I assumed her point of view so you can experience Inge's story much as I did — as a very close, after-the-fact witness.

Unlike many Holocaust survivors, Inge spent very little time in concentration camps. Hers is a story of a different kind of imprisonment.

I hope releasing Inge's story will help those who were close to her make better sense of her unusual behavior in her later years. Beyond that, I hope her story will help shed light on the experiences of the thousands of young children left behind in Europe during the Holocaust.

DAVID E. GUMPERT

Acknowledgments

You can't spend more than a decade researching and writing a book, as I did, without receiving important assistance from countless individuals along the way. So many people were so generous with their time, recollections, and research material that my biggest problem in writing this acknowledgment is that I can't possibly name them all. But I believe the roles of most will become apparent as you read this story. And to those I neglect to properly acknowledge here or later, my apologies in advance.

A number of professionals were unwavering in their support of this project during the challenging times I experienced. Pamela Mandell, a highly skilled editor based in Provincetown, Massachusetts, on Cape Cod, appeared in my life at one of my serious low points and gave me encouragement, technical insights, and harsh red-pen editing essential to bring the story to life. She also taught me important lessons about effective writing.

Elliot Glickler, a long-time friend and a French teacher in Newton, Massachusetts, slogged through seemingly endless pages of documents written in French to help me better understand both the places and people in Inge's experience. My mother, Leonore "Lilo" Gumpert, and my deceased father-in-law, Otto Sulzberger, did the same with German-language documents.

On the publishing side, I benefited from the advice of two individuals: New York literary agent Nancy Love and Omaha, Nebraska, Holocaust researcher Ben Nachman. The latter helped me make the connection with

Bill Eerdmans, Jr., of Wm. B. Eerdmans Publishing Company and all the wonderful people at this gem of a publisher, especially my caring and capable editor, Linda Bieze.

Then there were my friends who undertook the unenviable task of critiquing various revised and re-revised manuscripts during my journey. I understand well that giving an honest opinion to an author friend about his book manuscript is not the most enjoyable act of friendship. Yet Suzanne Reyes, David Satter, Laurel Tauby, Susan Weininger, Al Furst, Melissa Weininger, Joyce Rains, and Bonnie Weiss all handled the challenge better than I could have imagined and helped me finally produce something I was comfortable with.

Finally, there were so many individuals connected with Inge during her Holocaust years in Europe, who gave so much in the way of personal remembrances, as well as documents and photos, that I can only interpret their willingness to share with me as a tribute to their friend and my aunt, Inge Joseph Bleier. Most are people you will meet in the story that follows, while some were behind the scenes.

Arnold Frank of Brussels made available to me several hundred pages of an unpublished, hand-written memoir from his mother, Irene Frank, who served as a teacher to Inge and her friends during their years in southern France. Edith Goldapper Rosenthal, one of Inge's friends, also gave me access to her unpublished memoir. Ruth Schutz Usrad, another friend of Inge, made available her memoir, *Entrapped Adolescence*, published in Israel in Hebrew, via an English recorded translation. Hanni Schlimmer Schild, another of Inge's friends, allowed me access to her notebook containing the words of many songs the children sang in Belgium and France. And Jacques Roth, a friend of Inge, gave me important Swiss documents.

I relied as well on information contained in two books published in German about various aspects of the experiences of Inge and her friends: *Fluchtweg durch die Hintertür* (Escape through the back door, originally published in French as *la Filière*) by Anne Marie Im Hof-Piguet and *Die Kinder von Schloss La Hille* (The children of Château la Hille) by Sebastian Steiger. Both Anne Marie and Sebastian cared for Jewish children in France for the Swiss Red Cross during the war, and both also generously made themselves available to me for interviews.

Others connected with Inge allowed me access to their photos, some of which appear in this book. Regina Illman of Berlin was extremely helpful in getting me photographs from the collection of one of the adults who had been with Inge and her friends. Peter Salz, another friend of Inge in France, gave me several photos of Inge from his extensive collection when I visited him in Israel. And Walter Reed of Chicago, still another friend of Inge, helped me sort through and copy photos from his extensive collection.

Finally, I must thank Julie Bleier Hernandez, Inge's daughter and my cousin, for making available to me Inge's original sixty-six-page manuscript that inspired my efforts. Julie has been unwavering in her support of me during these difficult years of bringing Inge's story to completion.

DAVID E. GUMPERT

Introduction

D URING THE SUMMER of 2002, I attended a reunion of about 150 Holocaust survivors in Chicago. One by one over the course of three days, these men and women in their 60s and 70s told stories of leaving Germany as children and traveling across the Atlantic. The details varied. Some left directly from Germany. Others came from Portugal, after hiding in France. Some were greeted in the United States by relatives, while others went to live with foster families spread around the country. Some of the foster families were Jewish and some weren't. Some were caring and some abusive.

But these stories also shared a sameness. All the children had departed alone, or with a single sibling, and left behind parents, aunts, uncles, and cousins. More often than not, the relatives left behind perished in the Holocaust. These stories told of terrible sadness tinged by an important measure of redemption and virtue apparent in the lives these survivors had built and the new families they created. Two Harvard University researchers, Gerald Horton and Gerhard Sonnort, reported on their study of these and other survivors, and their results confirmed what one might expect in this nation of immigrants: By significant majorities, these survivors had achieved not only economic security but also, more importantly, significant personal satisfaction and happiness in their new homes. These individuals appeared to have moved past their sadness and achieved a semblance of closure.

As I listened to the stories and the report of the researcher, I couldn't help but feel envious. My family's story was much the same as theirs — of children who had survived while a parent and close relatives perished, of new lives reconstructed in the United States. But as far as we had come on the surface, our family had failed in the final analysis to achieve the satisfaction these others had because we hadn't gained closure. Simply too many matters remained unresolved.

In a very real sense, my family has been in a state of turmoil over the Holocaust since family life imploded beginning in 1936. Three generations now have spent long years obsessed with the Holocaust. My grandfather, Opa Julius, spent his last twenty years at it, my Aunt Inge more than forty years, and now I'm past the decade mark. While other families managed, despite all the pain, to put the traumatic events behind them, my family keeps reliving the past, wondering how certain events could have happened, what other events actually occurred, and what might have happened "if only." We're at once desperate for clarity and afraid of what we might discover.

The obsession becomes ever more difficult to accept as time goes on, and we are told the Holocaust is long over, literally and figuratively. Publishers tell us that "the market" for Holocaust stories is saturated and the public's appetite for the subject has waned, especially in light of the new dangers illuminated for us on September 11, 2001.

A big part of the public's disconnect, I believe, comes about because of the way in which people tend to imagine the Holocaust. People tend to think of mass murder, and the luck of the draw that allowed some to survive — those who hid in a latrine, or possessed musical skills, or married a Nazi. They sometimes neglect the more mundane aspects of life during the Holocaust, such as the challenge of communicating during wartime with family members scattered around the globe, reading too much or too little into thin letters and cramped writing, trying to figure out what was really happening in their lives and who was winning and losing the war. Then there was the psychological aspect, the grinding, endless stream of discouraging news that helped determine whether survivors should push on against ever-longer odds or simply give in to the discouragement and depression.

For my family, writing comes more naturally than talking. So my Aunt Inge and I have attempted to gain closure by writing about what occurred. We have been doing this since World War II ended, and *Inge* is the result. The writing has taken us so long because the events are so incomprehensible, the surrounding circumstances so murky, the outcomes so difficult to fathom. Will the shroud of uncertainty that has led to ongoing family tension, recrimination, even madness, finally be lifted? Possibly so.

And now to Inge's own story.

DAVID E. GUMPERT

Truth

[*February 1983*]

IT WAS THE SUMMER of 1959 and we were driving along the Pennsylvania Turnpike when my husband suddenly said, "Why don't you write a book about your life?" The image filling my mind was a happy version of *The Diary of Anne Frank*. By the time we reached Lancaster, this seemed a pretty good idea.

Of course, I now know better. How could I have been so naive, so stupid, to not have appreciated the Pandora's box I was opening? Besides, who would want to read such nonsense? Those initial written meanderings from back then really had been better off buried in the attic for all these years. But this urge to write is like the terrible itching of my scalp from the lice we used to get in France — it won't go away. No matter how many painkillers I take, I can't stop my crazed mind from always returning to that first draft and the events and people it conjures up, especially Walter and Mutti.

And then there is the photo of Walter and me. Each time I view it, it is as if I must shield my eyes from the sun. I want so much to destroy it — cut it into a million pieces or burn it. But I couldn't bear to be without it. So what choice does that leave me? It keeps eating a bigger hole in my heart, and now I suspect that there is little left. I'm pretty much skin and bones, and I can barely think a lucid thought.

Exactly when was the photo taken? Probably during the summer of 1941, since we're dressed for warm weather. Why is Walter wearing his

Dutch wooden shoes? I thought he had gotten rid of them by that time. How did I come by such elegant shoes and that pretty dress? Maybe Inge Helft loaned them to me, since she worked so hard to preserve her nice clothes. Why is Haskelevich in the photo between Walter and me? Did Haskelevich ask to join the photo, perhaps to symbolically place himself between Walter and me? He always seemed resentful of our relationship. Did I ask him to join the photo to avoid having to face the awkward moment of deciding whether to hold Walter's hand? Did Walter invite Haskelevich in for the same reason? Maybe the photographer, probably someone from the Swiss Red Cross, invited Haskelevich. And why is Haskelevich wearing a suit and tie instead of his trademark black beret and knickers? Or is it possibly not really Haskelevich at all, and rather some visitor from the Swiss Red Cross? It's so difficult to be certain, since I rarely saw Haskelevich without his beret.

Despite my delirium, certain things are becoming clearer. One is my craziness in thinking I could create a fairy tale existence here in Chicago — that if I had a husband, child, house, car, and gourmet food, it would light up the blackness.

Now with the darkness enveloping me, I know why my family members act as they do. I would probably cheat on Frank the way I suspect he is cheating on me if I discovered him, as he has discovered me, unconscious in the kitchen from drug overdoses every few weeks. And I would be like my daughter, Julie, going out as often as possible, looking for parties and boys and avoiding school work, if my mother lay in bed all day moaning and groaning and crying out for her own dead mother.

I don't know what gave me the idea that doctors could cure the oppression that is now part of my being — the skin infections and failing kidneys, the stomach and leg pains . . . and that I could take uppers and downers and endless painkillers without consequence. I am a nurse, after all, and I know. I just don't seem to learn.

I even took the advice that came to me incessantly from relatives and friends: I consulted with a psychiatrist, actually two psychiatrists. But they were as I expected — no better than the quacks I visited to cure my skin and kidney problems — two sides of a coin. "Let's talk about your past," they said at first. When I told them I didn't know where to begin, it was too complicated to just start talking about, they didn't persist. Well then, "We can come back to that," one said. "For now, let us not forget the many positive things in your life . . . how you advanced to chief nurse of obstetrics at a major hospital . . . how you've written two widely adopted textbooks for nurses . . . how you've earned a master's degree in journalism well after most people even think about school . . . how you created a new family." They almost had me convinced I was normal. No, I could tell from the sympathetic nodding of their heads that they didn't have a clue about what lay behind the facade. They just wanted me to keep coming back in hopes I would eventually say something rational, or irrational, I never could be sure. So one of the few smart decisions in my life was to take my leave of them — one after three visits and the other after four. Think of all the money we'll save in the process, I thought.

I suppose back in 1959, driving across the rolling hills of Pennsylvania in our purring Ford Fairlane, everything seemed possible. More than fifteen years had passed since the war, and I had assumed a real-person life. I trained as a nurse, advanced in my career, married a pleasant man from Austria (Jewish to boot). Having children seemed like a possibility. I deluded myself that I could get past the three earlier miscarriages and produce a child. I saw so many children being born every day at Weiss Memorial Hospital in Chicago and was certain I could do that. When it turned out I couldn't, I even turned that problem into an opportunity, adopting beautiful Julie when she was just a few days old. Looking from the outside in, I suppose it would seem as if I had accomplished my goal of starting life afresh. That's what I wanted everyone to think. But looking at it from the inside out — that was an entirely different matter.

I BEGAN LIFE in Darmstadt, Germany, in 1925. My father had a factory that produced soap and shoe polish, and he rode to work on a bicycle. My sister, Lilo (short for Liselotte), also had a bicycle. I did not have a bicycle, so every once in a while I swiped Lilo's before she left for school. I got to school on time, but how I had to watch out during recess! I never rode the bike home from school — Lilo was bigger and stronger.

We had much fun together, though. We spent many hours in our huge garden, trying to snatch apples off the trees by swinging high up on the swing, or teaching our cousins new tricks on the horizontal bar. In the evening, after we went off to bed, we harmonized "Wanderlieder."

My father's father, Hermann, lived just a block away in the "Louvre." He was a huge man — must have weighed over two hundred pounds. He was disabled from a stroke suffered a few years earlier, so we visited him daily. Our affirmative answer to his usual query, "Have you been good today?" always produced a big cookie jar. That was the time for Lilo to put on her charm — she always walked off with stuffed pockets. I had theorized at an early age the main reason my grandfather kept his grouchy housekeeper was because he needed her for baking our daily cookie supply.

One of my favorite pastimes was reading. I read for hours at a time — Dickens, Goethe, Marlowe. I also spent much time at various sports. We belonged to an athletic club for children and young adults, which met weekly at a meticulously maintained sports field. Here, being the youngest (I was only eleven) and having no bicycle were advantages. Invariably, the trainer picked me up and set me on his luggage rack for the bicycle trip to the club. Thus transported, I was the envy of the teenage girls among us because the trainer was not only about twenty, but also blond, handsome, and muscular. I did the broad jump and fifty-meter runs, and at several sports festivals I came away with second and third prizes.

Sundays during the summertime were a special treat. My parents met with the rest of the family at the home of my maternal grandmother, Josephine, and from there we began day-long excursions to the neighboring villages and mountains. There were leisurely walks where we could run and play to our hearts' content. On these excursions, I learned the distinguishing features of the various fruit trees, berries, and flowers — knowledge which would be indispensable just a few years later.

Oma Josephine was a diminutive woman and an organizer, a doer. When her father died in his forties, she took over as manager of his textile business and turned it into a thriving shop in the center of Darmstadt at a time when women weren't especially independent.

I always seemed to be the youngest child around. Lilo was three years older than I. My first cousin, Hilde Loeb, wasn't really a child; she was in her early twenties, but she was around a lot. Maybe because I was athletic, the older ones included me in their games and conversations. Hilde was very sophisticated and pretty and became my idol, or at least my first idol. When she talked to Lilo and others about one boyfriend or another or about the latest fashions, she didn't try to shoo me away. Instead, she seemed genuinely interested in me, in what I was doing in school. She admired my athletics, probably because it was not something she did well. Our paths would cross again years later, in southern France. And then many years after that, in the United States, she was one of the few people who knew what I had experienced. When she died a few years ago, she left me that much more alone.

Anyway, I have always enjoyed athletics. Until just a few years ago, when my kidney problems began acting up, I loved playing tennis. I think it's one of the reasons I married Frank. We had such good times playing tennis together.

Papa

SUBTLE CHANGES gradually crept into the carefree days of my childhood. I became more and more aware of serious discussions between my parents. More often than not, my mother sent Lilo and me out to do the grocery shopping because Jewish children were treated with somewhat less disrespect than Jewish adults. It was not until weeks later that we also noticed the signs placed on practically every store in Darmstadt, "JUDEN UNERWÜNSCHT" (Jews unwelcome). Attending school became more and more of a daily struggle. Everyone knows now about the ruthlessness and aggressiveness of the members of the Hitler Youth. But how was I as a child to understand the sudden rejection and insolence of neighborhood children who previously had claimed to be my friends?

My parents and their friends increasingly discussed "emigration," "America," and "affidavits." From 1936 on, events happened that would make any Jewish child mature rapidly. One evening late in that year, my father did not return home from work. He had been arrested.

Strangely, I wasn't as upset as you might imagine. I never felt especially comfortable with Papa. It's difficult to explain, except he just didn't seem particularly interested in Lilo or me. He was a big man — probably six feet tall and husky — and could have enveloped Lilo and me in his arms at once, yet he never hugged or kissed us (or even my mother, for that matter). In fact, his long face, interrupted by the carefully trimmed mustache, rarely relaxed or smiled. He seemed cold and distant, though sometimes I thought he was sad.

My most pleasant memories of him are associated with food. He did business with various butchers and often brought home succulent roasts and steaks. Mutti scolded him: He was being too extravagant, and besides, we shouldn't eat so much meat. But I loved the rare roasts and thick veal chops and tender soup meat. Years later, when there was nothing to eat, I dreamt about those wonderful pieces of meat. His softest moments came on occasional nights before we went to bed, when he would drop off a piece of chocolate to Lilo and me as he said his "Gute Nacht."

Papa often escorted Mutti to the opera on Saturday evenings — he in a starched white shirt, black suit, and tie, and she in a beige evening gown. He so tall and strong. She so small and elegant. Mostly, he was distracted and aloof, and Mutti sometimes tried to excuse him. "He's worried about the business," she sometimes whispered in an aside when he was uncommunicative.

Yes, the business. Always the business. To be technically accurate, it wasn't necessarily the business, but Papa's incompetence in running the business that created no end of problems for us. Certainly when it was running right, the factory was very important for us. We lived in the nicest part of Darmstadt, a pleasant, small German city, about twenty-five kilometers south of Frankfurt. It had elegant apartment buildings, carefully maintained parks, and streetcars winding through. The city's most distinguishing feature was the "Lange Ludwig," a fifty-foot-tall, narrow, black statue topped by Ludwig, Grand Duke of Hessen, which dominated the city center. Now it strikes me as a permanent reminder of German arrogance.

We had a large, airy house, three stories tall, with many bedrooms. It was on Alicenplatz, a wide street with lots of trees and flowers. In those days, owning a home in the city was a sign of special wealth. My clearest memory of our home is the cherry wood-paneled library on the first floor with lots of books where my father liked to spend his little free time reading and smoking cigars. We even had a live-in housekeeper who kept the house spotless, did the shopping and cooking, and babysat Lilo and me.

Papa's father, Opa Hermann, who later bestowed cookies on Lilo and me, was a shrewd businessman who grew the business from nearly nothing in the late 1800s, when it was run by his wife's family. It was an animal-fat rendering business, and I have no idea what drew him to such a dirty, disgusting business. But he built it into a thriving enterprise. The rendered fat was sold for use in things like shoe polish and soap. I visited the factory occasionally, beginning when I was six or seven years old. The low-lying white building sat right next to railroad tracks in a crowded industrial area. Though the area was only about three kilometers from our house, it looked to me to be an entirely different world — no trees and lots of dust and trucks and freight trains and uniformed workers.

There were about thirty employees, mostly women, who worked in blood-smeared white jackets, stirring huge vats of animal fat and packing containers for shipment. Most of the women were nice to me, and a few even gave me pieces of chocolate when I visited. But I hated the foul smells of the animal remains and the chemicals used to break them down, so when Mutti asked me if I wanted to accompany her on a visit I usually said no.

In 1932, when I was seven years old, Opa Hermann had his stroke and was unable to walk. After a few weeks, he was sent home from the hospital, partially paralyzed on one side of his body. He spent all his time sitting by his second-floor living-room window, watching the comings and goings of the neighborhood. Once, during one of Lilo's and my cookie visits, I marveled at a mirror he had attached outside the window so he could see more fully what was happening up and down the street. The upshot of Opa Hermann's stroke was that Papa, who had been assisting him, suddenly had to run the business. Unfortunately, he was totally inexperienced. Always lurking in the background, looking over his shoulder, was his father.

A man as domineering as Opa Hermann couldn't, of course, be completely passive. I heard bits and pieces of the arguments between him and Papa when we visited Opa Hermann's apartment or when Opa was wheeled into the library in our house.

"Have you called the Schmidt factory in Mannheim?" Opa would say. "Roland Schmidt told me he wants to do business with us. He needed a little more time, but now I hear his factory has expanded. He probably needs a new supplier."

On another occasion, he'd start in: "Why can't we get the Ruckens plant to increase its orders? Each month five hundred kilos. We should be selling them fifteen hundred kilos every month, a thousand minimum. Someone is getting that business. Gerhard Ruckens needs lots of personal attention. You need to inquire about his daughters, about his tennis game, about his stamp collection. He has many interests, and he likes to do business with people who share his interests, or at least want to talk about his interests. I couldn't care less about tennis and stamps, but I'd always listen to him babble on and on. I'd leave with a larger order."

He always pushed Papa in ways he seemed reluctant to go. Often the arguments degenerated into personal attacks based on Papa's less-than-observant approach to being Jewish.

Religion was an inconsistent matter in my family. My family was Reform Jewish, which means we weren't as strict about Jewish laws as other Jews. Thus, I was the only Jewish girl in my class who attended school on Saturdays. The other three Jewish girls in my class, who observed the Sabbath, came to me on Sunday to obtain their homework. (The German schools operated on a six-days-per-week system.) My mother's family was very liberal. In fact, my mother's brother, also Hermann, was married to a Catholic, Aunt Ida, who was my favorite aunt.

Papa's family was much more orthodox. His three sisters married into Orthodox Jewish families. Even though it was against Papa's upbringing, he worked on Saturdays. I think he did it strictly because he felt one day of rest was sufficient for him and this philosophy would not offend his Maker. But who knows? Maybe it was a way for him to get back at his overbearing father. As for me, I learned Hebrew and the Bible stories and actually liked those lessons quite well.

Papa's work habits had their desired effect, because when Opa Hermann was especially angry, he would hit Papa with religion. "You're working on Shabbat again? You have a big new customer? I hope you aren't working on the Sabbath to do paperwork.

"Do you still let Clara take you to that church they call a *shul*, with steeples on the sides? Do they still play the organ? And have a choir? That is no *shul*. You know what a real *shul* is. You were raised in one. Why don't you take her there sometime?"

I only heard Opa Hermann's accusatory questions. Here and there, he ended or began a question with *"schlemiel,"* the Yiddish word that roughly translates: "stupid idiot." I never heard Papa's answers, whether it was because he didn't answer or because he kept his voice down, I don't know.

After the stroke, Opa Hermann became more disdainful of Papa. I'm not sure if it was his frustration over his physical limitations and not being able to make all the decisions and run the business, or his disappointment in seeing his son fail to carry on as successfully as he hoped.

Opa Hermann wasn't the only one who became angry with Papa. Mutti was very quiet and unassuming, but sometimes I heard her accusations from the kitchen.

"You have to go to Mannheim again? You were just there last week.

Have you received any business from Mannheim in the last six months? Why is another trip going to make a difference now?"

Then, when he returned, there would be another set of accusations.

"Hildegard and Lotta and all your other employees get wurst and chocolate, and what do you bring your own family? Nothing. Those people stand around while the business crumbles and they receive the delicacies. And you ignore your own family."

I developed my own set of questions for Papa during those years of the mid-1930s. I was able to direct mine only to Lilo or to myself. It was obvious to all of us our fortunes were steadily deteriorating as the Nazis became ever stronger and more influential. Papa worked like a dog but the business didn't cooperate. It was hard to know how much of it was because of Papa's incompetence and how much because his customers wanted to avoid dealing with a Jewish business owner. Papa, of course, never discussed how badly things were going, but it was clear our standard of living was deteriorating. First, we rented out the third floor of our house as an apartment to a couple who had a child of five or six. He was a terror — I could hear the rumbling of him running back and forth overhead whenever I tried to study. Then the maid was let go. Then we started renting out rooms on our second floor to students at a nearby university. My parents' Saturday evening opera trips became more infrequent. The succulent roasts disappeared from our dinner menu.

While the source of Papa's business problems may have been hard to pin down, one thing was clear: When opportunities and problems presented themselves, Papa had an uncanny ability to make the wrong decisions.

The first example was what might best be called "The Uruguay Affair." In 1934, when it was clear that Hitler was in charge of the government and was making the Jews his regular scapegoat, one of Papa's suppliers arranged for him to be offered a job with a rendering business in Uruguay. When Papa brought it up one evening at dinner, a rare smile spread from his black mustache across his normally pensive long face. I think he appreciated the fact he was actually wanted by someone else.

I had never heard of Uruguay. But when I looked it up in the library, and learned about its long coastline and temperate climate, I thought I was reading about paradise. I didn't know Spanish, but since I was doing so well in my English classes, I was confident I could learn Spanish, too. Lilo and I talked and fantasized about swimming during the winter and making new friends and starting a fresh life in a place where they didn't hate Jews.

Over the course of several successive evenings, Papa and Mutti conversed at dinner about Uruguay and all the repercussions of moving.

"How can we take Papa with us? He is so frail from his stroke," said Papa.

Mutti worried about her mother. "How can we ask her to give up her business? I can't imagine her learning Spanish. She is becoming frail as well."

Papa again: "I can't get much for the business because our sales are declining. Yes, we can sell the house, but after we pay all the taxes and fees, I don't know if there will be enough to re-settle and live like human beings."

So many questions revolving around what seemed to me to be such a simple matter: Did we want to stay in Germany and have our lives continue to deteriorate or did we want to escape and start a new life full of hope?

Papa and Mutti never said they rejected the move to Uruguay. But after a few more evenings, they just stopped talking about it. I doubt anyone even stated that a decision had been made, but its finality hung heavy over the forced dinnertime conversation in the days that followed. They obviously concluded, as bad as things were in Germany, they'd just as soon stay with their established routines than upend their lives and those of their extended families to start over in a new country. And they didn't want the responsibility of having pushed others to leave and possibly be unhappy, or of leaving relatives behind who wouldn't make the move.

I knew in my gut it wasn't a good decision. I've always had good instincts about people and situations. I could see even then our lives were headed in the wrong direction. My best friend, Inge Vogel, had for no obvious reason stopped coming by the house to pick me up on the way to school. Yet I knew the reason. When someone pulled on my hair or pinched me from behind during a class, I was always scolded or punished by the teacher instead of the Gentile child who instigated things. I sensed the growing hostility would just keep getting worse and somehow we would have fewer and fewer opportunities to escape. Of course, I couldn't know Hitler would murder millions of Jews, but my instincts told me the entire atmosphere was unhealthy and likely to continue worsening.

So here we were at the end of 1934 having committed ourselves to remaining in Germany. What did Papa do in the New Year? He borrowed money to sustain his business. I'm not talking about regular bank borrowing. I'm talking about personal borrowing, from a Nazi of all people! I learned all this from my cousin, Walter Kramer, who was three years older than I (and the son of my father's sister). That made him thirteen years old, but even then he understood business matters on a level far beyond what most children know. He was a bookish type, a whiz at math, and a bit arrogant. And unlike me, he was terrible in athletics, to the extent that other children teased him as "gummeybopp" (rubber doll). Maybe that was why he said to me, with an air of superiority, that Papa's business affairs were much worse than anyone realized.

Walter told Lilo and me that the men of the family met in Frankfurt with some wealthy relatives and friends to discuss Papa's business problems and his need for cash to keep the factory going. When the meetings ended, the money didn't materialize — I imagine because these men didn't want to throw good money after bad. Walter described Papa sitting on the floor in an apartment hallway after the decision was made, moaning and crying like a baby about his failings as a businessman. I tried to imagine him, such a large man, slumped on the floor. Walter told us that to keep the business going after that rejection Papa ignored the advice of Opa Hermann, and borrowed money from our neighbor, Heinrich Gunter, a Nazi. Then, when Papa couldn't make his loan payments, Gunter demanded part ownership in the business. In this instance, I had to agree with Opa Hermann — Papa was a *schlemiel*.

Even as I write this, I can't believe what happened next. Papa became hooked on barbiturates, a significant expense that further altered his already impaired judgment. He commissioned Lilo and me as his couriers to pick up money he borrowed from relatives and then stop at our neighborhood pharmacy to purchase his pills. It was very convenient — we could pick up groceries for Mutti and narcotics for Papa ("sleeping pills," was the innocent label he gave them in instructing Lilo or me to make a pickup) — all in one trip.

I never knew how Papa arranged the prescriptions. I do know that Herr Woll, the professorial pharmacist, had a knowing look of disapproval on his pale face as he squinted through his thick glasses and handed me the plain-paper package with the drugs. It was bad enough in his view that we were Jews. But a Jewish drug addict!

I suppose I shouldn't have wondered about Papa's acquisition techniques, since I seem to have learned his lessons in obtaining my own drugs. It's not really so complicated — you just go to doctors and tell them you're having trouble sleeping or have a pain in the stomach or back and need the drugs. They quickly tire of the stories and the illnesses that don't get better. So, to get rid of you, they write the prescriptions.

Life marched on through 1935 and 1936 and, as expected, just kept getting worse. But the insults and discrimination were nothing compared to what occurred on the day when Papa failed to return home, November 10, 1936. That day, our lives completely crumbled.

As I pieced things together from Lilo, Mutti, and other relatives, a group of police came into the factory and announced Papa was being arrested for selling rancid animal fat, unfit for human consumption. They were uninterested in hearing Papa's protestations the fat not only wasn't rancid, but was intended for use in making shoe polish and soap. So, in front of his employees, the police handcuffed him and took him away. I would expect that part of the scene included insults about the thieving Jew trying to deceive his unsuspecting German customers. Mutti also told me that it was Papa's own employees who reported him to the police. I wouldn't be surprised if Heinrich Gunter egged them on. After all, who stood to benefit most from the removal of Papa from the business? Mutti seemed most upset about this. "After all he did for his workers," she cried. "He did for them before he did for his own family." The only saving grace was Papa was arrested by municipal police, not the Gestapo. This meant he was still part of the civil justice system, or what remained of it. Had the Gestapo arrested him, he probably would have disappeared forever.

Not that any of that really mattered to our lives. What mattered was that Papa's decisions made him totally useless to us as a breadwinner, not to mention that his life might have been in danger. It was difficult for me to sort out all of my many feelings at this terrible time. I knew I should feel sorry for my father, brutally arrested and locked up. Perhaps because Mutti never took Lilo or me to visit him, I could allow myself to push my feelings of sympathy aside. All the relatives kept saying, "Poor Julius. What did he do to deserve this?" I resented the sympathy they had for him. Why didn't they save some of it for Mutti, Lilo, and me? What would happen to us? How would we survive?

Departures

MUTTI TRIED to paint the best possible face on Papa's prison situation for Lilo and me, but the following days, weeks, and months became a continuous struggle for her. Like most German *hausfraus*, she had few job skills and little experience managing money. And now she was burdened with the dual responsibilities of caring for us and trying to prop up Papa's spirits. The latter was more challenging.

As part of German administrative efficiency, Mutti received various printed forms each time she visited Papa in jail. Mutti inadvertently left one form on her dresser just a few days after Papa's arrest; it showed his distinctive, scratched scrawl and his request for "permission" to receive various items: writing paper, a pencil, the Darmstadt newspaper, jam for his bread, and his shaving equipment. On a separate form, permission was granted for everything but the shaving equipment.

Even as an eleven-year-old, I quickly grasped the significance of that form. The trauma of the arrest combined with the withdrawal from his sleeping pills had pushed Papa over the edge. His jailers didn't want to give him the means for ending his own life (though I can't imagine why they'd object to one less Jew).

I know I should be blaming the Nazis for all of this. That's what everyone else does, right? For a long time, I tried to. Underneath it all, I blame Papa as much or more than the Nazis. The course of events was so obvious and he actually had a way out. Yet he chose to ignore the opportunities and chase after the problems, and then to try to escape the resulting calamity via drugs. In the process, he endangered his entire family. And he wasn't finished yet.

The Joseph family's downward spiral continued; in fact, it accelerated. We lost our house when Mutti couldn't make the mortgage payments. The court and bank officials tied yellow labels signifying bankruptcy on various pieces of our living room and dining room furniture that were being repossessed. We were forced to move into a dark, two-room apartment in a poor part of town, where we had to share a smelly hall bathroom with two other families. A year after, in late 1937, Papa was found guilty of his "crimes" during a show trial that attracted lots of newspaper attention in Darmstadt. He was sentenced to three years in jail and, despite Mutti's pleas that he be kept in a nearby prison, was sent off to a prison that was a four-hour train ride from Darmstadt.

Now, the two main figures in my life were Lilo and Mutti. Lilo, as I've already suggested, was bright and attractive, a busty brunette in the making. She could also be charming and dramatic, if a little scatter-brained and dreamy-eyed. She possessed our grandmother Josephine's musical aptitude and could quickly sound out "Wanderlieder" and other popular melodies on the piano, to the delight of relatives we visited. I stood quietly off to the side while Lilo performed and answered questions about what she was doing in school. If anyone inquired into my life, it was usually to ask Mutti about my eyes and my glasses. I have been nearsighted since I was very young, and in Germany that was a bigger problem than it should have been because people seemed to believe that a pill or a treatment existed to cure any physical shortcoming. So Mutti endlessly carted me off to optometrists and opticians for various eye exercises and "treatments" (like sitting in a darkened room for hours), which, of course, did no good except to make me a source of sympathy.

Anyway, Lilo was the family favorite with most of the relatives. By 1937, she was fourteen and obsessed with going to the United States. And I mean obsessed. It was all she could talk about — going to the United States and finding romance with an American and getting married. She knew the names of American movie stars like Bette Davis and Greta Garbo. She even knew about Joe DiMaggio and the New York Yankees. Not that she understood a thing about baseball. Lilo's obsession wasn't entirely a pipedream, because Papa had an American cousin, Robert Joseph, who lived in New York City and was a prosperous businessman. It wasn't easy at this point for a Jew either to leave Germany or to get into another country (unlike in 1934, when Hitler was practically pushing Jews out the door and other countries were less resistant).

But if nothing else, Papa's arrest in late 1936 convinced Mutti, and presumably Papa, that Hitler meant business in all his diatribes about the Jews. So during the course of 1937 and 1938, Mutti and an aunt put in motion the procedures necessary for Lilo to leave. There were letters back and forth to the United States and to Jewish organizations and seemingly endless government forms.

Finally, in late June 1938, Lilo got what she wanted. I learned about it from her screams shortly after the mail arrived one morning. "America! America! I'm going to America!" I rushed into the living room where she was hugging the precious piece of paper and put my arm around her.

The elusive affidavit from the cousin — really a guarantee from him that Lilo wouldn't become a ward of the state — had come through, and Lilo was on a list to take a ship from Hamburg on July 14. Mutti, Lilo, and I spent the better part of the next two weeks shopping for new clothes for Lilo and visiting our many relatives so Lilo could say her good-byes. Don't ask me where Mutti got the money. Perhaps Oma Josephine arranged discounts from her textile business. Anyway, it was as if Lilo had celebrity status. She was carrying the family banner to America and she basked in the glow.

What a farce the whole drama was. Four years earlier we passed up an opportunity for all of us to leave the country in dignity as a family. Now, it was a major source of celebration when one person got to leave on a rush basis.

I really was happy for Lilo. But I was also unhappy for me. Why didn't Mutti try to get me sent along with Lilo? I kept asking myself that question, even today I ask it, and I must admit I don't have a good answer. I remember Mutti telling me once, "I can only ask Robert [Papa's cousin in America] to take the responsibility of one of you at a time. When you are a little older, I will try to make the same arrangements for you."

Which brings me to Mutti. Physically, she looked a lot like her mother, my Oma Josephine — diminutive, dark blond hair always fashionably set, just a little over five feet (even her hands were small), but with an interesting, some might say pretty, face.

Emotionally, she was much more difficult to fathom. She was cultured — the opera trips with Papa were clearly her idea. And she was as much the worried mother as any caring mother could be. She always kept after Lilo and me to eat our vegetables and to wear warm clothing when it got cold. She was always concerned we look our best when we visited relatives and friends, and sometimes she made a huge production out of selecting cloth from Josephine's store and sewing it into dresses for us.

But while Josephine was an outgoing, take-charge person, Mutti was much more quiet and withdrawn. Almost a loner. And that may help explain the closeness of my relationship to Mutti, since I am a loner as well.

When Papa was sent off to prison, and Mutti was as upset as you would expect, she and I drew close. I was desperate for some reassurance that however bad things were for Papa, they would be all right for us (doubtful as I was deep down), and Mutti was my only hope. I may have played the same role for her. I had a way of comforting her that Lilo didn't have. So while Lilo was dreaming her dreams of going to the United States, I was tending to Mutti, massaging her temples and placing cold washcloths on her forehead when her migraine headaches came on — usually after returning from a visit to Papa in prison. I held her hand and lay quietly next to her. My simple presence seemed to calm her.

"You have the magical cure," she joked with me. "With your special treatment, I will be rid of this headache in no time."

I believe her reliance on me may help explain why Mutti didn't push to get me sent to the United States. Then she would have been all alone and worried sick about both her children being off on their own. I can only surmise she still didn't fully comprehend the dangers we faced by remaining in Germany. She must have convinced herself that as a twelve-year-old, I was too young to be sent off alone and once she got Lilo sent abroad, she could wait for a time until I reached Lilo's age. Unlike Papa, Mutti wasn't selfish.

One of the most difficult things for Mutti to do was simply to put food on the table. There were no jobs for Jews, and even if there had been, she didn't have any special skills. So she was reduced to selling silverware and other possessions and begging and borrowing from relatives and friends. I vividly recall one relative in Frankfurt who sent us beautiful homemade cakes. Wonderful, except sometimes that was our only food, together with hot cocoa. I liked cake as much as anyone, but it's not very satisfying when it is your only food for dinner.

Mutti found herself leaning ever more heavily for financial support on a cousin of Papa's, Gustav Wurzweiler. He had become very rich trading in the world's depressed stock markets; apparently, he had a knack for spotting the few good stocks. Each month, Mutti visited him at his home in Mannheim, about a two-hour train ride away, and nearly always she returned teary-eyed and headachy.

She always brushed off my questions of concern, but I once over-heard her telling her sister, my Aunt Martha, "He always makes me feel as if I have to beg for the money. Each time, Gustav waits for me to ex-plain that because Julius is in jail and our money has already gone to pay the lawyers and the business debts, we need his help to buy food and clothes. Gustav knows all this, but he always makes me repeat it. He acts as if he can't understand how someone else can get into financial diffi-culties. Then, once I have finished explaining why we need the money, he always asks me to tell him how much I need. He knows how much I need, but even after I tell him, he gives me about one-half or three-fourths of what I ask for, and I feel so awful. He knows I would never ask for more than the minimum we require." So after a time, we were in a position where we couldn't live with Gustav and we couldn't live with-out him.

After Lilo left in July 1938, I, too, began fantasizing. My fantasies were stoked by Lilo's first few letters describing the glamour of life in America. She spent her first two days in New York before being sent by a Jewish or-ganization to Chicago to live with a foster family.

July 25, 1938

Dear Inge,

I am now on a train to Chicago, where I am going to live. I have spent the last two days in New York, and you wouldn't be-lieve what it is like. When we left the boat, I almost kissed the earth because I was so happy to be here. After we went through customs, we were seated in a taxicab — can you imagine, there was a radio built into the cab. But soon there were many other things that made an even deeper impression on me. That night, I met Robert and Selma Joseph at their apartment on Park Avenue. It is quite spacious and very beautiful. At eleven that night, we went out because they wanted to show me New York at night. We went up to the top of the Rockefeller Center Building. We had a sight from up there one can hardly describe in words. There were millions and millions of lights flickering, there were thousands of colored lighted advertisements, there was the noisy traffic hardly lessened by the late-night hours, there were the skyscrapers dark and silent and mighty, something to be afraid of, to be wondering of the technique of our century. It was the greatest and deepest impression of anything I've ever had.

The next day, they showed me New York by daylight. Selma bought me two lovely dresses at a wonderful little shop. I was so impressed by all the new and beautiful things I had seen that day that I could hardly eat dinner. After dinner, they took me out to Radio City Hall. Was there ever something more beautiful and luxurious? I don't think so. After we had seen the movie "Algiers," and a stage show with the "Rockettes" dancing girls, we went to a restaurant for some refreshments. When I returned to their apartment, I was very tired, but I could hardly sleep because I had so many new impressions to think about.

Inge, I can't wait until you can come. You will love it in the U.S.

Love and kisses,
Lilo

How I envied Lilo her freedom and safety. I hoped more than anything that I'd be leaving before long, certainly well before I reached fifteen. I had this vision of myself in the United States, wearing bright red lipstick and dark red nail polish just like the movie stars I saw in posters and magazines.

On a day-to-day basis, life wasn't actually as terrible for me as it was for Mutti and Papa. I was now attending school at the Liberale Synagogue, our spired temple that Opa Hermann correctly pointed out looked like a Russian Orthodox church. At the start of the school year, Lilo and I, and all our Jewish classmates, learned one weekend via the local newspaper that a new law had been passed that meant we couldn't attend the public school any longer. We were being thrown out. Getting away from the harassment at the Goethe School, and into a place where the students and teachers were friendly and respectful, was actually a relief for me.

I didn't expect much from the new Jewish school, even though I had enjoyed my Sunday School classes. I didn't think they could teach more than Bible stories. But amazingly, the teachers at the synagogue school were as good or better than the ones I had had at the Goethe School.

The one who dominated my mind, and imagination, was Fräulein

Goldschmidt, who taught us English and French and who had a preference for fashionable wool skirts and shawls from England. We called her
"Go" — a gesture of informality in our formal society that she actually
welcomed. She was a woman in her late twenties or early thirties, and I
hung on her every word as she described trips she had taken to England
and France. For me she embodied sophistication — in her erect posture,
the careful styling of her soft brown hair that dropped just over her shoulders, and her special attention to walking, sitting, and crossing her legs.
Her femininity was in stark contrast to us girls, who were at an age when
we seemed to bounce around in herky-jerky style and all our clothes
seemed ill-fitting and gave us an unkempt appearance. I could easily imagine Go fingering the latest fashions in expensive shops in London and
Paris.

Fräulein Morgenstern came once a week from Frankfurt to teach
math, physics, and chemistry. Professor Jacob was the school's principal
and promoter of classical Roman and Greek culture. I wasn't much for
philosophy and history, but I actually enjoyed his discussions about Plato
and Thucydides. Fräulein Loeb, a small, dark-haired woman, taught us
needlework and, as we stitched, a bit of Yiddish here and there. And Herr
Lowenthal, the elderly cantor, taught us Hebrew. Behind his back, we
made fun of him and his old-man ways. I never cared much for learning
Hebrew or for the Zionist philosophy that seemed to justify our learning
such a strange language. But maybe because all of us were such outcasts in
our society, we now seemed more closely bonded and eager to learn than
in earlier carefree days.

Hitler must have heard I was enjoying my new school, because it
didn't take long for him to get rid of this one entirely. Four months after
Lilo left for the United States, on November 9, 1938, the bleakness of our
future became crystal clear. That evening, Mutti and I turned out the lights
in the living room and sat silently listening to the shattering glass of Jewish storefronts and the screams of Jewish men being hauled off by the
mobs or the police. We didn't have a telephone, so we couldn't communicate with relatives. It was Kristallnacht. I felt terribly vulnerable, wondering whether the mobs would come up to our apartment and haul us off.
But something told me that was unlikely — there were enough men to
keep them busy. All I could feel was numbness.

Later in the evening, when it seemed the crisis had finally ended, except for the smell of acrid smoke, we could see the glow of fires lighting

the sky. The next morning, we learned from relatives that gangs of Germans had set fire to the Liberale Synagogue. So much for school.

By now everyone had gotten the message, loud and clear. Hitler was deadly serious about getting rid of the Jews. We were supposed to be smart people, but in this situation we certainly were slow learners.

Emigration became the major purpose of life among the relatives and friends of my family. The only problem was now that we were finally ready to leave, no one wanted us. And I mean no one. Not America, England, Canada, and none of the European or South American countries. Actually, a few people were still escaping to China, but it was supposed to be a miserable place to live, with as many daily dangers as in Germany. The quota numbers and requests for visas became exercises in futility for many people.

Nevertheless, Mutti went through the motions to acquire quota numbers at the American consulate for us. She corresponded with our relatives in England, Belgium, and America, imploring them to send us visas. Living in Nazi Germany in the late 1930s was for us like living with a rope around our necks. The only vital question was: "Will it be possible to leave before the rope will be drawn tight?"

The one ray of hope for me was the newly forming "Kindertransports" to England and Belgium. After Kristallnacht, these countries opened their doors just a crack, but only to children — no adults allowed. So Mutti applied for me to obtain one of those treasured exit permits, to England or Belgium.

First, I would need a child's passport. That was a special experience for a thirteen-year-old, to go to the local police station and apply for the passport. Any tiny illusions I might still have held about policemen being protectors were finally buried. It started after I filled out the request form. "Noch ein Jude" (Another Jew), smirked the policeman I had given the form to, as he handed it to a comrade. I was directed to a special room packed with other children and teenagers waiting for their passports. If anyone spoke, a woman at the front shushed them. For about an hour, I had to stand at the back since there were no seats. The room was cold and drafty. Each time a policeman poked his head in to call a Jewish-sounding name, he snarled to emphasize its Jewishness. "FeldSTEIN, KatzMAN," and so forth. My name got the same treatment ("YoSEF") and the man who was about to hand the now-priceless passport dangled it a few seconds in his hand as if he might still withhold it. I bit my tongue through all these humiliations, determined to complete my business and leave.

We received a scare just after Mutti filed the Kindertransport applications, when we learned the applications for England and Belgium were ultimately handled from the same Jewish organization office. Might she have confused the Kindertransport officials by filling out two applications? She was visibly upset when she learned from a friend about the possible error. Mutti didn't really care whether I went to England or Belgium; she just wanted me out of Germany. She moved swiftly to avoid any chance of a mix-up by contacting Gustav Wurzweiler. He had moved to Brussels a few months earlier, probably because of the difficulties of trying to do business in Germany as a Jew. Fortunately, he was able to secure me a place on a Kindertransport to Belgium. At the time, we didn't appreciate the critical difference between going to England and Belgium.

During the first week of January in 1939 we received the news I was to leave for Brussels on January 11. That left about five days to be spent with Mutti, who busied herself preparing my clothes and other belongings.

Now it was my turn to be the center of attention during frantic days of shopping and visiting with relatives. If I was going to live with Gustav, I'd at least need a couple of new dresses and blouses. But the laughter, hugs, and kisses that punctuated Lilo's departure were largely missing now. Perhaps because Belgium was only a few hundred kilometers away, my departure was less impressive than my sister's. In fact, it was more likely a sore reminder to my relatives that Belgium was as far as any of us could hope to go, and then, only if you were one of a few lucky children.

Luxuries

VERY EARLY on the morning of January 11, Mutti and I took a taxi through the dark, empty streets to the train station in the center of Darmstadt. The dark cold outside accentuated the dank interior of the dimly lit train station. The plan was for Mutti to travel with me on the train as far as Cologne, a large city near the Belgian border. From there I was to travel with other Jewish children from around Germany who were part of the Kindertransport to Brussels where Papa's cousin Gustav was expecting me.

The train ride was routine as we passed through the hilly countryside of farms and medieval castles, but for me it was a journey into another realm. It had turned sunny and crisp outside, but in my mind everything was shrouded in a cold mist. Mutti carried on conversation in a normal tone, as if she were merely escorting me to a relative's for a few weeks away.

"Don't forget about your blue dress if Gustav has guests over to his apartment.

"Remember, you have two heavy sweaters, so be sure to wear one whenever it is below freezing outside.

"Try to eat at least some of whatever they serve, even if you've never seen the food before. Gustav is a gourmet and you don't want to insult him.

"Be sure to write at least once a week."

The only hints that this could be a long separation came in two comments that have always stayed with me. One was a piece of advice I doubt Mutti even realized the implications of. "Now, I sewed all your dresses with extra material folded in, so they can be let out as you grow."

The other was more blatant. She launched into her monologue, which I had heard a number of times, about Lilo, and why, at the young age of sixteen, she was hanging around with older German-Jewish boys, some in their late teens or early twenties, in the United States. What especially bothered her was that these boys seemed to be "below" Lilo in social class. Don't ask me how she knew any of this. But this time, instead of asking her rhetorical questions about why Lilo didn't use better judgment, she honed in on me.

"Inge, I know you are only thirteen and won't be going out with boys for a while. But when you do, make sure it is with boys who are from your kind of family, whose parents are educated and cultured. Otherwise, you will be inviting unnecessary conflict."

I didn't know if she was speaking from her own experience, implying that Papa was below her, or if she was just projecting frustration with Lilo. I nodded my agreement.

As we pulled into the huge station at Cologne, she tried to brighten. "We'll be together before long, all of us, in America." The reality we both were keenly aware of was that this could be the last time we would be together . . . ever. I couldn't fully comprehend the ramifications of that last piece of awareness. As the train pulled out of the Cologne station, she stood motionless on the platform, in her distinctive pose of right hand on right hip. As I watched her diminutive figure grow smaller and smaller, I already missed her, and I knew I would miss her more. I never imagined how big a hole her absence would carve into my being. Years later, I spent hours in a drug-induced state calling out for her.

I must also admit, I really must, that as the train left Cologne and rolled toward Brussels with several dozen other children, I felt a little bit like the cat that swallowed the canary. Finally, I was out of Germany. I was on my own. No, it wasn't America, but Brussels was glamorous . . . and it was free. As a thirteen-year-old, I didn't really understand that its closeness to Germany made it extremely vulnerable. All I could think about was the possibility that I might see movie stars.

LIFE IN BRUSSELS was different from anything I ever had experienced. The glittering city was as glamorous as I imagined. I had met Gustav only once before in Germany. I could immediately see his resemblance to Papa, his first cousin. Although he was a bit smaller, Gustav's rectangular face, small eyes, and slicked-back black hair reminded me of Papa.

All I knew about him was he was very rich and married to a Belgian woman by the name of Loulou. By the time I arrived, they had been married about seven years. They were very nice to me. Gustav and Loulou met me at the train station and presented me with a gift-wrapped box of fancy chocolates. I couldn't imagine they were doing this for a child. They allowed me to spend my first night at the Hotel Albert with the other Jewish children who had just arrived in Belgium from Germany as well as Austria. The hotel had thick oriental rugs and glass chandeliers in the lobby, and the women on the elevators all wore bright red lipstick and had dark red fingernails. I doubted they were movie stars, but I felt as if I were already in America! I shared a large room with one other girl, though that first night I was so excited I could barely sleep.

With the instinct of a child, I realized very quickly that neither Gustav nor Loulou had the slightest idea about childrearing — they treated me as an adult and continued to give me all the chocolate I wanted! They immediately enrolled me in a fancy girls' school and, because I had little trouble learning to speak French, I easily made friends with the girls in my class.

Gustav was always dressed impeccably and lived in the newest building on Avenue Louise — a spacious five-room apartment that easily accommodated his large, dark-wood furnishings from Mannheim. On the same floor, he maintained a separate two-room apartment for his parents. He was very fussy about etiquette, and when I was in his presence I always tried to act the lady. I remember one afternoon, when Gustav took me shopping in his car, I bumped my head several times on the dashboard because he abruptly stopped the car at each street corner. All we had purchased were a book, some fresh vegetables, and a pound of cherries, but coming from a place where a dinner of scrambled eggs was a special treat, this event was something to be savored. So after the car was parked, I excitedly offered to carry the two small packages upstairs. Gustav scowled at me. "The maid will come down to get the parcels," he said.

What sticks in my mind now was his tone and the way his thin lips curled in displeasure. It was the first time I had seen him this way. I sensed his contempt for me and what he perceived as my inferiority. I also fully appreciated the effect he had had on Mutti every time she asked for money.

Loulou, on the other hand, came across as much more relaxed and open, laughed at her husband's excessively formal style and mannerisms, and wore her red-blonde hair loose to her shoulders.

After a short time with Loulou (I soon called her "Lou"), I found myself as entranced by her carefree ways and sophistication as I had been by Go. Though she was probably in her early or mid-thirties, she seemed much like a teenager. Soon, she and I were treating each other like longtime friends. Once I planted a dozen or so large stones at the foot of her bed. I lay in my bed for what seemed hours, awaiting her reaction. Sure enough, just when I could wait no longer, I heard her shouts and screams. She came dashing out of her room and into mine, shouting: "Inge, I'm going to kill you!" We both laughed hysterically.

However, Lou and Gustav were alike in one way. They always dressed very fashionably — Cousin Gustav in a gray or black suit, vest, and subdued blue silk tie and Lou in the latest French designer skirts, blouses, and suits. They wore beautiful clothes even on days when they weren't leaving the apartment. On Sunday afternoons they donned long-sleeved whites for tennis at an exclusive Belgian club. Overall, I was enjoying my new life and I let Lilo know in a letter:

February 9, 1939

My dear Lilo,

You probably received my letter and I hope that within the next days I will also get a letter from you. You cannot imagine how fabulous it is here. I started school already on the third day, a high school like your Eleonorenschule in Darmstadt. I am studying French, Flemish, history, geography, sciences, morale, arithmetic, hygiene, diction, crafts, gymnastics, household, singing. Tomorrow we have swimming. I am happily looking forward to it. I already know French quite well. Last week we wrote a French work and I had zero mistakes and the teacher wrote "tres bien." We get bulletins every week, which is a type of report card, and in everything I have a five, or tres bien. That is the best one can have. And I don't even study all that much. We have school from eight in the morning until noon. At ten o'clock there is a fifteen-minute recess. Then in the afternoon again from two to five, except on Thursdays and Saturdays.

Lou is adorable. I like her better than Go, who is already history with me. I could not have imagined that this would happen so fast. Gustav is so nice to me, you cannot imagine. They give me money and say I should come to them with any problems, and if I need anything I should just tell them.

Lou and I often act foolishly. I wouldn't have believed that she is still so young. She is also very pretty, and is so amused when I address her as "Aunt." How do you like the name "Luzi"? That is the name that Gustav calls Lou by. In the beginning I didn't know what he was talking about.

Sunday we go to the movies. This Sunday I saw "Queen Victoria," a fabulous film.

Today I was examined by the school dentist. He gave me a form to fill out with the questions of when I got my first tooth, when I started walking, and when I started to talk. I think they are crazy. I should know those things?

I am falling asleep here.

Love and kisses,
Inge

My letters to Mutti were similarly filled with the impressions of my new life, but I must have written quite a bit about the private arguments and battles taking place in Gustav's home, for she reprimanded me not to report any gossip. I was amazed and promptly wrote back explaining no one read my letters before I mailed them, but to my annoyance, she never replied to this.

It took me weeks before I appreciated the wisdom of Mutti's refusal to be drawn into gossiping. What a fool I was. She understood much better than I that not only might my letters be read, but that her letters to me could be read as well by an inquisitive Gustav or Loulou rummaging through my drawer. This realization dawned on me in a public incident that still makes me shudder.

Once Sunday afternoon I was enjoying a plate of still-warm apfel charlotte drowned in whipped cream at a coffee house with Gustav and a male friend of his. I don't remember why he asked me along — maybe Lou wanted me out of the apartment. In any case, there on the table next to my apfel charlotte was a sealed letter, ready for mailing to Mutti.

"So what are you writing your mother about me now?" Gustav asked. He sounded nonchalant, but he was grinning deviously. As I took hold of the letter and muttered about it being a routine note, he suddenly reached over and grabbed it out of my hand. Almost in the same motion, he pulled out a small pocketknife and began opening it. In that moment, I remembered I had recounted how Gustav angered Lou one evening by failing to invite her along to one of his business dinners. I pulled the letter out of his hand, saying, "It is full of girl talk."

People in the coffeehouse turned to stare at us. I could feel my face becoming hot, which meant I was probably turning red. Gustav laughed hysterically at my discomfort and humiliation. All the rest of the afternoon he teased me. "So you are writing secrets about me. . . . They must be important secrets that you won't allow me to read them. . . ." Despite his crude effort to joke, I had the feeling he was seriously concerned about my letter.

The two of them certainly provided a treasure trove of gossip. For example, Lou and Gustav had separate bedrooms. One day, Lou, clad in a slip, answered the phone in the living room just as Gustav walked in. Lou shrieked and motioned for him to leave. I was not exactly raised in a nudist camp, but I could not see anything terrible in Gustav seeing her in a slip. I became even more confused the following Sunday. That is when they had a house guest over for the weekend — an artistic-looking man with unruly, wavy brown hair. Lou took me along for a walk with the guest on fashionable Avenue Louise, and I had to look many times before I was sure Lou and this man were kissing.

After that, Lilo's story about Gustav and Lou struck me as true. When Lilo first recounted it, I thought it was another case of her imagination running wild. According to Lilo, on their wedding night seven years earlier, Gustav saw a scar on Lou's abdomen. After much denial and avoidance, Lou finally acknowledged the scar was the result of a hysterectomy done several years earlier. Gustav was furious because that clearly meant the marriage would be childless. He was enraged, but not enough to annul the marriage.

But the question that gradually impinged on my thinking was how this marital arrangement would affect me. I sensed I would become a target of Gustav's pent-up rage. I just didn't know how.

There were so many opportunities for tension with Gustav. He was a man of strict religious traditions, and that led us into difficult territory. I asked him why he was so observant that he refrained from riding on Saturdays and kept to a strictly kosher diet. He never could explain why certain rituals important many hundreds of years earlier, such as the sanitary rules of not eating certain fish and meats, were still observed in the twentieth century.

"This is the Jewish law and it must be obeyed as it has been written," he stated on more than one occasion.

His beliefs created problems for me. He insisted I attend Hebrew lessons on Sunday mornings given by a rabbi known to him. It took almost an hour by streetcar to get there, and by the time I returned, it was after one o'clock in the afternoon. I had nothing against the rabbi; in fact, I found him to be a very nice man. I only objected to the time — Hebrew lessons on Sunday mornings caused me to miss many Girl Scout events. Gustav wasn't sympathetic to my frustration and sometimes became annoyed with my complaints. "If you had had the right preparation in Darmstadt, none of this would be necessary," he once said in an obvious dig at Mutti and Papa.

I received clear signals of his real view of me one evening at dinner when he inquired about my day at the exclusive private school for girls (École Fernand Cou) in which he had enrolled me. It was a place where girls were required to wear stockings, white gloves, and hats. I was not especially comfortable with all the formality, but it was certainly a big improvement over my school situation in Darmstadt. So that evening, I recounted a class discussion about current news events during which the teacher expressed hope that Great Britain's Prime Minister, Neville Chamberlain, would be able to negotiate successfully with Hitler. Gustav sneered, as if it were my comment rather than the teacher's. He then launched into a discourse about Germany's war preparations and the naïveté of England and the United States. The main question, he instructed me, was which countries would Hitler attack first? It was obvious Gustav had thought a great deal about it, and he expected the worst.

"What will happen to us if there is a war?" I asked, afraid to hear the response. Gustav hesitated and looked at me quizzically, as if I had caught him off-guard with my logic.

"I have begun my own preparations. Luzi and I will be more prepared than the British and Americans." Then he abruptly changed the subject by commenting to Lou about rising prices of rents and furniture.

It was obvious that, in the event of war, I was not a part of their plans. Afterward, I found myself mentally trying to paint the best face on the situation. Maybe it was because I had lived with them for only a few weeks. Perhaps Gustav didn't think of me as a permanent member of his immediate family. Maybe he would change his mind.

Payments

GUSTAV DEFINITELY had it in for me. But I must say, he cleverly handled the situation. He told me at dinner one evening that, as much as he and Lou loved having me around, they were worried about my safety, since they traveled frequently to Switzerland and Spain. They didn't want Mutti worrying about me, either. And surely I'd be better off living with other children my age. And so on and so forth. The plan was for me to live for a few weeks with a nice Jewish family who had a daughter my age, and then I'd move into a Belgian children's home just outside Brussels. They made the home sound like a privileged retreat — a place run by the wealthiest Jews of Brussels who provided a home away from home for German and Austrian children like me who had been sent away by their parents.

I wanted so desperately to believe him, yet my gut told me something else. I nearly drove myself crazy trying to figure out what I did to deserve being kicked out of Gustav's home. Yes, they traveled a lot, but they had a full-time maid to give me meals and, at thirteen, I was independent enough to get to and from school. Did he perceive me as becoming too close to Lou? Perhaps he saw me snicker when Lou shooed him out of the room? Or maybe it was the coffee house incident with the letter.

Rubbing salt into the wound was the feeling Gustav communicated that, despite my being a burden, he would still provide for me. I was to continue attending the fancy school. He would send me money every few weeks "and anything else you need." I would be out of his day-to-day life, but he would use his money to arrange things so he could tell Mutti he was tending to all my needs.

I became more upset when he inadvertently let slip that Papa's sister, my Aunt Ida, and her husband Josef, had just left Germany for Palestine a few days earlier. Mutti almost certainly knew nothing of this, since she had made no mention of it in any of her letters to me recounting relatives' and friends' progress exiting Germany. A few months earlier, another of Papa's sisters, Beate, had made it to England. It was as if Papa's relatives were easily slipping out of mainland Europe, while Mutti and I remained stuck in place.

As I read a letter I had written to Lilo, I was reminded how powerless I was, and how frustratingly unwilling Mutti was to try to help her own cause.

February 22, 1939

My dear Lilo,

Just now, before I left for school, I received your letter of February 1. I hope you received my letter, too. I am very happy when I get mail. All of last week I did not go to school because I had the flu. But don't write that to Mutti; she only knows that I had a cold. Gustav is in St. Moritz skiing. Yesterday I received a package from Mutti with chocolates for Lou and marzipan for me. Yesterday I also received an upsetting letter from Mutti.

Dear Lilo, our relatives are bastards. It is sad to say this, but unfortunately true. Today Ida and Josef are going on the boat to Palestine, and they did not tell Mutti about it. If Gustav hadn't told me, she would have no idea about it. And Papa's "caring" sister Ida did not leave anything for her brother, who is in jail and has nothing — and whom she could help. This terrible gang, they should have it very bad and can never have it bad enough! Gustav is more decent in that respect — he sent Mutti 100 Marks through Mr. Block (Lou's father), which surprised me because he didn't say a word about it to me. I have talked with him for hours, trying to figure out a way for him to help Papa. He has a friend who is a doctor where Papa is imprisoned. Now I am upset with Mutti, because she doesn't let me know if the friend of Gustav can do anything to help. But no, she doesn't write it to me, and not to you, either. I know how it is in Germany, worse than in hell, but no, always such consideration from Mutti. She no doubt writes Gustav the most beautiful letters and makes no demands.

Dear Lilo, please let me know how to make a leather book

cover, which I want to give to Lou for her birthday in May. Explain it in detail so that I can understand it. I will then ask Mutti to send me the leather, and if you have a puncher, you can send it to me. I will return it to you as soon as I am finished.

> *Write soon. Many kisses.*
> *Inge*

Within days of mailing the letter, I was sent off to live with a family in Brussels, a family with the last name of Feuerstein. I don't remember much about my experience with them, except they seemed like a normal, well-off family, living in a bustling, middle-class area of Brussels with lots of shops and restaurants. There were a pleasant mother, father, and daughter, Julia, who was about my age. She and I got along fine. We went to movies together and out for ice cream. At some point while I was there the Feuersteins acquired a Ping-Pong table, and Julia and I played endless games. I loved Ping-Pong. I think that introduction was a big factor in my decision to obtain a Ping-Pong table for Frank's and my first apartment in Chicago, even though we outraged some friends and relatives by turning our dining room into an amusement area.

The routine of living with what seemed to be a normal family and going to school was agreeing with me. There were smaller frustrations here — our mail routine and my expectation I'd need some more summer dresses, as I noted in letters to Lilo.

> *March 7, 1939*

My dear Lilo,
I really could be very angry with all of you. Tomorrow it will be eight days since I heard from Mutti, and fourteen days since I heard from you. I am not going to mail this letter until you write.

> *March 8, 1939*

Finally this morning I received a letter from Mutti. She cannot write so much any more now, since evidently Robert Joseph has taken on the guarantee for Papa to go to England.

I have a big request for you, but you don't need to do it if you cannot. Do you have by any chance a better type of summer dress you could send me? I would be simply too happy, because in Germany I had only two, a green one for school and a blue one that I wear already now because it is the only somewhat elegant dress that I own. I also have two old summer dresses, one I got from Edith in Frankfurt, which is so terrible looking that I won't ever wear it, and then a white one which is already too short for me. We go out so often and here in school I also need to be dressed well.

I really didn't want to write it to you because I don't know if you have a dress that you don't need. I actually don't get any allowance, and the money that Lou gives me on occasion I need for stamps. Lou told me that I should tell her if I need anything, but a dress is expensive and it would be better if they gave the money to Mutti. If you cannot do it, forget about it, but if you can do it, I will return it to you. If you cannot do it, please don't write to Mutti that I don't have a dress, for she has enough worries.

You would be the best human being on earth if you wouldn't let me run around naked. (It really isn't that bad.) I envy you that you can earn money. For me, this is impossible, since no one here would hire a thirteen-year-old girl.

Last Sunday Julia and I went to the ice-skating rink and watched the skaters. Then we went to an ice cream place and ate ice cream. Then we went to the movies and saw an American movie, "Always Good-bye." It was very nice. Afterwards, we went for dinner to Julia's grandparents. It was Purim. The Feuersteins are not religious at all; they go mainly on Yom Kippur to synagogue.

Perhaps that light-blue dress with the red scarf that is too tight for you? I know I have no shame, right? And I really have chutzpah. Now I am satisfied. I am in a really good mood today, do you notice? If I get no mail from you tomorrow, I will mail this anyway, otherwise there will be more pages.

Regards and kisses,
Yours,
Inge

In my overall satisfaction with life in the Feuerstein family, I wondered whether, or rather hoped that, Gustav had forgotten about the refugee home for children. But after I was with the Feuersteins for about three months, I received the news from Gustav about the children's home for refugees. Actually, he had Lou deliver the news, on a warm Sunday afternoon in early May, as the three of us were eating lunch in an elegant restaurant when Lou suddenly said, "You will need to leave the Feuersteins shortly because that was a temporary arrangement." I was caught by surprise. She continued, "But we have arranged for you to live in the place we told you about, where you'll be much better taken care of. It is the Home Général Bernheim. It was established by the Jewish community here especially to help children like you. You'll be with other children your own age and you'll be well provided for."

"Why can't I stay with the Feuersteins?" I asked, looking at her, then at Gustav. "I get along with everyone in the family."

"They will be having two other relatives moving in, so they won't need the money any longer," Lou said, sipping at her coffee.

I remember wondering, what does money have to do with the Feuersteins? Then it dawned on me — Gustav had been paying the Feuersteins for my room and board. They no longer needed the money and were kicking me out.

I felt as if I had been punched in the stomach. I also felt like a fool for not having realized money was part of the arrangement. Worse, I now understood everyone wanted to be rid of me. My face flushed hot with anger. Words tumbled from my mouth, directed at Gustav. "You don't care about me. You never cared about Mutti. I hope that Hitler will come to Belgium, so you will feel what it is like!" As the tears welled up in my eyes, I pushed my chair from the table and ran from the restaurant.

I wandered the streets of Brussels' old center city area, where artists and musicians congregated. I did feel a tinge of relief about the home for refugees, but by putting me into such a place, something akin to an orphanage, they were putting me completely out of their lives. This was the end of the line — after all, where else could they possibly discard me?

The coldness of the ornate, pale yellow government buildings in the ancient city center made me chilly despite the warm, late-spring air. What I would give to be able to return to Mutti's apartment and lie next to her in bed, arranging a cold wash cloth on her forehead to relieve one of her headaches. Or to commiserate with Lilo. I knew from her letters she was having trouble adjusting to life in the United States, living with a foster family in Chicago who sometimes didn't give her enough to eat. I even felt guilty about Papa rotting in jail. At least I could wander about freely. All the members of my family were in different places and undesirable situations, and there was little likelihood we would reunite anytime soon.

Late that night, when I returned to the Feuersteins' apartment, Mrs. Feuerstein was still up. "We were worried about you," she said. "Why were you so upset?"

I half expected her to hug me, but she just stood looking at me. Why should this time be different from the others? "I suppose I didn't want to move again," I said flatly.

"You will like it at the Home Général Bernheim," she said. "I have heard wonderful things about it; all the children there are very happy."

"Yes, I am sure I will," I answered, and excused myself to go to bed.

The next day at school I confided in my closest friend in Belgium, Frieda Steinberg from Austria. She was someone I likely wouldn't have been friends with back in Germany. She was very much the artist, not to mention quite opinionated and outspoken to boot, but here at our fancy girls' school we were among the few Jewish children, and we were both without our parents.

My story startled even Frieda. She knew about Gustav's wealth and arrogance, but when I got to the part about Hitler, all she could say was, "You really told him that?"

With that, I began sobbing. "Yes, I told him that. I hate him!"

To deal with the pain of those events, I wrote to Lilo:

May 14, 1939

My dear Lilo,

Please don't send any more letters to me here at the Feuersteins', but wait until I write you because tomorrow or the day after I will go to a children's home, and I don't have the address. I will write you then in detail because, thank God, I don't have to stay at the Feuersteins' any longer. Lou will call the Committee tomorrow, and then I will be transferred to the local children's home. Oh, how happy I am. Nothing has happened, nothing at all, but Mrs. Feuerstein has to take in two relatives and there is no longer room for me. They are sort of stupid, so I am glad that

I will get away from there. So wait for my letter. Did you receive the package?

Many kisses,
Yours,
Inge

Lou took me shopping for new clothes at one of the elegant boutiques on a side street off Avenue Louise. My instinct told me the fancy dresses, gloves, and hats she insisted on purchasing wouldn't be appropriate for the refugee home, but then my instinct also told me she was buying the clothes to soothe her guilty conscience.

Then came the Sunday in June when Gustav drove me in his Mercedes to the end of a long block of plain, brick row houses on the outskirts of Brussels. A six-foot-high brown brick wall interrupted by a wooden door dominated this end of the street. When Gustav opened the door, we found ourselves facing a huge three-story house totally different from its neighbors — it appeared quite new and had the airy look of a villa with Mediterranean-style shuttered windows. A small, black-lettered sign over the front door was the only special identification: The Home Général Bernheim.

The home was administered by a Belgian couple. First I met the "better half," Elka Frank. She was a slender woman with limp, brown hair whose smile revealed slightly buck teeth. She was in her mid-to-late twenties and neither her rumpled brown dress with frayed collar, nor her lack of makeup, did her appearance any favors. But she was personable and tried to make me feel welcome.

"I'm Elka Frank, the director of the Home Général Bernheim, and you must be Inge," she said breezily as she opened the door. I immediately noticed she had a strange way of directing her gaze up past my head, off into the sky, as she spoke to me. "We're just sitting down to lunch, so why don't you join us? I'll have my husband, Lex, bring in your suitcases."

A husky, brown-haired man appeared. Apart from his wrinkled work pants and work shirt, he had a disheveled, almost vacant, appearance. And he was totally serious. If ever there was a time to crack a smile, it was now, when he greeted Gustav and me. Yet his gaze betrayed not even a hint of fun or pleasure. As if suddenly remembering niceties, he shook Gustav's and my hands, and I felt the calluses on his palms.

"The weather seems to be warming up," Alex remarked, an awkward effort to make conversation.

"Yes, it does," Gustav said, sighing, as if he couldn't wait to escape. If Gustav meant to intimidate Alex, he appeared to be succeeding, because silence ensued and there was no eye contact.

Elka now turned to her husband, her smile gone, and addressed him with impatient dismay. "Well, what are you waiting for, Lex, the suitcases to carry themselves? Mr. Wurzweiler doesn't have all day."

As Alex turned awkwardly to collect my suitcases, Gustav seized the opportunity to beat a hasty retreat. "I think you'll be in good hands here, Inge. I know the Franks will take good care of you. Now remember what I said about calling us if you need money or anything else. We'll be in touch with you in any event." He grabbed my hand and shook it, saying, "Goodbye, young lady."

I entered the Home Général Bernheim and followed Elka down its long dark entryway to the expansive dining room where thirty girls were sitting around an oversized dining room table eating lunch. I realized almost immediately that I was, unfortunately, correct about the appropriateness of the new clothing Lou insisted on. There I stood, dressed in a tailored navy-blue suit, white blouse, and round straw hat, wishing more than anything I could somehow, like Cinderella, be transformed back into rags. While Elka introduced me, I watched helplessly as the girls glanced at each other and giggled, covering their mouths to keep from laughing.

Ranging in age from seven to fifteen years old, they were dressed even worse than I had expected in badly matched and ill-fitting blouses and skirts that were likely donated.

Elka tried her best to break the ice. "Inge," she said, "tell everyone a little bit about your background." But before I could say anything, she explained I was from Darmstadt and that I had an older sister who had gone to America. She spoke about my involvement in athletics while in Darmstadt — information she no doubt received from Gustav and Lou. Without warning, she suddenly stopped talking and looked at me.

I took my cue. "I was a member of an athletic club and did best in the broad jump and fifty-meter run. I placed second and third in one big meet, and won some other prizes in smaller meets."

More snickering. I sat at one end of the table and joined them. I ate a slice of bread smeared with strawberry jam from one of several bowls.

The fresh French bread was clumpy in my dry mouth, and I forced one slice into my churning stomach.

By the end of lunch, I heard three girls across from me giggling. As one glanced in my direction, I caught the word "Dipples," meaning track prizes or diplomas — also my new nickname.

Visas

I HAD BEEN BRANDED as the rich girl with the expensive clothes who wanted to be superior to everyone else. The penalty was isolation and silence, interrupted by occasional teasing and giggles. Day after day, week after week. It was as if I were enclosed in a shell and the shell kept getting thicker. Elka tried to be pleasant, but she was powerless to break the barrier between the other girls and me. I suppose if I had reached out, I could have been friends with some of them. But something in me didn't want to reach out. It was too much trouble. I just wanted to be alone with my sadness and self pity, and my rage at Gustav for sending me away and for seeing me as an inconvenience.

Two noteworthy events stood out during this time of empty languishing — one following naturally from the other. On a humid morning in early July, Gustav telephoned with a thunderbolt of news: Papa had been released from prison and expelled from Germany. He would be stopping in Brussels in a few days on his way to England.

My mood instantly brightened. It had been nearly three years since I last saw Papa, and it was as if I had forgotten that he still existed. Could he somehow rescue me from the misery of this refugee home?

Three days later, Lou picked me up and drove me to Gustav's apartment. When I asked her about Papa, she hesitated. "He had a difficult time in prison," she said as she drove. "He will need time to recover." I wasn't sure exactly what she meant. Once we arrived, it took me only a few seconds to understand and realize that Papa wouldn't be doing much rescuing.

The big, burly six-footer I once knew was now a ghost of his former

self. He had lost at least fifty pounds. His black hair had thinned considerably, and what remained was mostly gray. His always-serious demeanor
now had a flat edge. In the nearly three years of his imprisonment, he had
aged fifteen or twenty years. Slowly, very slowly, he pushed himself out of
Gustav's easy chair to greet me. He slouched forward as he stood. He
smiled slightly as he gave me a tentative kiss on the cheek, barely touching
my arms. He actually looked proud as he looked me over and remarked,
"You have grown so."

I wanted to ask him what had happened to him, but I didn't know how
to frame the words. Since Papa had just arrived, Lou and Gustav were on
their best new-guest behavior. They insisted on driving Papa and me
around Brussels on excursions. I barely noticed the historical sites,
churches, and stores they pointed out. Just the sound of Gustav's voice ir-
ritated me, with his phony sincerity, trying to impress us with his knowledge of the city's architecture and history.

What grated on me even more were Papa's abject subservience to
Gustav and the rich man's thinly veiled contempt for his first cousin. Did
Papa's presence remind Gustav how near each of us is to failure? What's
worse, I couldn't even be sure if Papa noticed what was happening. Maybe
his cousin's behavior felt comfortably familiar — so similar to the way his
father had treated him. (By this time, Opa Hermann had died from another stroke.)

As if he were trying to impress Papa with how well I was being cared
for, and perhaps rub Papa's nose into his own pathetic circumstances,
Gustav dug his hand into his pocket and pulled out a wad of cash for me.
Not wanting to further Papa's humiliation, and remembering Lilo had just
sent me a few dollars, I declined to accept it. "Lilo sent me money from the
United States. I have more than enough," I answered.

"Your sister should save her money for when you all get together in
the United States," Lou said.

To my dismay, Papa took Gustav's side and scolded me for accepting
money from Lilo. I didn't even bother to explain that I never asked for the
money. My older sister took it upon herself to send me a few dollars that I
had exchanged for francs.

When Papa and I were alone briefly, he reinforced Lou's words.
"Loulou is right, you know. You and Lilo shouldn't be sending money back
and forth. Hold onto it. You can always get money from Gustav." What a
lost cause Papa was.

I kept waiting for him to say something about me going to England with him or at least speculate about when I would join him. Finally, by the second day, without his even hinting at the possibilities, I brought up the subject myself. Papa was surprised by my question. "Oh, poor dear one, don't you know there is no way for me to take you? I only have a visa for myself."

"What about Mutti?" I asked.

"Mutti doesn't have a visa either. The authorities have said it could come within a few weeks. But there is a problem of money. She needs many marks for an application fee, and we don't have the money. She will try to borrow it. If she can make the arrangements, she will then join me."

Isn't that what Gustav was for? It all seemed so hopelessly complicated. It was unclear to me how Papa had obtained the money for his visa, or if he even had needed the money, since he was being expelled. He talked on and on about affidavits, exit numbers, and visas, and about his cousin Robert Joseph in New York and his older sister Beate Oppenheimer in London. In any event, the plan was for Mutti to join Papa in England and for the two of them to go to the United States. Only at the end of his long explanation did he add, almost as an afterthought, "Then, we hope to get you over to America as well."

A wave of nausea rolled through my stomach. Gustav and Loulou would be heading for safe harbors. Papa, Mutti, and Lilo would be happily reunited in the United States. And where would I be? Rotting in a refugee home outside Brussels? Why did no one seem to care about my fate?

That Tuesday afternoon, Papa accompanied Gustav when he drove me back to the home. As I gave Papa a quick tour of the facilities, my stomach churned in anxiety. How wonderful it appeared. The spacious dining room and living room with pretty oriental rugs, and the first floor sitting rooms with their flowery, cushioned upholstery — so comfortable. Why should he feel any urgency about getting me out? I was well-off and secure here in Belgium, at a time when many people were living in uncertain and even miserable conditions in Germany and Austria.

No! No! I wanted to scream, but I kept my mouth shut. Papa was so frail and, in any event, powerless to do anything about the situation. So I was cordial to Papa when, standing outside the home, he gave me a good-bye kiss on the cheek. The fact that I might never see him again seemed immaterial.

As I turned back into the Home Général Bernheim, tears welled up in my eyes. Fortunately, the other children were away at school or on walks. I was alone with my misery. I trudged up the stairs to the room I shared with four other girls in a dormitory on the second floor. As I neared the top of the stairs, I saw a door I had never noticed. Unlocked, it opened onto a narrow set of wooden stairs leading up another flight, apparently to the attic on the top floor.

I don't know what made me go forward, but I tentatively walked up the narrow staircase. The attic had the stale and musty smell of a museum, accentuated by the dim light. One section was filled with furniture covered with white sheets. Piles of books were scattered about. From what I could tell, most were specialized texts about agriculture. One of the other girls had said that Alex Frank studied agriculture and that he and Elka had spent several years on a kibbutz in Palestine before returning to Belgium.

Not that any of that mattered. The reality was there was nothing here for me in this house or in the whole country of Belgium. I was overcome by a feeling of hollow emptiness unlike anything I had ever before experienced. It is a feeling I have unfortunately become reacquainted with in the last few years — I don't know what to compare it to, except that it is familiar, like an old shoe you know doesn't fit quite right but you wear anyway, and sure enough, you get blisters.

Why, I asked myself, did I always come out on the short end of the family hierarchy? The answer seemed obvious. Lilo was engaging and pretty, but I was withdrawn and . . . well, unruly mouse-colored hair, a beak-like nose, and a flat chest say the rest.

Dirty white curtains hung over the windows on either side of the attic. I approached one facing out from the back of the house. As I pulled back the curtain, I was amazed at how much higher it was than the window of my second-floor dormitory. A jump from here into the garden of sunflowers and tulips below might just provide the relief I needed.

My hand was filthy from holding the latch for a long moment before I unlatched it. The window creaked as I pushed it open, hopefully not loudly enough to attract any attention. The fresh air cooled my face made wet by tears. I lifted my right foot out the window and felt for the ledge outside.

A voice made me start. It was a deep girl's voice. "Jumping won't solve anything. You'll only make your family very unhappy." I drew my foot in, wiping at my face as I turned around. The voice belonged to one of the girls from my dorm room, Ruth Schütz. Ruth was the only one of the girls who had been marginally civil to me since my arrival. She hadn't spoken much to me, but neither had she joined the others in laughing and giggling each time I walked into the room.

"How did you know I was up here?" I asked, embarrassed, not knowing what else to say.

"I heard footsteps over our room. I had never before heard any noise from up here, so I thought I would take a look."

"I was just poking around," I explained. "The books up here look awful. They're all agriculture textbooks."

Ruth ignored my explanation. "What's upsetting you? Is it the way the other girls are treating you?"

"No, they're just stupid. My father said good-bye. He's leaving for England."

Ruth then inquired about how he got to Brussels and why he wasn't taking me along. I explained about the arrest, visas, and affidavits.

"Well, at least you got to see your father," Ruth said. "The last time I saw my father was in Berlin and the Gestapo was cutting off his beard in our apartment and dragging him away. I tried to hold onto the car that took him, but the police pushed me away. We could find no information about what happened to him or where they took him. It's as if he vanished."

I felt bad for Ruth, who now seemed to be fighting back tears of her own. She turned and walked back toward the attic stairs. "Do me two favors," she said, turning her head. "First, don't do anything stupid at the window. Then, wash your face. It's filthy."

The urge to jump out the window had passed, replaced by a sense of relief at having been able to share some of my pain.

When I returned to the dorm room after stopping in the bathroom to clean up, Ruth and two other roommates, who had just returned from school, were sitting on their beds. For the first time since my arrival at the home, conversation didn't dissolve into giggles the moment I entered.

One of the girls, Inge Helft, continued with a tale about another girl who lived in the home, who had been sent to live with a Belgian family. "She doesn't want to go and I don't blame her. If they try to put me with another family, I'll run away."

Inge H., with her dark, almost olive complexion, looked as if she might be fifteen or sixteen. In fact, she was a silly thirteen-year-old, immature and overindulged. She told us she was an only child and her father owned a large department store in Saxony. Her parents put her on a train to Belgium in late 1938 and, since arriving in Brussels, she had lived at the Home Général Bernheim, with a brief interlude at the home of a Belgian family.

Because that family had nothing for her to do, she spent her days writing letters to her parents and other relatives still in Germany. After two weeks of total boredom, she persuaded the Jewish Committee to bring her back to the Home Général Bernheim. In the interim, her father had been sent to Dachau, contracted dysentery, and died. Her family now consisted of only her mother and her.

The second girl, Adele Hochberger, had a strikingly pretty face, high cheekbones, and brilliant blue eyes enhanced by long eyelashes and long, straight black hair. She was another giggly-type, with her own depressing tale. She had been sent away with her one-year-old brother, David. He was now in an orphanage in Brussels. Her older sister, Gisele, had managed to travel to Palestine.

"And what happy circumstances bring you here?" Inge H. asked, looking at me.

I felt self-conscious as the three sets of eyes turned to me. I wondered exactly what Ruth had told the other two about the attic. "I was living with my father's cousin and his wife. They traveled a lot and couldn't look after me."

"In other words, they didn't want to be bothered," Inge H. summarized. Very perceptive, I thought, but I shrugged my shoulders. I didn't want to share the nasty details — Lou screaming in her slip or Gustav teasing me in the coffeehouse. Even though the other girls had had similar experiences of rejection, I feared they would mock me for getting kicked out of a rich family's home.

For the first time since my arrival at the home, though, I felt camaraderie. When the call came for the ritualistic afternoon snack, I joined my new-found friends in wolfing down several of the yummy sandwiches Elka Frank served most afternoons — a slice of bread covered with a thin layer of chocolate.

That evening, I wrote Lilo this letter:

July 7, 1939

Dear Lilo,

You probably meant very well when you sent me the money that you earned yourself, but you are really dumb. You should really know that we have to save and keep all the money for when our parents come and start a new existence in America. We need all the money possible. And you should understand that they can use the money better in America than to send it to me because I have everything. I have written you many times that I have enough money. Don't send me any more. If you want to send Papa some money, go ahead.

If you could see Papa, you would see how serious life is. You cannot imagine what he went through. I now understand how important it is to study and learn so that later on we can be of assistance and help our parents. In our present situation, we must do everything in our power to help them.

I hope that you have a nice vacation. Papa will leave on Thursday for England, first to London and after fourteen days to Aunt Beate. Stay well and many thanks for your good intentions.

Love and kisses,
Inge

I can't believe what a wonderful job I did of concealing my true feelings. I am very skilled at rationalizing things. Or maybe I just didn't want Lilo to know what a terrible letdown Papa's visit had been.

Gypsies

WERE THOSE first weeks at the home simply my "adjustment period," as psychologists might put it? Though Ruth and I never discussed it again, I had the feeling that while she probably told the others about my being upset and encouraged them to end their abuse, she likely hadn't revealed the goriest details of our encounter in the attic. Maybe they just tired of being mean. Or perhaps the attic event made me seem less standoffish. Whatever the reasons, I began over the next few weeks and months to befriend the same girls who had been my tormentors.

The summer of 1939 seemed like endless silliness. We spent hours playing dodge ball in the back yard. The other girls always wanted to be on my team because I could throw the large rubber ball hard and accurately, and I was quick enough to get out of the way when the ball was thrown toward me. When it rained or was cold outside, groups of us sat on a rug in the home's living room and played a game called "five stones." The object of the simple dice-tossing game was to be the first person to accumulate five stones. The game becomes mindless after a time, but it kept us occupied.

The best day of the week was Friday, when one of our caretakers, Mademoiselle Lea, took us on walks through nearby fields of wheat and barley. A large-boned, blonde Flemish woman, Mademoiselle Lea was one of the few non-Jews involved with the home. She was rather strict, ordering us to walk in single file, but she made the walks interesting by instructing us in how to identify the birds we saw and heard and teaching us songs. One of them, a French folk song, stuck in my mind, even after all these years. We sang it as we stood on a wooden bridge that crossed a small, meandering river near the home. The words were strange and ominous, but in French, with the pretty melody, it was a special pleasure to sing together.

> Listen, listen to the fire,
> from which emerge secret whispers.
> These are glowing embers
> that bring us bad messages.

Mademoiselle Lea's rigidity occasionally brought out the mischievous in us. Once, as she was organizing a Friday afternoon walk, several of us decided to be "unavailable." Ruth was hiding out in a sitting room, pretending to do homework. Inge H. was in the dormitory, supposedly with a sore throat. Dela hid in a bathroom. I announced I had to find Dela and joined her in the bathroom.

Mademoiselle called out the names of all the girls who were supposed to go for the walk. One of the girls loudly called out my new nickname in a singsong voice, "Inge Irain." Hearing her, Dela and I began to laugh hysterically in the bathroom. I caught myself, and whispered to Dela to quiet down, but she only laughed harder.

Sure enough, there was a knock on the bathroom door and Mademoiselle ordered us to join the group. For weeks afterward, Dela and I got even more joy from recalling the incident and arguing about whose fault it was Mademoiselle discovered us.

That incident emboldened Dela and me to try our most serious bit of mischief. Above Elka Frank's office on the first floor was a bedroom with a small hole in the floor that allowed us to hear everything said in her office. One evening, when it was raining, we organized a little trick, pouring water through the hole as other girls poured water from other rooms next to pipes. Elka, as we expected, thought the roof was leaking and called one of the lady donors who arranged for a workman to immediately come over amidst great excitement. Sensing we would be discovered, we confessed that it was all a trick. Elka was pretty upset with us and ordered that we not have dessert for four days. But after two days, the affair was forgotten and our cook, Frau Glora Schlesinger, kindly woman that she was, just began serving us dessert again.

The weirdest day of the week was Sunday. Many of the children, like me, had relatives or family friends in Brussels. Occasionally, Gustav and Lou picked me up on a Sunday afternoon and took me with them on their shopping excursions and out to a restaurant for dinner. As full of hate as I felt toward Gustav, I must admit I was still attracted to Lou. I idolized her fashionable clothes, her flowing strawberry hair, her worldly ways, and her ongoing interest in me, or at least what seemed her interest in me. It was as if she reverted to adolescence when we spent time together, and invariably we dissolved into giggling about some silly thing — a funny name or a strangely dressed man walking on the street. Even though we were forbidden by Elka to wear makeup, Lou gave me some — a small bit of bright red lipstick contained in a round steel holder and black eyelash mascara with a broken brush applicator. Then she and Gustav would return me to the refugee home and I would feel rejected again, even though it really did feel like home and I looked forward to seeing my friends.

The worst Sundays were when we were left to the devices of the Committee, which was comprised of a dozen or so wealthy Jewish women who oversaw and financially supported the home. Two names I remember are Madame Goldschmidt, who headed the Committee, and Madame Wolf. We always knew when one or another of them was around because they invariably arrived in a big, black limousine driven by a chauffeur. They wanted to be nice to the girls who didn't have relatives or friends available, so sometimes they decided to bring individual girls for visits to their own homes or out to a museum and restaurant.

Several times one or another of them pressured Dela to join them in their homes for "recreation" — playing with their children. But invariably it upset Dela.

"Their children have so much," Dela would tell me afterwards, "and I have nothing. I don't even have money to buy postage stamps to send letters to my relatives by airmail."

Based on my single Sunday experience with the Committee, I had to agree with her. On one Sunday, my hostess was a heavyset woman in her thirties, who arrived after lunch with her equally heavyset husband and their nine-year-old son. They wanted to take me out for ice cream and cake. We drove into Brussels and went to a small cafe. The little boy refused to stop whining about a mosquito bite he had scratched open, and the parents argued endlessly about how to deal with it. The father maintained the boy had to learn not to scratch, and the mother kept saying that they ought to apply medication to the bite. I sat there feeling as if I were invisible. None of them spoke to me, and I ate my vanilla ice cream and apple strudel in silence. After we finished, they drove me back to the Home Général Bernheim. I had learned my lesson and so, whenever Elka Frank asked me if I would go on one of those Sunday outings, I told her that Gustav might be stopping by or that I had school work to complete. I was much happier spending time with a book.

Ruth discovered a Zionist youth group that met nearby on Sundays. There she learned French and Hebrew folk songs and discussed political issues concerning Palestine. I had little interest in politics, though, and declined her overtures to come along.

I drew closest to the other girls late at night, after we had gone to bed and the lights had been turned out. Inge H. and Hanni Schlimmer, the fifth girl in our room, laughed and laughed, seemingly at anything. The dumbest joke could keep them giggling forever. Sometimes we speculated about the relationship between the home's supervisor, Elka Frank, and her husband, Alex. All of us were in complete agreement: Alex was a bit creepy in appearance and demeanor. "I wouldn't want to sleep in the same room, let alone the same bed, with him," said Inge H.

Opinion was more divided about a Russian man who seemed to be a friend of the Franks and came around on Sundays to do odd jobs and repairs — Elias Haskelevich. He was balding and very much the man about town with his black beret and knickers. He loved to tease me about my studies and my reading, saying I was far too serious. The implication was I should be more carefree, like him.

He made his point most emphatically the previous Rosh Hashanah, when he arrived at the home all dressed up in suit and tie, carrying flowers and a bottle of champagne. He proceeded to open the bottle and share it with Lotte Nussbaum and me. Lotte was, like me, an introvert, except perhaps even more so.

"I am going to show you what fun is all about," Haskelevich said as he poured our drinks.

Elka came by the living room as we were sipping our champagne and was aghast. "These children are only fourteen, and you give them champagne, and on Rosh Hashanah?"

"Well, it is the New Year, is it not?" Haskelevich answered, a look of mock innocence on his round face.

She just shook her head, sighed a deep sigh, and left us. We proceeded to get tipsy and giggle, and Haskelevich seemed pleased that he had loosened us up.

But others of the girls felt uncomfortable around him. "Do you notice the way he looks at us older girls?" Ruth sometimes asked. "He's probably already in his forties, and still, he gives us these very serious looks. He should be looking at women his own age. How come we never see him with a grown woman?"

Frau Schlesinger, our cook, was the one person we all agreed we liked. Sometimes, when I confided in her, she gave me a special treat like a piece of chocolate or candy. It didn't take long for us to compare notes and realize she spread those special treats more widely than we realized, but she had a way of making each one of us feel as if she alone were benefiting from her largesse. Inge H. had a special attachment to Frau Schlesinger because, I think, she reminded Inge of her mother. Somewhat overweight, with her brown hair pulled in a bun, Glora looked like everyone's idealized mother — usually smiling in her stained, white apron. She always inquired about whatever problem we had shared with her the day or week before. Frau Schlesinger was married to a quiet, thin man, Ernste, and they had a son, Pauli, who was about six years old.

What always struck me during our late-night discussions was even though none of us knew each other back in Germany and Austria, we all had friends in common. Dela's family in Berlin was close to a brother of Herr Lowenthal, our cantor in Darmstadt. Since Dela and Ruth both came from Berlin, they had many mutual acquaintances and family friends. Some nights we talked for hours, trying to see how many connections we could make among our families and friends. One name prompted a recollection of someone who might know the first person and so on. Sometimes it seemed that, if we reached back far enough through the generations, we would discover we were all related.

Sadly, though, all the fun could never compensate fully for the void of not having our mothers and fathers around and for the anxiety we felt about their safety. The emptiness was most pronounced on weekdays right after lunch when Elka passed out the day's mail. Whenever I had a letter from home, a wonderful feeling of joy swept over me. I clutched it tightly to my chest and quickly staked out one of the living room's easy chairs, where I could savor the pleasure of slowly opening the envelope and reading and re-reading each phrase from Mutti or Lilo. The days that brought me no mail left me feeling desolate, and the rest of the day dragged on forever, longer and lonelier than I could bear. And if I received no mail for several days running, I began to wonder if something was wrong at home or with Lilo in the United States.

Once, when I hadn't received mail for several days, I became very upset and wrote this to Lilo before going to sleep:

February 22, 1940

Dear Lilo,

I'm waiting impatiently for mail from you. Please write me. You have no idea for how long I wait. And you do not know the longing I have for you. And you know even less, my dear Lilo, how much I love you.

Every one of our family is alone now in a different country. What crime have we committed? Oh, my dear Lilo, you do not know how I'm looking forward to our reunion, to getting together again. It could be years yet. I'm not homesick any more, but when I think of you, my dear big sister, I have much longing and I go crazy over it. But now, that's finished. On Monday, I will write to you again how it was on Sunday, and then, I hope, I will have mail from you and Mutti. For now, good night and a big kiss.

Love,
Inge

Lilo was a disappointment to me. I knew she had her own problems, but at least she was living in the country where she would eventually settle. Papa was due there shortly. And she had an ocean separating her from Hitler. Later, when we reunited and she shared this and other letters with me, she explained that because she moved so frequently during those days, letters often took weeks to catch up with her. But I never did get over the hurt.

My new friends and I were like Gypsies. Our mothers and fathers were in Germany and Austria, our sisters and brothers scattered about in Belgium, Poland, Palestine, Britain, and the United States, and we were not sure where we'd be living next weekend, next month, or next year.

Worse yet, because we weren't considered adults, we were dependent on unpredictable supervision and arbitrary decision-making by adults we barely knew. Consider Ruth's situation. Her mother was unable to obtain any news about her father after the Gestapo hauled him off. Ruth arrived at the Home Général Bernheim in early 1939 with her eight-year-old sister, Betty. Then in the fall, her mother arrived with her youngest sibling, four-year-old Bronia. Ruth's mother was in a situation similar to Papa's, only worse. Ruth's mother had a visa to enter England as a housekeeper, but she had been unable to secure one for anyone else, including Bronia. Understandably, she didn't want to leave such a young child, and for a time she considered trying to smuggle the little girl into England with her. Eventually, Ruth and the Franks convinced Ruth's mother that the plan wouldn't work and she would likely not be allowed into England, endangering both Bronia and herself. She finally decided to travel on to England alone, leaving Bronia at the Général Bernheim home. Once in England, she reasoned, she could work to get visas for her three children to join her.

Because there was nothing for Bronia to do at our home and there were no other children her age, the Franks arranged to place her in a Brussels orphanage. When Ruth visited her sister after several weeks, she was shocked to find Bronia malnourished and so upset that she had begun wetting her bed. The headmaster of the orphanage said Bronia "didn't behave," and he punished her by locking her in a darkened room several hours each day. Ruth argued forcefully with our home's Committee members to get Bronia moved. They promised to look into the matter, but nothing ever happened.

These temporary situations weren't tenable. How would they be resolved?

Parachutes

B UZZING AROUND in the background was the war. Hitler invaded Poland on September 1, 1939, just before we were due to start school. In
the days immediately before and after, Brussels deteriorated into a panic.
Air-raid sirens sounded, presumably for "practice," and army trucks rum-
bled through the streets. All the coffeehouses closed down for a few days.
The newspapers were full of stories recounting political debates about
whether to put foreigners, like us, into special detention camps, though it
seemed as if the idea had been rejected.

Our Friday afternoon walks were put on hold, and Elka warned us to
stay close to the home. "You could be mistaken for Germans if people hear
you speaking German among yourselves," she said. "Belgians are terribly
afraid of the Germans, and we are hearing more stories of Germans being
attacked in the streets."

It seemed only a matter of time before the rest of Europe would be
consumed in Hitler's madness. The quiet routine surrounding our home
provided some measure of reassurance. Later in September, as the war
frenzy subsided, the older girls enrolled in various vocational schools
around the area. Ruth and four other girls attended a sewing school that
Ruth hated because it was both strict and boring. She had to memorize
lessons about sewing techniques, and her exams were to recite the lessons
and keep neat notebooks of what they copied from the blackboards.

My days at the fancy girls school were over — probably because it was
too far away — so along with Dela, Inge H., and several other girls, I attended a school that trained its students in accounting, bookkeeping, and

secretarial skills. It was a far cry — in appearance and quality of students — from École Fernand Cou. It had stuffy, overcrowded classrooms and less-than-eager teachers. I'd say it was even a level below my old Goethe School in Darmstadt in appearance and teaching quality. Yet for all its problems, it was far more challenging and fun than Ruth's school. The math was certainly new and interesting.

Because Dela and Inge H. had trouble learning the accounting and math, I spent many hours helping them complete their homework.

"Why do we have to learn this stupid stuff?" Dela sometimes asked in exasperation.

"Social workers don't need to know accounting and mathematics," agreed Inge H. "I know that's what I'm going to be, so why do they make me take this?"

"We may not get to do what we want right away," I suggested. "We have to be prepared to help our families earn money once we are all reunited."

Inge H. was skeptical, as always. "Do you really think we'll ever get back together with our families?" she asked. It was clear she didn't expect an answer from any of us. The implications of her questions were increasingly ringing true. I was getting tired of spouting the party line. But I did enjoy helping them. It made me feel useful.

The war seemed to lurk everywhere, though, intruding itself whenever we might begin to feel comfortable. News reports suggested Hitler's invasion of Poland was just the beginning. Speculation was rampant on where Hitler would strike next. Holland? France? Belgium? That made my two personal questions loom ever larger: How would I get out of Belgium and to the United States? And how would Mutti get out of Germany?

Neither question offered much for me to attach hope to. Mutti was in contact with Papa's cousins in New York City who had arranged for Lilo to go to the United States, but they ran into continued dead ends trying to get Mutti out. Her letters reflected a growing sense of desperation. One of them, from April 1940, was indicative of this:

> *My dear Inge,*
> I hope you continue to enjoy your school. You are very fortunate to be away from here, as life gets harder day by day.
> My efforts to emigrate are moving at a snail's pace. Each time

I think I am making progress, another problem comes up. After I filed an affidavit from Robert Joseph at the American consulate, I was informed that the American embassy in England needs to receive the exact same papers from Papa there. Each time I go to the American consulate here, they seem to have a new rule or two.

I hate to keep bothering Robert about these details, because I am afraid it may make him angry. I am also exploring traveling from a Japanese port, but that costs an extra $300. I would have to ask Robert for that money, which would be just another bother for him. I am trying to get all the papers together in advance so that he wouldn't have to be bothered with all the details and would then just send the money.

This week, Mr. and Mrs. Wartensleben left via Russia. But most people are having the same problems I am having. While it had always been difficult to make arrangements, that is no comparison to how it is today. Mr. Mann, who sells train supplies, could not get his visa because of a one-day delay, and now he has to start with his affidavit from the beginning. Uncle Hermann has nothing as yet, and is looking for a new affidavit.

I am also worried about Lilo. As you know, she has a boyfriend who is several years older than she. I don't think it is right at her age to go with only one boy. I can understand that she is so alone and wants to be with someone. But she has her whole life ahead of her. Maybe you can write her to be reasonable. She doesn't listen to me.

I hope that you are eating well, and that you have enough clothes as you grow. Please let me know about how your courses are going.

Many kisses,
Mutti

I had so many awful feelings as I read her letter. No way out. No one cared. She was a prisoner in hell. I was a prisoner a level above hell, but a prisoner nonetheless. On top of it all, she was worried about offending Robert Joseph. I wanted to tell her to stop being such a fool. She was in hell, and she was worrying about irritating the one slim hope she had to get out! And Papa and Lilo? It felt as if they didn't know or didn't care, or both.

On May 10, 1940, we were awakened by strange, loud noises. It was worse than any thunderstorm. Looking out our dorm room windows, we saw flashes of lightning but wondered why they were so much closer to the ground than normal lightning. That's when we saw the skies full of white parachutes.

Ruth and I rushed down to the kitchen, where we found Glora Schlesinger already there, wearing her familiar white apron. But she wasn't preparing breakfast. Her normally cheerful face was drawn and her lips were set tight. "The Germans are attacking," she said, simply.

A cryptic radio announcement told us German bombers were attacking the city. Elka told the twenty-five of us to move quickly to the basement. As the full impact of what was happening sank in, my heart began pounding heavily. My stomach churned. I wanted to just run away, anywhere.

I tried to take a few deep breaths as I joined the other girls in silently negotiating the creaky wooden stairs into the Home Général Bernheim's spacious basement which, like its attic, was strictly for storage. There were a few cushioned chairs covered with sheets, and a large tattered oriental rug covered part of the floor. A huge, coal-burning furnace dominated one side of the cellar.

We all sat quietly on the floor and listened for more bombs and air-raid sirens. I don't know when we had been gathered together so quietly before. A low chatter was usually the best we could do. When the booming became more distant and the air-raid sirens sounded less frequently, the mood relaxed, and some intermittent chattering broke out. Certainly the fact that Elka was spending more time upstairs than downstairs suggested the danger wasn't as close as we had initially feared. But one thing was certain: The Germans were coming. Even if they didn't arrive at our home this day, they would arrive before long.

At about mid-morning, Edith Goldapper, a girl from Austria, announced that she was going to try to telephone family friends with whom she had stayed when she first arrived in Brussels. That's when I realized I ought to call Gustav. Several other girls with relatives in Brussels decided they would also try to contact their families. The next time Elka came down to the basement, we crowded around her and begged for permission to use the phone.

Hadn't Gustav always told me to call if I had any problems? If this didn't qualify as a problem, I thought to myself, what did? Surely Gustav would know how serious this was. If the situation was as severe and threatening as it appeared to be, perhaps I could meet him and get away.

Unbelievably, I reached Gustav's apartment on the first try. His maid, Berta, answered the phone. Normally friendly and talkative, she was now short and nearly curt. No, Gustav wasn't there. He and Lou, along with Gustav's parents, had climbed into his Mercedes four hours earlier and taken off. That would have been at the first sound of bombs falling. Did they tell you where they were going? No. Did they tell you when they would be back? No. She said only that she helped them load several suit-cases and boxes; she assumed they would be gone for a while.

As Berta answered my questions, I felt a gnawing sensation in my stomach. I tried to hide my tears from the three girls who stood waiting to use the phone after me. I didn't want them to see how upset I was. Gustav had made his rejection final. He would try to save his and Loulou's skins, but would do nothing to help me. I was on my own.

On my own, but not alone. Edith and the other girls had no better luck. In one of the cases, no one answered the telephone. In another, a maid related a similar quick-get-away tale. Even Elka struck out as she tried to reach several members of the committee — they, too, had disap-peared.

Ruth, who had more to worry about than herself, was distraught. She was desperately trying to get through to the orphanage where Bronia was placed but couldn't even make a connection. The telephone lines to that part of the city had been destroyed.

"What am I going to do about Bronia?" she kept asking me, tears streaming down her cheeks.

I wanted to comfort her, but I didn't know what to say. "We must be patient," I said. "There's nothing you can do now. We have to see how things will develop. Maybe later you will be able to get to Bronia."

In the early afternoon, Elka allowed us to come upstairs to eat cheese sandwiches Frau Schlesinger had prepared using some dried-out French bread left over from the previous day. My mind focused in on a detail: I hoped the crisis might make her and Elka forget about administering the tablespoon of cod liver oil each of us was required to take every day. But neither of them forgot and each of us had to take our daily dose, despite groans all around. After lunch, Mademoiselle Lea herded everyone back down to the basement.

I remained upstairs a little longer than anyone else because I was the last one in line to use the bathroom, and when I emerged I could hear Elka on the telephone at the end of the long hallway. She was in tears.

"You must find a way, Max. I cannot be here with twenty-five Jewish girls when the Germans come marching in. . . . Yes, Madame Goldschmidt has been in contact and says she knows people who can help. . . . I don't care what kind of train you find for us. . . . Yes, a freight train would be fine. . . . Yes, I understand that everyone wants to leave Brussels. But Max, these are children."

I was pretty sure Max was a relative of Alex Frank, perhaps his brother. He had been at the home several times with Alex. I was not sure exactly what Max did, but I had a vague recollection of Alex's boasting that he was an official in Belgium's government. I always discounted the possibility he might be someone important since he was related to Alex. Alex had already left. The night before, when the Belgians realized that an attack by Germany was imminent, he'd been called back to active duty in the Belgian army.

When I finally returned to the basement, everyone's mood was noticeably more upbeat. Hanni Schlimmer, someone who loved to sing and make up songs, was pushing everyone to join her in one of our favorites, "Cod Liver Oil." I'm not sure who wrote it, but we all knew the words by heart and sang it to the melody of the Three Penny Opera.

> And the shark, he has teeth
> and he has them in his face.
> But in his stomach he has cod liver oil,
> but the cod liver oil you cannot see.
> Madame Frank comes with the bottle.
> Many scream, "I am too fat
> and will burst if I take it,
> and that would be unfortunate."
> Some scream, "This will taste terrible
> and I will vomit, ach."
> The ones who have some sense
> wash it down with coffee.
> But all the children of the Général Bernheim Home
> get marrow in their bones
> and will be famous around the world
> because they are big and strong.
> The moral of this story:
> Don't scream when you get cod liver oil

because you will be big and strong
and even longer than this poem!

That evening, we brought our blankets down to the basement for sleeping. The bombing had stopped. But we really had no idea what was going on in the outside world. Were German soldiers marching into Belgium? How long would it take them to reach Brussels? What would happen to us when they arrived?

I kept my fears to myself, but Inge H. didn't. "I wonder when the Germans will arrive," she blurted into the silence as we all lay on the basement floor waiting for sleep. Her question hung in the air. No one answered. We could only wait.

For four days our new routine continued. Upstairs for short periods to eat, take cod liver oil, and go to the bathroom, and the rest of the time lying around the basement, reading, talking, singing, and wondering. The booming bombs fell mostly at night, and it seemed to us that they were further in the distance than they were when the first bombs fell. On the third day, Ruth pushed us to sing her favorite song. She had learned it at one of her Sunday Zionist meetings:

Everybody in this world has his own house
where he is at home.
Each nation in the world has its own country
and that is where it is at home.
But only one group in the world has no homeland.
Wherever it is, it gets thrown out,
and before the world, every day stands
the eternal Jewish problem!
Jew, whereto, where is your place in this world?
Where can you live without fearing the tomorrow?
The world is so big,
For you it is so small.
One country is still available —
but you cannot go there.
One door is still open,
But for you it is closed.
There is no place in the world
for a Jew like you.

Hunted

THE BOOMING of bombs continued in the distance, but we had no way to know exactly what progress the Germans were making. Finally, at about ten o'clock on the morning of the fourth day since the start of the invasion, Elka Frank bounded down the stairs to the basement. Her eyes were shining with excitement. She did not need to resort to the usual clapping of hands and yelling to attract our attention.

"I have good news! We have received permission to board a train that's leaving Belgium. A bus will come for us in an hour."

She instructed us to put on as many layers of clothes as possible, to put shoes, sweaters, and food into our rucksacks, and to be ready at 11 A.M. In the kitchen, Frau Schlesinger had a treat for us. She had opened a dozen or so giant bars of chocolate and half a dozen large boxes of cookies. These were items we wouldn't have room to carry, she said, and there was no way she was going to leave them for the Germans, so we were free to stuff ourselves. And stuff we did. Never had I eaten so many sweets at one time.

As I savored my fourth butter cookie, I could not escape the feelings rushing through my mind and down into the pit of my stomach: disgust with Gustav for leaving me to the Nazis while he made his way with Lou to America, anger at Papa for not somehow arranging for me to leave Brussels with him, and total helplessness in a swirl of events completely beyond my control.

The extraordinary treat tasted sweet but was full of bitterness, like the bitter herbs we eat on Passover — a sendoff into the desert of the unknown. Yes, we were wandering Jews and it was time to move on. Who knew where? In this scene of my pathetic drama, there would be no forwarding addresses for Mutti, Lilo, Papa, or anyone else who might care even a little about what happened to me.

We must have made a comical sight standing outside the home about to board the old school bus on that warm morning of May 14. Each of us twenty-five girls was wearing a winter coat, and everyone walked with an unfamiliar stiffness: Under our overcoats, each of us wore two or three sweaters, two or three pairs of pants, and one or two dresses. I was sweating profusely.

Inge H. stood out from the rest of us. In addition to her rucksack, she had packed a huge black suitcase and it bulged with her clothes. When Elka saw it she tried to convince Inge that she wouldn't be able to carry it around.

"Where are we going?" asked Inge H.

"We're not exactly sure, but we will probably have to walk some distance," Elka explained. "This suitcase will be a burden to you."

"I have important family things in here — special clothes and photos. It is very important that I take them."

Elka apparently decided not to press the point and simply to let events take their course. She didn't mention the suitcase again.

Only on our way to the train station did Elka tell us that we would be leaving for France. The trip through downtown Brussels was very disturbing. Deep holes marked some of the streets and many windows and walls were shattered.

No one asked Elka any follow-up questions, not even the obvious question: Where in France were we going? It was a good thing. As we were to find out, Elka didn't know, either.

For Ruth, however, the destruction we saw was terrifying confirmation of her very worst fears. Elka tried to reassure her that Bronia would be taken care of by the orphanage. Besides, there was no way we could take the time for a detour to find her. We would have to leave Ruth's little sister behind.

When we arrived at the old main train station, we discovered why we hadn't seen people on the streets. Everyone was at the station, or so it seemed. As their parents stood in long lines trying to buy train tickets, children sat on bulging suitcases and trunks that lay strewn about the main floor. Everyone was shouting. Mothers were trying to get their children to behave. The men in line loudly protected their places, challenging anyone who tried to push ahead. I watched as several men cornered conductors and other rail workers, waving wads of currency before their eyes, hoping to obtain a prized seat.

Elka directed us to a far corner of the station and instructed us to remain there. She would check on our arrangements. I hoped she wouldn't take very long. I was hot from all my clothes, but the sticky station floor discouraged us from getting too comfortable or re-packing our rucksacks.

It seemed at least two hours passed before she finally returned. As upset and disgusted as I was about my situation, I was relieved to spot her. She was smiling, with strands of unruly hair matted to her sweaty forehead. She directed us through the swirl of people to a platform. We would board a train, she told us, but not the kind of train we were used to. Indeed, the cars on this platform were all freight cars with huge, sliding wooden doors and straw on the wooden floors.

Elka located our car and herded us in. Herding is a good way to describe what was going on: A sign over the car's entrance read, "Maximum: ten horses." About a dozen girls were already in the car. But the freight car was so enormous that, even with thirty-five or forty girls, it wasn't terribly crowded. With no window, however, it was dark. Only a few slats near the floor allowed us to see out and get some air.

One look at the other girls had us moving quickly to the opposite side of the car. Those other girls were, for the most part, younger than we were. They were about nine to eleven years old, and their clothing was shabby and disheveled. Most disconcerting, however, was that most of them were scratching their scalps and bodies.

Lice, was my first thought. The word spread among the Home Général Bernheim teens and children: The other girls were under the care of the Salvation Army and they appeared to be Jewish.

I truly had hit bottom: I was in a dark freight car designed for animals with other people whose skin was crawling with lice. There was no place to go to the bathroom. Not a shred of privacy. I just wanted to escape this nightmare — faint or even fall through the floor.

THE FREIGHT CARS departed Brussels shortly after we boarded. Some of the time the train ran very smoothly; at other times, it just crawled along. Over the hours my disgust gradually gave way to a level of acceptance. As the train moved slowly along, each of us picked a spot for sitting and sleeping. I stayed close to Dela, Ruth, her sister Betty, and Inge H. At night, Ruth and Betty, aching with worry about their younger sister, curled up together. I was glad now that Elka had advised us to take the extra clothes. My winter coat served as a welcome mattress, and my extra pants served as a pillow.

It was late in the evening when we suddenly heard the same booming noise that had awakened us a few mornings earlier. Some moments later, there was a terrific explosion seemingly next to us. Our car seemed to shudder and the train jerked to a stop. Trapped, like dogs or pigs, children were screaming and crying. We tried to see through slats in the boxcar, but outside, everything was dark and still. One of the very youngest girls, one of the lice group, tried desperately to put a bright face on the situation. "Maybe," she said hopefully, "it's fireworks. The French must be welcoming us."

One of the other of the young Salvation Army girls was crying hysterically, clinging to me, her body shivering with fright. I held her tightly, forgetting, for the moment, the lice, and I crooned to her, "It is nothing. It will be all right. You'll see. We'll start moving again. Just relax." Trying to comfort her actually made me feel a bit less afraid for myself. Other than the occasional sounds of men moving past our car toward the back of the train, there was silence.

SOMEHOW THE WORD got around that one of the center cars had been hit by a bomb and people had been killed. Now I'd become a target for bombing attacks by the Germans. We were truly hunted animals. I remember thinking: Maybe they'll hit our car and put an end to this.

Hours later, without explanation or announcement, the train began moving again. We must have been close to the French border when the attack occurred, because we entered France during the early morning hours that followed.

The French people welcomed us with open arms. At each station where we stopped, we were received with friendly words and heaps of cheese and tomato sandwiches. At these stops, we also became acquainted with the famous French "toilettes." They were constructed in such a way we had to use all our concentration not to fall into them. There were two foot pedals, one on each side of an opening, on which we were required to balance. After our mission was complete, we pulled a chain that brought forth a flush of water. The first time I did it, I failed to step aside and was doused with water. The other girls had laughed at my clumsiness.

The reminders of war kept intruding on our attempts to entertain ourselves. Once, when our train pulled over onto a siding to let an oncoming train pass, we could see through the slats the other train's open freight cars and the wounded soldiers lying on stretchers inside. We saw blood stains seeping through arm and head bandages. The soldiers were British. At one point, as their train slowed, some of the soldiers started to sing "It's a Long Way to Tipperary," and we joined in. Before we reached the end of the song, though, the train picked up speed and moved beyond us.

On and on the train rolled. The weather was becoming warmer, and the air inside our freight car turned beastly hot and stuffy. I started to remember the toilette dousing with some fondness, hoping I'd have another opportunity soon. But the train stopped much less frequently, mostly in the middle of the countryside, giving us just enough time to leap out, find trees, relieve ourselves, and jump back onto the train. Night blended into day and day into night. Oh, how disgusting I felt, living in the same clothes for so long. My hands were filthy from the train floor, and my hair was matted and gnarled. At the Home Général Bernheim, I had grown used to daily showers as an antidote to the lice intermittently cropping up among the girls.

As the swaying train rolled on, its speed varying from fast to slow to fast again, some of the children started to get motion sickness. Skinny Ilse Wulff, who was a year younger than I, was the worst, crying hysterically and vomiting into a pail in a corner of the freight car. Dela, feeling nauseated and dizzy, had a hard time as well.

Between the crying and throwing up, Elka Frank was becoming ever more frazzled. Ilse's moaning had become more persistent. In the dimness of one early morning's light, the usually mild-mannered Elka completely lost her self-control. To me, the moaning had become something like background noise, but Elka was unable to ignore it, and in the twilight of my semiconsciousness, I heard her shouting at Ilse, "Stop it! Stop it this instant!" Sitting up, I froze in place. Elka was kicking Ilse as she lay moaning. "Just shut up!" Elka screamed. "I can't listen to you any more!"

I stepped toward Elka and urged her to move away from Ilse. Just as suddenly as she lost herself, Elka regained her composure. "I just wish this trip would end," she said to no one in particular. "I can't stand it any longer."

FINALLY, ON THE seventh or eighth evening of travel, when it seemed as if none of us could bear to be on that train a moment longer, we arrived at a small village about forty kilometers southeast of Toulouse, France's southernmost large city.

No, that's not quite right, we didn't just arrive, we were received. Despite all the chaos of the exploding war, it turned out the French had done some important advance preparations to handle large numbers of displaced civilians.

We were ordered to take our belongings and leave the freight car. During the course of our trip, additional refugee girls had been added to the car, increasing our numbers to about fifty.

As we climbed out of the car, we gaped in astonishment. Out of a freight car not far behind us came about fifty boys. They were from a refugee home for Jewish boys in Brussels that we had heard about when we were there but had never visited. So tired and disoriented were we that we had barely enough energy to carry ourselves and our rucksacks, let alone introduce ourselves or otherwise get to know each other.

Together, we walked into a small building that looked like a meeting house. Several women served bouillon in ceramic tea cups. They were there to welcome us. A heavyset man with a beret got up and said he was "extending the hospitality of all of France. Long live France!" I was impressed with our treatment, given the fact we were Gypsies. It was significantly more consideration than I had received from Gustav.

A rumor spread among us that we would be staying in a beautiful nearby château. Our hopes soared as we were directed to walk to Seyre, a village six or eight kilometers away. As we trudged slowly and tentatively on this warm, not altogether unpleasant, spring night, Inge H. realized her poor judgment in bringing the large suitcase. Crying hopelessly, she tried to drag it along the dusty road. After some cajoling, I finally managed to convince her she should dispose of certain items — a pair of dress shoes, a lace shawl, a party dress, and other fancy clothing. "I don't think you'll be needing those things," I told her. Looking around at the dark countryside, she couldn't help but agree. Finally, the case was light enough that she could haul it.

The village of Seyre had about one hundred inhabitants in its eight or ten beige, stucco buildings along the main street, and most were old men and women with children. The young men were all at war, trying to repulse the German invaders. So our group of boys and girls from Brussels effectively doubled Seyre's population.

On our walk into town, we saw a huge, white château illuminated by the moonlight on a small hillside. My heart leapt in anticipation. But then I heard the Frenchman who had greeted us tell Elka Frank, "We wanted to have you stay there. But we were ordered to save it for French soldiers. You will be staying just down the road." He didn't describe where we were headed, which I should have realized wasn't a good omen. We walked down the dusty main street of Seyre to a long, gray, two-story building. As the first few girls entered, they gasped and covered their mouths. I soon learned why: The place smelled like a barnyard. The girls were directed to climb a flight of narrow stairs. The boys stayed downstairs.

The dusty wooden floor was covered with straw. Disappointed but too exhausted even to complain, we all silently removed our coats, peeled off the extra layers of clothing, and lay down. I fell into a deep sleep.

Plagues

I WAS BACK in the abyss — probably further down than during those first weeks at the Home Général Bernheim. It was as if I had climbed out of a deep hole and, just as I was emerging into the sunlight, was kicked back in — only this time the hole had become deeper and blacker. I'm not sure I can find the words to describe the total sense of confusion, chaos, and devastation. At least in Brussels I had my creature comforts. Here in Seyre . . . we lived like animals. I had been condemned to a barren wilderness.

That first evening, as we climbed from the freight cars, I worried our biggest challenge would be learning to live with boys. My experiences had been limited to all-girl talk. In endless bedtime conversations at the Home Général Bernheim we discussed the kinds of boys we imagined falling in love with. Dela and Inge H. amazed me. Already, they had decided exactly the kind of men that interested them: height, hair color, facial features, and so forth (all variations on tall, dark, and handsome). Because I didn't have anywhere near such a clear picture, I had much less to contribute, although once we talked about how the man in my life would be strong and decisive, in contrast to my father. In any event, I anticipated terrible awkwardness and embarrassment being with the boys, especially because I was so filthy and unkempt.

During those first hours of apprehension we trudged the six or eight kilometers from the rail station to Seyre in near silence, until gradually I forgot to think of us as adolescent boys and girls together. We had too many other things to worry about.

Often during those early weeks I remembered a phrase from our prayer books at the Liberale Synagogue back in Darmstadt. In it, we asked God to protect us from "pestilence, war, and famine." I also remembered the Passover Seder and the recitation of ten plagues God visited on Egyptians to help the Jews survive the Pharaoh — vermin, frogs, hail, locusts, and so on.

We had our own chronicle of pestilence and plagues. First, we had so little in the way of basic "stuff." For toilet paper in our little outhouse out back, we were reduced to scrounging for leaves. For soap, we had to use sand we dug up along the road. Our only clothes were what we wore and carried onto the train. I tried to wash my things once a week, but often there wasn't enough water. So sometimes I had semi-clean clothing, but mostly I alternated among the same few dirty things.

We didn't know where our next meal would come from or even if it would come. The only food in even somewhat ample supply when we arrived, or at least that we could afford to purchase, was corn meal. Mornings and evenings we had some variation of corn meal gruel. Sometimes it was corn meal with onions, while at other times it was corn meal sweetened with molasses. At midday, the main meal was usually a stew of some kind. Sometimes it was a stew with bits of real meat and vegetables, but more often than not, it was made of foul-smelling animal intestines served with slices of stale French bread. I don't know exactly how Glora Schlesinger did her cooking, because all she had were a few pots and a fireplace in the barn. Because we had no furniture and few utensils, eating became a primitive, humiliating experience, because we had to eat the slop standing up or sitting on the floor.

Nearly all of us contracted skin sores — probably because we slept on hay that wasn't changed and became ever filthier as we brought in dirt from the outside. Our diet, devoid as it was of vegetables and fruits, certainly didn't help. Within a few weeks, nearly all of us had white blisters on our arms, legs, backs, and even in our mouths. My case was among the worst.

Elka Frank, recovered from her freight car breakdown, worked tirelessly to help us. She rubbed our sores with cool yogurt that she acquired from area farmers. As soothing as the yogurt felt, it was as inadequate as a few pails of water would have been for dousing a house fire. We were severely hampered by the difficulty of bathing. There were, of course, no showers or baths. We had only the water we could draw from a town well, and we had few pails or other utensils. We were fortunate if we got to wash ourselves thoroughly every four or five days; then we tried to use any leftover water to wash our clothes.

As soon as one skin sore hardened and the scab fell off (leaving an ugly scar), several others appeared to take its place. Sleeping on the prickly straw made the pain of the sores nearly unendurable. Each night I tossed and turned, trying desperately to find a comfortable position. I even had sores in my nose and my mouth. Only breathing in the cool air offered relief, so I alternated breathing through my nose and mouth.

Those skin problems never entirely disappeared from my life. As I write this, the leg sores I recently developed have failed to heal and even drove me into the hospital for two weeks.

In those days, though, I had to actively pitch in and partake in all the "cures." Just when we could no longer tolerate the skin problems, we were hit by lice. First, the younger children got them, but gradually we older girls were infected as well. As hard as I tried to resist, I couldn't help but scratch. Elka managed to acquire small amounts of gasoline, which she combed through everyone's hair. That provided short-term relief but it never completely rid us of all the lice, and within a day or two, new lice hatched to torment us. I'm not sure which was more repugnant — the itching from the lice or the constant smell of gasoline in my hair.

After the lice epidemic had been with us for a week or so, Elka made a drastic decision: Everyone would receive a haircut — a complete haircut. My hair was rather unruly, so I didn't care so much, but for the girls with pretty curls or long hair, the event was traumatic. Dela was especially upset about losing her black curls. "Even my mother wouldn't want to look at me now," she sobbed after Elka had shorn her locks.

After everyone's hair had been cut, we stared at one another in shock. Gradually, then, everyone began to laugh. Now little differentiated boys from girls. After a few days, we forgot about how silly we looked with our nearly bald heads. Or maybe we were happy to be rid of the lice.

Then in early and mid-June we were visited by yet another form of pestilence — French soldiers. Hitler's war machine was pulverizing mighty France. Most of the military action was taking place in northern France, far from us. But for the beleaguered French soldiers whose command structure was rapidly disintegrating, southern France gave sanctuary from the fighting.

Leaderless French soldiers headed south, some of them finding their way to our village. In the early evenings and nights, when the soldiers got drunk, we older girls had to watch ourselves. Once, just after dinner, as it was getting dark, three soldiers caught up with Dela and me on the main street. They put their arms over our shoulders; I recoiled from the stale smell of alcohol on their breath as they told us we could all go into the woods and "have a good time." Fortunately, Dela and I had the presence of mind to keep walking and we broke away just as we reached our barn. We hurried in and pushed the door shut behind us. They didn't try to follow.

For the most part, the male adults with us managed to fend off the soldiers but, for a time, we were virtual prisoners in our abandoned goat barn. Going to the outhouse after dark became a terrifying experience, and we had to nail wooden boards across our windows to keep the soldiers from getting into our building during the night. The boards kept the soldiers out, but they also kept the beastly summer heat in, and the warm, moist air exacerbated our ever-present sores, making sleep nearly impossible.

The most difficult ongoing problem we had to confront, though, was our main supervisor, Gaspar DeWaay, or "Uncle Gaspar," as he was known to us. I have no idea how he came by the name "Uncle," because there was nothing endearing or avuncular about him. All I can remember about his wife, Lucien, or "Aunt Marie," as she was known to us, was that she was pregnant and very close to giving birth.

I couldn't understand how the boys of our group had, for a year or more, endured Uncle Gaspar as the supervisor of their refugee home in Brussels. He was their equivalent of our Elka Frank. Maybe in the more relaxed atmosphere of Brussels he had been a compassionate person. Maybe the combined pressures of our refugee problems and his pregnant wife were too much for him to handle. Whatever the causes, it didn't take us long to realize he was our most terrible scourge.

A slender man in his thirties, he had wavy, blond hair and wore thick eyeglasses. He looked fairly ordinary, but his thin lips reminded me of Gustav because they rarely showed even a hint of a smile. Someone said that prior to taking over the boys' home, he had been a streetcar conductor in Brussels. I had no difficulty envisioning him as a conductor, ordering people to pay their fares and to sit quietly. He never spoke to any of us children individually, nor did he greet us nicely as a group.

On the contrary, he regarded all of us with contempt. The worst of his hostility seemed to pour forth at mealtimes. Prior to each meal, we were forced to line up in rows, three across, in front of the abandoned goat barn that also housed our dining hall. As we stood and shuffled, he stood motionless in front of the door, arms folded, waiting for a complete and enduring silence. This was easier demanded than done. Some of the children, after all, were only five, six, and seven years old.

Finally, when everything was to his liking, he nodded and opened the door to the dining area. We filed in and sat on the benches that some villagers had, after a few weeks, donated to us. Here we sat in silence with our hands folded behind our backs. When all was to his liking, he said, finally, "Bon appetit," and we began eating the disgusting gruel.

But Uncle Gaspar's terror didn't end there. He had other rules about mealtime and eating. He insisted we speak only French. He explained that if we were mistaken for Germans, the French, who were at war with Germany, might well victimize us. Some of us had learned French while we were in Brussels, but many of the children, who hadn't spent much time in Brussels, spoke only German. Gaspar's rule condemned them to eating each meal in total silence.

Uncle Gaspar also demanded we eat everything on our plates, wiping up any leftover morsels with our bread. Given the foul-tasting food and how young many of the children were, the requirement to eat everything was sometimes an unrealistic demand. It didn't help anyone that while they fed us disgusting gruel, Uncle Gaspar and the five other adults, who ate at a separate table, enjoyed such delicacies as jam, butter, and eggs.

For anyone who had the misfortune to be discovered breaking a rule, the punishment was severe. Ruth's younger sister, Betty, had a particularly difficult encounter with Uncle Gaspar. One evening Betty sat at the dinner table with Ruth and me listening to another of the older children tell a story about the Nazis' harassment of his father. When he described something she didn't understand, Betty, out of habit, asked, "Was?" (pronounced "vas," meaning "what" in German). All of us were so absorbed in the story we failed to notice Uncle Gaspar, whom we had dubbed "The Panther," sneaking up behind us. He had overheard Betty's single word of German.

To punish her, Uncle Gaspar sentenced Betty to a week of eating only bread and water — alone, in a storage room. Terribly upset, Betty sobbed hysterically, but Uncle Gaspar could not be moved. Betty had to serve her punishment.

Ruth was angrier than I had ever seen, but she decided she would fight

Uncle Gaspar by cunningly outmaneuvering him. She devised an elaborate scheme to collect extra food for Uncle Gaspar's dog, Rouge. "Oh, I love Rouge so much," she cooed to Uncle Gaspar. "I have set aside some of my serving and some other children who love him have also saved food for him." Perhaps blinded by love for his dog, Uncle Gaspar willingly overlooked the rule about eating everything off our plates. Instead of giving the food to the dog, however, Ruth took it to Betty.

With offending boys, Uncle Gaspar was even worse. On several occasions he took boys to an adjoining shed, ordered them to pull down their pants, and beat them with a stick. We could hear their screams and see them leave the shed with tear-stained faces. Uncle Gaspar's reign of terror reached a climax one evening in late June. The youngest of the children, three-year-old Manfred Manasse, refused to eat the pumpkin-based gruel that was our meal that night. Manfred was an independent little boy whose floppy brown hair gave him a chronically unkempt appearance. That evening, he refused to be intimidated by Uncle Gaspar. The dining hall grew suddenly silent as everyone's attention shifted to the confrontation between the three-year-old and Uncle Gaspar.

"You must eat it," Uncle Gaspar said, his arms folded as he towered over the little boy.

"No," said Manfred. "I don't like it."

"You will be punished," countered Uncle Gaspar. "This is your last chance."

One of the older boys sitting at the same table as Manfred, Jacques Roth, offered to eat Manfred's food.

"No," said Uncle Gaspar. "He must eat it himself. That is the rule."

Jacques was my age, fourteen, and short. But he had broad shoulders. I sensed he was strong. At some point as the tension built, Elias Haskelevich, our handyman from Brussels, placed himself between Jacques and Uncle Gaspar. With no warning, Jacques and Haskelevich were rolling on the floor, with Jacques holding his own against the older man who was attempting to restrain him. Several other boys rushed over to break up the fight.

As Jacques and Haskelevich each shook and rubbed his arms, Uncle Gaspar, without a word, turned and left the dining hall with Aunt Marie. Within days of that incident, Uncle Gaspar and Aunt Marie departed without notice. All kinds of conflicting stories circulated about what happened. One teen said the two of them were spotted silently slipping away from Seyre very early one morning in a wagon loaded with bags of corn meal, sugar, flour, clothing, and pots and pans. Rumor had it that they had purchased those goods with money provided by French relief agencies and, rather than feed us adequately, they had hoarded the purchases for themselves. Another version had it that the couple headed back toward Belgium because of German-inspired orders that non-Jewish refugees return to their country of origin. In this version, the couple actually turned over unspent funds provided by the Committee to Madame Goldschmidt, who was also now hiding out in France.

Regardless of which story was true, the fact was that Uncle Gaspar had been our leader. Who would step into the breach and take charge now?

Community

A FEW WEEKS after our arrival in France we were joined by Alex Frank, who was no longer needed by the now-defeated Belgian army. He was an extremely bashful and awkward young man and no one paid much attention to him at first. But after Uncle Gaspar and Aunt Marie departed, he let us know in no uncertain terms he was in command from now on. Not his wife, but he. If the army ever has made a man out of someone, well, here he was. From now on there was going to be discipline, order, and cleanliness, but with a human face.

In one of his first acts as director, Alex gathered us together in the dining hall and announced, "I expect you to remain silent at mealtime until you have been given permission to speak. I also expect you to speak only French at mealtimes because it is very important that you learn to speak French so we fit in better here. You may speak German when you are alone among yourselves. There will be no more beatings. Anyone who disobeys the rules will be separated and will eat alone. You are each able to show individual responsibility.

"The oldest among you will care for the younger ones. Because not everyone has decent clothing, we ask each of you to put your dirty clothing into a common laundry pile and we will distribute the clothing evenly among you. Those of you older children who have skills like science and arithmetic can help teach those who don't. For those of you ages nine to twelve, my mother, Irene, will teach regular morning classes."

He grouped us according to age, boys and girls separately, into three classes: the three- to eight-year-olds in one group (named the "Mickeys") and the nine- to twelve-year-olds ("Les Chamois") and the thirteen- to sixteen-year-olds ("Le Grande") in the two other groups. Two girls and two boys from the older age class helped in taking care of the younger children.

Alex's firm leadership provided important comfort and reassurance. I never talked politics with Alex — I had little to say — but according to some of the children he was an avowed socialist. From what little I knew, it seemed he had the perfect opportunity to practice what he preached.

Aside from politics, he was intent on giving us more responsibility, implicitly trusting we would rise to every challenge. He established relationships with the area farmers, appealing to their sense of charity in an ongoing effort to coax badly-needed, reasonably-priced food and supplies from them. His agronomic training must have helped. He managed to obtain an ongoing supply of corn meal along with intermittent supplies of milk, eggs, and butter.

He took pleasure in promoting communal activities of every sort. Among the memorable ones were the special baths we took to relieve our skin sores.

A local doctor had advised Alex to treat our ongoing affliction with hot sulfur baths, and somehow, he was able to scrounge up three huge steel tubs, more like vats, along with sulfur. Glora Schlesinger and several of us girls heated buckets of water over the fireplace in the "kitchen." It took us more than two hours to prepare the baths.

The truly objectionable part of the bathing, apart from the foul smell of the sulfur, was that each tub of water was supposed to serve fifteen or twenty children. On different evenings, girls and boys had their turns. That was fine for those who were at the head of the line, but by the time the fifth or sixth girl got to the tub, the surface of the filthy, sulfured water had white scabs floating on it. We developed elaborate competitions and games to determine the order in which we would bathe by spinning a stick attached to a board. Needless to say, many arguments broke out about whether the stick was pointing at this one or that one, but we worked it out.

I was usually nauseated by the time it was my turn. Yet Elka Frank coaxed each of us into the tub, telling us, "Your skin will feel better, I promise." Yes, my skin did feel better for one or two days, but that hardly seemed long enough to compensate for the experience.

With Alex in charge, we were able to relax much more than we had with Uncle Gaspar, and we grew closer as a group. Several of the children were amazingly talented. Hanni Schlimmer, one of my roommates in Brussels, whom I had known as a skinny, chatty girl, turned out to be a talented artist. On one of the inside walls of our main building she sketched large colorful drawings of Mickey Mouse, Porky Pig, and Felix the Cat. Where she obtained the marvelously bright red, yellow, and blue paint I didn't know.

Edith Goldapper was another flighty adolescent with special abilities. Despite being only fifteen, her thick eyeglasses, high-pitched voice, and busy-body demeanor made her seem a much older woman. Nevertheless, she loved to organize performances of skits and plays that diverted our attention from the difficulties of daily life.

She took the lead in putting together poems, scripts, and roasts. She helped organize one roast, in honor of Elka Frank's twenty-sixth birthday, that had everyone hysterical with laughter. Among Elka's other peculiarities, Edith managed to capture her way of looking skyward and the way she dominated Alex. Something may be lost in the translation from German, but here are some of the lines:

> One celebrates a phenomenon today,
> By a famous astronomer . . .
> The stars are magnificent so
> One doesn't need a telescope,
> The view goes on endlessly
> Looking for new stars.
> But watch out,
> Because when she continues in this vein,
> She will end up
> Like "Hans-guck-in-die Luft" (Hans look up in the air).
> At the table she screams, "Behave yourselves!"
> The girls listen, amused,
> And the more she screams,
> The noisier they get . . .
> She loves to fish to make cod liver oil
> And holds a record in fishing.
> Where shall she get the fish now?
> She fishes in the pots and pans.
> But which fish does she catch now?

There is no sign of any fish.
She fishes for beans in the water;
One has to get used to that.
But when Mr. Frank comes home,
All the beans have been eaten.
She tells us in no uncertain terms
That he shouldn't be told about it.
As a housekeeper she excels,
A Viennese cook first-class . . .
Salted water is not only in the ocean,
But it gets served as gravy in Seyre . . .
But since it is her birthday today,
We congratulate her and wish her the best,
And hope that she will continue to
Swing her cooking spoon always happily!

Elka took it all in good style, laughing at the barbs. She was a very decent person. Unfortunately, after our arrival at Seyre, she experienced ever-worsening stomach problems, and her birthday was no exception. No one could figure out what caused her chronic pain and nausea, although based on my nurse's training, I would now guess that she was suffering from Crohn's disease or colitis. She felt miserable even when she was able to eat such luxuries as eggs and jam. Most of the time she endured the pain but, as time went on, she sometimes lay in bed for days.

Relaxation

T HE OLDEST group of children took turns doing the chores of cooking, cleaning, and laundry. This took care of the morning hours. Between the hours of 1 and 3 P.M. everyone took siesta, and for very good reason: The summer climate of southern France was extremely hot. One village custom was to drink red wine with lunch and during much of the day, since the well water had to be boiled before drinking and red wine was nearly as plentiful as water. During our first few weeks, local farmers laughed when they learned we were boiling water and very generously gave us wine as a substitute.

So not long after Alex Frank took charge, we were drinking wine with our lunch, and plenty of it because of the unaccustomed heat. Lying down after lunch was my greatest pleasure of the day. I have never again been able to feel so comfortably drowsy, day after day.

The few adults with us had enough worries trying to get us fed and taken care of that they had little time to devote to our individual well-being. Everyone was glad the little ones slept so well in the afternoon and the older ones did not grow restless. This blissful living went on for about six weeks. Then one day, near the end of the summer, we were out of wine and the farmers had no more for us. The Germans occupied northern France and all food was being rationed, above all, wine.

Now, in the midst of my misery, I understand I had discovered an escape — and a link to Papa. I remember those hot summer afternoons and that "comfortably drowsy" feeling. I don't know why drinking wine later in life didn't produce the same results, but I kept searching out new tranquilizers and painkillers to achieve them. Nothing worked like that red wine in an old barn in a tiny French village. Maybe because the pain had moved too deeply into my being.

In any event, three other adults are worth mentioning. The first two were Mademoiselle Lea and Monsieur Leon, both Belgian. The former helped tend to us in Brussels and was single. Monsieur Leon helped in the boys' home. He told us he was married and had a seven-year-old son. He was tall and skinny with a dark mustache, and he always wore knicker-bockers. If our life in Seyre was summer camp, they were the counselors for le Grande and organized our games and get-togethers. They taught us an amazing number of songs and delighted in discussing intricate political and social situations, though I grasped little of their meaning.

But their activities extended beyond the political arena. A number of us kept running into Monsieur Leon at night on our way to the outhouse, which was behind the girls' sleeping rooms and on the same path leading to Mademoiselle Lea's room. He invariably ducked at each unwelcome encounter.

The oddest thing about Mademoiselle Lea's behavior was its unbelievable hypocrisy. One of her notable acts, aside from leading us in games and other such activities, was to set us straight about our co-ed environment. Not long after we arrived in Seyre, over the space of several afternoons, she called each of us teenage girls into her room for a "private" discussion. She cleverly asked each girl to promise not to divulge the substance of the meeting to anyone else so that word wouldn't spread to the younger children or the boys.

"You must know that boys can be very aggressive," she said, opening our private discussion. "They can be especially aggressive with girls in ways that are not appropriate. You must be on your guard, and must avoid leading them on, and discourage them if they try to take advantage." She looked at me as if to try to determine whether I comprehended her barely cloaked message. I must have nodded or otherwise looked as if I understood, because she quickly concluded, "Not that I am worried about you, Inge. I know you are very responsible."

One day, Mademoiselle Lea and Monsieur Leon departed, without even a good-bye. Now all the non-Jews were gone. That left the rest of us — truly a small tribe of wandering Jews. I was quite fond of Mademoiselle Lea and Monsieur Leon, but I had learned to avoid becoming emotionally attached to them so that when the inevitable day of their departure arrived, I would be prepared. Now there were just five adults: the Franks; our cook Glora Schlesinger, her husband Ernste, a kind of handyman, and Elias Haskelevich, our part-time handyman in Brussels and provider of champagne the previous Rosh Hashanah.

Maybe because of his Russian origins, Haskelevich spoke French and German with a peculiar accent. He was about forty to forty-five years old and bald. In spite of his looks, his bearing was very youthful. He wasn't especially disciplined about schedules, but he did keep in good shape by participating in our activities — sawing wood, carrying pails of water, starting cooking fires, and bicycling each day to a neighboring village nineteen kilometers away to fetch supplies. He also amused us with his endless stories, such as those about his days as a student in Russia and later in Austria, when there was "real discipline." His strange encounter with Jacques Roth was quickly forgotten and he was equally popular with the boys and girls, because we felt he really liked us. Also, he was the only person available with whom we could discuss anything important to us.

Haskelevich endured our privations better than perhaps anyone else. While we all smelled of the barnyard from infrequent bathing, Haskelevich smelled of a flowery cologne. And where our group was totally destitute, eking out a subsistence dependent on government handouts and charitable farmers, Haskelevich had an endless supply of cigarettes enabling him to continue chain-smoking.

Yet he had sensitivity, too. I remember one day when the two of us were hauling water from the well, he inquired casually about my parents. I told him about Papa's arrest and expulsion from Germany and how Mutti was still there trying to arrange an exit.

"Your mother must be very persistent," he said, tending to the cigarette perched between his lips as he tried to keep from spilling precious water. "No one wants the Jews in their country. She and your father will need to be creative. I'm sure he'll try to work with your relatives in New York to get you and your mother out."

It had been so long since I confided in an adult and received a sincere and gentle response. I just hoped he wouldn't suddenly disappear, at least for a while. I doubted he would leave, though, because he was Jewish and there weren't too many other places for him to go. Also, our community afforded him a more important role than he likely had ever had before. From what I could determine, he had held a variety of low-level clerical jobs before the war.

Sometime during this late-summer period shortly after the non-Jewish adults departed, my older cousin, Hilde Loeb from Darmstadt, appeared briefly on the scene. She arrived with a tall, handsome man, Walter Lieberg, who would eventually become her husband. They were on their way to Lyon, from where they hoped to depart to the United States. Hilde must have had good reasons for me not to accompany her, because I know she would have tried to help if she could. I also believe that by this time I was so discouraged about the possibility of emigrating that I didn't take rejection as personally as I did when Papa rebuffed me. Hilde did say she'd try to send word to Mutti about my whereabouts. She also promised she wouldn't tell Mutti about how horrible our living conditions were. Mail service had ended by this time, so I gave Hilde this letter to mail to Lilo:

August 11, 1940

My dearest Lotti [I sometimes called her Lotti, also short for Liselotte],

I hope you are well and that Hilde has been able to get this letter to you. I await mail from you anxiously, though it seems that little or nothing is getting through at the moment. Can you imagine, it is already four months since I last heard from you. How are you? Are you still with the same family, and do you still go to school? Please write me extensively because you can hardly imagine how happy it would make me to get mail from you. I have heard nothing from Mutti or Papa, or from Gustav.

Could you do something, anything, for my immigration? It is terribly difficult to get a visa from here to go to Portugal. Then I would need the American visa to go by boat to you. I have almost no hope at all anymore to come to you. Do you have any news from Mutti and Papa?

I have heard that Kent (England) has to be emptied of all foreigners, so Papa is probably no longer at his old address. I don't have hope at all that Papa is not interned. If he really is in a camp that would be terrible; someone would need to help him at once. Perhaps you could find out his address. We left Brussels in such a hurry that I didn't take any addresses along, otherwise I would already have written to Aunt Selma in New York.

I haven't heard from Mutti for more than three months. I hope that in a few days I can write directly a card to her. Please inform Mutti right away that I am well and give her my address. Those poor parents, neither of them know how and where the other one is, or where their children are. Mutti was supposed to receive her visa last September after Papa received his in July.

Here everything is covered with lice and fleas. It seems that all of France is filled with lice and fleas since all the refugees have arrived. Fortunately, I don't have any of either right now; I put all kinds of stuff on my head, petroleum and other stuff, so that I don't get any. Lilo, you cannot imagine conditions here!

We are told that we may eventually go to a different part of France and then we probably will have to work in the fields. Can you imagine what that means for me? I had envisioned my future so much differently. I want to work, but I want to work in a profession. Being a secretary is now out of the question for me. Now I am thinking perhaps I will be a baby nurse. If all that is lost now, can you imagine how I feel?

Now I have to close. We get once a month a ration card and are not allowed to have money. Please don't send anything.

My dear Lilo, I kiss you and send you love,

Inge

Curiosity

HASKELEVICH'S FAVORITE child was the youngest member of our tribe, three-year-old Manfred Manasse. He saw to it that Manfred received all the milk he needed and any choice morsels available. For some reason, Manfred still wet his bed and pants sometimes. On such occasions, Haskelevich held Manfred in his arms and reproached him angrily: "You are a little pig!" Manfred wasn't about to be insulted in front of us all. His response? "You are a big pig!" That line became a standard refrain among us.

Manfred's bed-wetting problem gave me rare opportunities to look beyond my own misery and help relieve the misery of others, even if only in small ways. More significantly, I realize now, the bed-wetting problem sowed the seeds of my relationship with Walter Strauss.

One morning, while I was helping to supervise the youngest children, I noticed Manfred innocently playing a game with several other children in a field behind the goat barn. The children from les Chamois, the middle group, were staring at him, covering their mouths to keep from laughing. Someone had taped a hand-written sign to his back: *"Je suis un pisseur"* (I am a pisser).

I nonchalantly grabbed the sign from his back and tore it up. I was about to ask the group who had played such a mean trick, but I quickly realized no one would tell me, and so I never did discover the culprit.

But my action caused a ripple effect. In our small group, where gossip was nearly as valuable as food, word about the sign spread instantaneously. Inge H. was terribly upset by the incident because she had a secret she had shared with me: She had a bed-wetting problem. I became aware of it in Brussels when one morning shortly after my attic incident, I commented about the smell of urine in our room. She was the only other person there and turned beet-red. "Please don't say anything," she pleaded as she tore her bed apart and pulled off the stained sheet. She told me she had suffered this problem occasionally since she had left home some months earlier. I felt terrible for her and agreed to keep her situation confidential.

Later during the day of Manfred's sign incident, I discovered Inge H. sitting under a tree behind the main building. "My problem has started again," she said, through tears. "I'm so afraid it's going to get worse now, and everyone will find out. If they put a sign on a three-year-old, what will they do to me?"

I reassured Inge H. her secret was safe and I would try to help her keep the problem from public view. But what to do about Manfred? Jacques Roth, the boy who fought with Haskelevich, came up with an interesting idea.

As a group of us older children sat around after dinner one evening, Jacques said, "What if I offer Manfred the opportunity to sleep in my bed for a few nights? My guess is that he'd be so honored to sleep with the older boys he wouldn't dare risk the humiliation of wetting the bed."

Walter Strauss challenged Jacques. "If you are wrong, then the humiliation would be complete, and he might never be cured of his problem."

I found myself studying Walter as he spoke. On this fall evening of 1940, for the first time I took serious note of him. Yes, I had seen him around. It was impossible not to notice Walter, since he seemed to be everywhere at once — hauling water, gathering wood, helping Alex lay hose from the well to our kitchen. And when Alex's mother, Irene, requested assistance teaching math and science to the younger children, Walter was one of the first to volunteer.

Because Walter simply did things without congratulating himself or otherwise calling attention to his efforts, it was easy to take him for granted. I believe that is what I did, because I have no recollection of the first time I saw him. He was just there and everywhere.

But that evening at dinner, I became consciously aware of his special presence. He was slight of build with straight black hair, a mop of which sometimes fell over his forehead and into his eyes. His soft, boyish features and freckles made him look even younger than his fifteen years. Maybe that was why I was startled when he made intelligent, mature observations.

Also startling were my fascination with, and feelings for, Walter. I had never really thought too much about specific boys, but on this evening, for the first time, I felt a kinship and admiration — an attraction — for Walter.

Anyway, despite Walter's counterarguments, Jacques decided to go ahead with his plan for Manfred. He had been acting like a big brother to the little boy, especially since the incident with Uncle Gaspar and Haskelevich, and he was convinced that Manfred would rise to the occasion. Manfred, of course, was thrilled to spend time with the big boys. Nobody mentioned anything about wet beds, and all of us arose the next morning holding our breaths. Jacques came in to breakfast with the good news: Manfred had stayed dry all night.

As a reward for his accomplishment, Manfred got to sleep in Jacques' sleeping area again. And once again, he succeeded. By the end of a week, Manfred returned to his own sleeping area, full of confidence. He never again had a problem.

I found myself feeling not only good about this particular turn of events, but also more positive in general about our lives. Not only had we accomplished something important, but suddenly Walter was more prominent in my life, or at least in my mind. I found myself watching him and increasingly admiring him. He demonstrated wisdom and maturity beyond his years.

Once, in the kitchen, Walter happened to hear Frau Schlesinger complaining to Alex there was so little milk that trying to spread it around to one hundred children made each serving meaningless. "Why not just give the youngest children the milk?" asked Walter. "They need it more than the rest of us anyway." Alex took the suggestion.

Walter spent hours teaching mathematics to the middle group of children. He always found clever ways to motivate them. One day he promised to teach them to play chess after they completed their lesson; they were so excited they learned quickly and then raced to complete their assignments.

I shouldn't make him out to be a saint, though, because he wasn't. His endless willingness to give of himself made him impatient with those he felt weren't doing likewise, sometimes too impatient. I recall how he challenged Inge Berlin, one of the older girls among us at seventeen. Inge, very serious and religious, had only joined us in Brussels for the train ride south. One of her responsibilities in Seyre was delivering food from the kitchen to our "infirmary," a room in a building down the main street where the sickest young children could lie undisturbed. Walter was convinced she was taking some of the food for herself and told her so. She tearfully denied his allegations. While most of the children believed Walter — already, he was clearly a leader — I was uncertain. Inge struck me as an honest person. We never did learn more, and fortunately, that controversy quickly faded away.

Though Walter and I often spent time together, mostly in groups, we rarely spoke. We worked together during the day and often sat together after dinner, but for the most part, the boys and the girls didn't really mix. Individual relationships between boys and girls still hadn't formed, and I think that was due to our preoccupation with survival. But also, most of the teenagers were still quite young, and we felt shy and awkward. I know I did.

As summer turned to fall, our lives assumed a certain routine. The village idiot proved to be a continuous delight. Apparently, only we had enough time and energy to enter into his silly game. He looked awful — small of stature with a horrible-looking face topped by a swollen nose, which he rubbed as he shouted: "Eh château, eh château!" We had to answer him by shouting back the same.

Vast fields of corn and potatoes and lovely, sloping vineyards surrounded our living quarters. During our long walks, we discovered fields covered with blackberries. These were not the regular bushes I knew from Germany but low-growing plants holding the sweetest berries I had ever tasted. We spent hours picking these blackberries, which became an important side dish with our meals. One day Ruth and I discovered a group of trees with delicious-tasting fruits that turned out to be fresh, ripe figs. I had never tasted anything but dried figs, so this was a rare treat.

Dread also filled these fruit-picking exercises, however. As the days of fall 1940 grew shorter and the nights colder, we realized obtaining food was going to present an ever-greater challenge. Thanks to the demands being made by the German occupiers to the north, the local farmers had less and less to offer Alex. And the blackberries and figs steadily disappeared from the landscape.

Alex started taking the older children on walks through the surrounding woods to look for thistle and chestnuts. Of course, thistle grew everywhere, but it was prickly. "There's always at least one place on the plant that is a bit less prickly," Alex coached us. "Grab it there, and don't let go."

And what happened to the thistle? Why, it went into vegetable soup, of course. One of Frau Schlesinger's scrumptious recipes. Sometimes, we ate the vegetable soup as a main course with bread, and sometimes we ate it as an appetizer to a chestnut or corn meal stew. The not-so-funny joke was that if you bit into a sweet-tasting chestnut, you were biting into one with a worm. Occasionally, Alex found us a few eggs. But what should have been a special treat disgusted most of us because he insisted we eat the eggs raw. "When they are raw, you get the full nutrition," he argued. "With so little to eat, we must take advantage of every bit of food."

But the question on everyone's mind didn't concern our autumn diet. What, we all worried, would we eat when the thistle and chestnuts had disappeared?

Gratitude

D URING THE FALL of 1940, we continued to live in total isolation. None of us were in contact with our parents, whether they lived in Germany, Belgium, England, or northern France, because the postal services were censored and extremely slow or nonexistent if one didn't know the exact address of one's family. Our families were often on the move, either trying to stay a step ahead of the Germans or being herded by the Germans from ghetto to ghetto, or to a concentration camp. The last I heard from Mutti, just before we departed Brussels, Darmstadt's Jews were being expelled from their homes and forced to live in smaller and smaller neighborhoods. The tiny apartment Mutti and I shared now housed Mutti and four of her relatives. More people would likely follow into the cramped quarters, unless that neighborhood was declared off-limits for Jews. In that case, Mutti would have to move, and I presumed she already had.

Each afternoon, during what had been our mail time in Brussels, an empty feeling overcame me. No longer could I look forward to any letters.

In October, mail finally began to appear again and even then only intermittently. But it was enough to let us know that things were even more bleak in the world we had left behind than in our world. I corresponded initially only with Lilo, who sent me an August letter she had received from Mutti. She had received word from Lilo, before my August letter sent via Hilde, that I was okay. However, Mutti had neither any inkling about the nature of my circumstances nor knowledge of Gustav's whereabouts. She assumed I was with Gustav, not an unreasonable assumption. She remained as desperate as ever to escape Germany. In her letter to Lilo, Mutti wrote:

Darmstadt, August 26, 1940

My dear Lilo,

On Friday I received your letter of 8 August, and you can imagine how happy I was that you heard from dear Inge and Hilde. The main thing is that the dear child is well. I hope you will be successful in bringing Inge to America. It would be greatly calming for me. I have hopes that the Committee will help.

I have not yet contacted Robert about my passage. I heard that new regulations will be made, but the American consulate does not call anyone at this time. I hope that my papers are in order now. Perhaps Robert will give an affidavit for Inge, but then he has to take care of her. I cannot mix into anything from here — I hope you will do it right and, most important, that you will be successful. When you write to Inge give her my best greetings. I hope she is well taken care of and that she has enough clothing, etc. I am very happy that Hilde is nearby and takes care of Inge, and Inge can go to her with any problems.

Dear Lilo, you know that I had been receiving DM 200 (Deutschmarks) every month from Gustav. For the last few months I received nothing; perhaps it would be possible for Inge to ask Gustav to continue to send me the money. It would be a great help for me, because then I could pay many things when I will be leaving here, such as railroad ticket to the boat, baggage. Perhaps Gustav can see to it that I will continue to get the money.

Did you get mail from Papa? I am glad that you are reasonable about your boyfriend; don't let anyone turn your head, and don't go out so often with him. Write to me once about your school. This week I received a card from you dated April 19, so slowly the mail comes in. So please, dear Lilo, confide in me what is in your heart. Give best greetings to Inge and Hilde. She should not worry about us.

Many kisses, Mutti

In certain respects, I realized, I was better off not having any news. In Seyre the war news that reached us sounded grim and very much in favor of Nazi Germany. Having to deal as a group with so much uncertainty helped keep us well behaved teenagers, I am convinced — but we probably became more serious and thoughtful than would have been normal for our age.

I drew closer to my best friends, Ruth and Dela. Ruth was dark-haired, solidly built, but pretty all the same — amazingly independent in her thinking and much more mature in her outlook than the rest of the girls. She had become ever more of a committed Zionist as a result of her Sunday afternoon program in Brussels; her ambition was to eventually live in Palestine.

Dela was the opposite of Ruth. She was of slighter build and the product of a sheltered family life. She was interested in the simple things and pleasures of life. She took our primitive living conditions much harder than Ruth or I — perhaps because she was more optimistic and sensitive. Dela and I sometimes talked for hours about our past family lives, and in Dela's eyes, we would eventually resume these lives with few changes.

On the one hand, Dela wasn't especially smart or intellectual; on the other hand, she was much more open with her feelings than I was. She regularly bemoaned our fate while I tried to minimize the problems, even though I secretly agreed. I must say, though, I was not naive enough to expect we would pick up with our former lives.

The endless conversations she and I had about our growing-up years helped pass the long afternoon rest times. Since each of us was a second child, we played a "can-you-top-this" game and compared tales of older-sister abuse — and how we got even. I entertained Dela with stories about the fun I had swiping Lilo's bicycle. Dela's story of sweet revenge stayed with me. She loved dolls, but when her older sister, Gisele, once received an exquisite hand-made doll for her birthday, she refused to allow Dela even to hold it. Gisele sat in front of Dela, dressing and undressing the doll, humming with pleasure for hours on end.

But Dela got even: One day she swiped the doll and hid it. Dela denied her sister's accusations — even when Gisele tearfully recruited her mother and father to pressure Dela. For several days, Gisele begged Dela to tell what she had done with her doll. Finally, Dela agreed to look for it, but first she extracted a promise that if she found the doll, Gisele would share it. A few days later, Dela "found" the doll deep in her sister's closet. She remembered her own collection of dolls — even their names — and she took joy in describing their pretty, handmade outfits in infinite detail.

One topic of conversation, however, gradually dwarfed everything else: food. Our biggest worry with each passing day was whether there would be enough to eat. To compensate for our empty stomachs, we found ourselves conversing endlessly about the food of our early childhoods. Dela loved to talk about the special dinners her mother cooked for her (since there were so few foods that Dela enjoyed). Sometimes Ruth joined our conversations and recalled the wonderful Shabbat dinners she had enjoyed with her sisters and parents. For her family, much more observant than mine, the Sabbath was a time of family togetherness and discussion about Palestine. Ruth's father read several Yiddish newspapers in order to keep himself apprised of events there.

"What I would give to smell the chicken roasting in the oven for Shabbat dinner," Ruth dreamed. "And the noodle pudding was so rich. Sometimes, for tea, my grandmother made a linzer torte. I can still taste the raspberry jam."

I, too, could imagine, and nearly taste, the foods they described. And because we were hungry so often, the descriptions nearly drove me crazy. But I never told them to stop, and sometimes I contributed my own recollections of succulent roasts, along with my favorite meal: Jagerfrühstuck (hunter's breakfast), a kind of omelet of scrambled eggs, fried potatoes, and sausage.

DURING THE LATE FALL of 1940, we experienced a stroke of luck. The Swiss Red Cross, whose offices were located in Toulouse, about forty kilometers northwest, heard about our difficulties and, at Alex's instigation, decided to assume responsibility for us. I don't know what would have become of us otherwise, but we all realized that we owed our immediate survival to them.

Little did I anticipate the lessons in power and compromise we would encounter down the road. But at that especially difficult point in time, Alex Frank had pulled off a huge coup by obtaining the support of the Swiss Red Cross. Many of the children disliked him, his wife Elka, and his mother Irene for their various idiosyncrasies, but as I saw it, the fact that he willingly sacrificed his own authority for our welfare demonstrated his true colors. He could have continued his personal efforts to obtain handouts on our behalf, and probably we could have continued our subsistence existence for a while longer. But he clearly saw the handwriting on the wall — the shortages created by the war would squeeze us unmercifully.

I understood the significance of Alex's decision the first time I saw Maurice Dubois, the head of Secours Suisse aux Enfants (Swiss Red Cross for Children) office in Toulouse. He drove up to our dusty outpost in a bright red Bugatti. In our poor village of Seyre, the sleek, French sports car couldn't have stood out more if it had come from another planet. And Maurice himself was quite a sight. He must have been six feet tall, but his erect posture made him appear even taller. He was dressed in an elegant, beige wool suit with knickerbockers — the first man I had seen in suit and tie since seeing Gustav more than six months earlier. Noting his wavy blond hair and sharp Nordic features, Dela turned to me as we watched him chatting on the street with Alex and observed in a loud whisper, "He looks like a movie star." She had no argument from me.

Certainly the contrast between Maurice and Alex couldn't have been more stark. There was no mistaking the debonair man from the city for Alex, the disheveled, vacant-eyed refugee. Whatever understanding Maurice and Alex arrived at produced immediate, tangible results. What a welcome change to suddenly have powdered eggs and huge wheels of cheese from Switzerland. And that was only the beginning. One day in late November, several wooden crates appeared. The assorted used jackets and coats filling the crates arrived just in time for winter. The boys, unlike the girls, had left Brussels literally with only the shirts on their backs. But we all needed more clothing.

While the food and clothing were welcome, our lives were still far from luxurious. We weren't hungry as often as we had been earlier in the fall, but neither were we eating eggs every morning or meat roasts at dinner. Corn meal continued to be our staple, but now Frau Schlesinger had more ways to dress it up.

The price for this largesse? I had just turned fifteen in September, and already I was a cynic. Unfortunately, I had been around enough adults to know they rarely give you anything for free. Since we had no money, the price would need to be extracted in some other form, right? And indeed, the first payment in our debt of gratitude came due very shortly with the approaching Christmas holiday.

About once a week, Dubois stopped by to check with Alex about our needs and to discuss what the Red Cross might supply. One day early in December, immediately following Dubois' departure, Alex called about thirty of the older children together. He wanted to tell us about "a potentially sensitive situation."

The Swiss Red Cross, it seemed, was intent on providing us with a "real" Christmas that would include gifts and, far more important, a special meal. Alex couldn't say what exactly the meal would be. but I'm sure that, like me, all the other children had visions of such forgotten treats as wiener schnitzel, roasted chicken, potatoes, and even pastries.

One of the girls, Lotte Nussbaum, brought us all back to earth. Lotte, my companion when Haskelevich sprang his Rosh Hashanah champagne treat in Brussels, was a couple of years older than I and, though pretty with blond-brown hair, painfully shy. She had just re-joined us in Seyre. Although she lived with us at the Home Général Bernheim for a short time, she had been living with a family in Brussels when the Germans attacked in May. Somehow Lotte managed to get to France on her own and was held in a French refugee camp for several months until Alex found her, got her released from the camp, and brought her to live with us in Seyre.

"For us, as Jews, to celebrate Christmas and the birth of Jesus would be a sacrilege," she said as forcefully as her soft voice would allow. Despite her shyness, she continued. "Why," she asked, looking directly at Alex, "don't we celebrate our own holidays? We have such beautiful holidays. You never even mention our holidays."

I was startled by Lotte's outburst and amazed by her eloquence. Moreover, I realized with a start I hadn't even given a thought to Yom Kippur or Rosh Hashanah, the holiest Jewish days. They had passed two or three months earlier without our notice.

Ruth spoke up. "We owe it to ourselves and to our families to try our best to remember our Jewish heritage."

Ruth had been our only Jewish conscience until the moment Lotte stood up. In the evenings, after dinner, Ruth taught us the Israeli folk songs she learned in Brussels. And from time to time, she organized Friday evening services which, during the summer, we held in a grassy area out back. We recited the Sh'ma, the Kiddush, and a few other prayers. Usually ten or fifteen children joined in. For me, those services provided a special, warm feeling, a reprieve from our steady focus on survival.

Apparently, our infrequent services had had little impact on most of the children. The opponents vociferously denounced Lotte and Ruth. One of the boys insisted just because we were taking gifts and eating good food didn't mean we were becoming Christians.

Inge Berlin sealed the matter. Despite her run-in with Walter Strauss over her delivery of food to the infirmary, she was highly respected as a serious-minded person. Her devout background may have lent her additional credibility. "We can feel in our hearts any religion we want," she argued. "Laws about food and religion are neither necessary, nor possible here. We cannot follow them anyway. Besides, Christmas is a civil festival that is special for children. I think also it's quite possible that if we reject their generosity we might insult the people who are trying to help us."

I didn't comment because I had mixed feelings. Many of the arguments Inge Berlin and others presented sounded to me like well-crafted rationalizations to justify our lack of Jewish observance, not to mention everyone's desire for a good meal. Still, I couldn't see letting ourselves get overwrought about a Christmas dinner. We had so many matters to worry us. Since when could we afford the luxury of making idealistic pretensions about our religion?

We never took a formal vote but the consensus was clear: We would welcome the Swiss Red Cross celebration. Still, I must admit that the decision made me uncomfortable. It was as if we had sold our souls, or at least a part of our souls. It wasn't quite Faustian, but the story of Faust's deal with the devil did cross my mind. Even today, I am ashamed because I realize now our decision that December day in 1940 was the first step down a slippery slope toward abandoning our religious faith, not only for us as a group, but for me personally. Wasn't our religious faith the reason we had been condemned in the first place? And wouldn't holding onto it be a way to fight the tyrants?

A few days before Christmas, Alex and several of the older boys marched into the woods and cut down a tall pine tree that they hauled back to the dining room. We all helped decorate it with a metal star and small wooden hearts painted red and blue, all sent by Dubois.

The day before Christmas, Dubois and his American-born wife, Eleanor, arrived with a few other adults from Toulouse. After smiling and inspecting the tree, they unloaded one hundred small packages wrapped in white tissue paper from their bags and placed them under the tree. Alex wrote a child's name on each package and lit candles that he placed on special holders attached to the branches. Late in the afternoon, with dusk settling quickly on our village, he summoned the rest of the children with a bell. Everyone gazed in awe at the beautiful spectacle of candles lighting the pine tree, but when the young children began to finger the packages, Alex shooed them away.

Our next payment to the Swiss Red Cross came due on that Christmas Eve, when Dubois gave a talk which extolled Jesus and indirectly criticized Jews. "This is a special time of the year. We pray that we might have the strength and goodness of Jesus Christ. I know that not everyone worships Jesus Christ, and that includes many of you here. But even if you don't worship him, you would do well to learn about his kindness and goodness and try to make him part of your lives. That is part of what we do at the Swiss Red Cross. We try to build Jesus Christ into our daily lives. If more of the world followed his teachings, we wouldn't have the terrible things going on in the world that we see today. I pray for all of you. And now I hope you will enjoy the celebration we have put together for you."

While our reward wasn't the wiener schnitzel and kartoffelcharlotte we all fantasized about, what followed was a very nice meal: special black and white sausages, which Dubois told us are called "blood sausages," mashed potatoes, and apple sauce. For dessert there were poached apples and pears and even a selection of pastries from Toulouse. And we were all allowed to eat as much as we wanted. And eat we did. Most of us had two or three helpings of everything. It was as if I were trying to eat enough for the next few weeks and months when I feared there wouldn't be enough. Everyone was so absorbed in the food no one stopped to talk.

Having a full stomach improved everyone's mood considerably and after we had stuffed ourselves, Dubois and his wife led us in song. One of the older girls stepped forward to play a Bach cantata on her flute, and later we all joined in singing "O Tannenbaum." The only sour note, so to speak, came when Dubois invited Lotte to sing "Silent Night."

"I understand you have a beautiful voice," he said.

I wondered whether perhaps Alex tipped him off about Lotte's opposition to the Christmas celebration. Lotte, after all, was no more talented a singer than any of several children. In any event, Lotte refused with an emphatic "No!" She did, however, maintain a semblance of cordiality. Inclining her head, she said softly, "This is the first time I have participated in a Christmas celebration and I want to thank you for helping provide it."

My efforts to eat enough for the next few weeks proved correctly motivated. That celebration provided the most pleasant memories we would have for quite a while. Almost immediately after Christmas, winter weather moved in with ferocity. The local farmers told us that year's winter was considerably colder than is normal in that southernmost area of France. We had heavy snows and temperatures fell below freezing.

Except for the kitchen with its fireplace, no other buildings had any heat. To conserve wood for the fireplace, Alex ordered us to be in bed by 8 P.M. Each of us had one rough wool blanket. That sufficed during the cool fall nights, but in that terrible winter, one blanket wasn't nearly enough. To keep warm, we girls slept in groups of three, wearing our winter coats and sweaters, wrapping our feet in old newspaper, and covering ourselves with our three blankets.

I slept with Dela and Ruth. Oh, how we froze. In the morning, when we awoke in the dim winter light, we could see our breath. My hands and feet were always cold.

Sometime during January 1941, Ruth, several other girls, and I came down with terrible fevers, apparently the result of jaundice. We could do nothing but lie in our sleeping areas, chilled with fever. The stronger girls took turns caring for us and bringing hot soup.

Being so sick seemed almost like being on the freight train again. Day and night blended together as I slept and hallucinated. I believe an entire week went by before my fever finally broke and I began to feel like myself again. But toward what outcome?

Giving

A s MISERABLE as life was for us, I found myself feeling gradually less sorry for myself as the winter wore on. I was still numb in a certain sense — I knew I didn't belong here in southern France but, rather, in the United States or England. But I was learning that, as difficult as my life was, it was even more difficult for the Jews who were being sent to concentration camps. Here, in early 1941, regular mail delivery was finally being restored, so some of the children were able to make contact with their families. I still heard nothing from Mutti, aside from occasional letters she wrote to Lilo that Lilo forwarded to me, and in those she divulged little about life in Darmstadt, preferring instead to focus on the rest of the family.

February 13, 1941

My dear Lilo,

I am happy that you spent nice days in New York with Papa. In the meantime, I received several letters from him and it seems he got used to everything, but his work seems to be rather hard. Dear Lilo, wouldn't it be better for you if you would stay in Chicago for the time being, as you say that living and working conditions are better there than in New York? But do only that which Papa wants you to do. Do you already have a job prospect? Does the Committee still pay for you? And where would Inge live if she comes to the U.S.?

I am presently taking a course learning how to iron, mostly

men's shirts and laundry. Next I shall take a course in spot cleaning. I am studying my English, but it is not yet very good.

Does Papa still eat his meals at Aunt Erna's, or was that only in the beginning? Is his clothing adequate, since he took only old things with him?

Today we have real spring weather after much cold, and I am writing you with the windows open. Mrs. Oppenheimer has died — in a hospital in Frankfurt. Her husband, who never paid much attention to her, carries on terribly now. All of a sudden his eyes are opened.

This week I sent a telegram to Papa because Stuttgart needs his earnings statement. I need to go grocery shopping now, so I am closing with greetings and kisses.

Mutti

P.S. I am learning how to play bridge from Doris Brill.

The idea of Mutti working as a laundress was almost as disheartening as her inquiring about where I would be living in the United States, but it was positively upbeat compared to the news other children were receiving. Walter Strauss reported that his older brother, Siegfried, had written him from a concentration camp in France, desperately seeking food and warm clothing. Another boy, Walter Kamlet, received word that his parents were in a concentration camp in Germany. Walter K., who was two or three years older than I, was our resident intellectual. He was at once arrogant and distant. He claimed he was an accomplished pianist, and who could challenge him? We had no piano. With his high forehead, narrow face, deep-sunk eyes, straight-combed-back-hair, and wire glasses, he certainly looked very much the intellectual.

As difficult as I found it to relate to Walter K., I sympathized when he approached Alex with copies of the letters he had received from his parents. "Isn't there something we can do from here? Can't we send help?"

One evening shortly after that, Alex joined a group of us after dinner and posed our dilemma: "We are hearing more and more about relatives who have been sent to special camps in France, Germany, and Poland. They have little to eat, and they need warm clothing. They are begging us for help. We have little enough ourselves, but we have more than they do. I want to hear suggestions from you about how we might help them."

The answer seemed obvious, and I immediately spoke up. "We should send them some of our things. Now that we have food from the Swiss Red Cross, we could share our marmalade, egg powder, and sugar."

Lotte Nussbaum quickly agreed. "Even though we would have less to eat, it is worth the sacrifice. We can have rice milk instead of real milk. Perhaps we can skip a meal or two. And now that we have some extra coats and long underwear, possibly we could send these as well."

At some point in the course of that discussion, I became aware of a different Walter Strauss than I had seen before. As the other children, one by one, voiced their support for my idea, I noticed Walter was watching me. And the expression on his face, a look I had never before seen, suggested both agreement and, it seemed to me, affection.

Of all the children, only two boys opposed the idea. One said, "Why should we go hungry so that people we don't even know can eat?"

His objections were quickly shouted down. "Heartless egotist," somebody scolded. "We only hope that you will never wind up in a camp and be hungry."

Before our meeting broke up, Walter stood up to voice his gratitude. "I know that many of you don't have relatives in the camps, at least not yet. I want you to know how much your sacrifices mean to me and the others who have relatives in captivity." His eyes moistened and I wondered if he was going to cry, but he didn't. A couple of his friends gave him pats on the back as our meeting broke up. Though he and I hadn't exchanged a word, I felt a sense of closeness.

The next day, instead of real milk and fresh bread, the older children ate only rice milk and stale bread for breakfast. We had our regular lunch of gruel, but we saved at dinner by eating just dried bread and water. We all felt good when, after dinner, Alex recounted to us how much we had saved. We would be able to send several pounds of powdered milk and eggs, along with some disinfectants, to relatives in camps.

We repeated our semi-fasting days several more times over the next few weeks. After about three weeks, we began to receive letters from the camp residents, thanking us profusely for our generosity. I certainly felt gratified and I know others did, too. Even Dela, who had trouble looking outside her little world, seemed touched. "I feel as if I've helped members of my own family, even though, thank God, nobody from my family has been taken to a camp."

Then, toward the end of February, the semi-fasting days came to an abrupt and unheralded halt. No one noticed right away. One afternoon, during our literature "class," I learned what happened. That winter, Alex's mother, Irene, who had been spending most of her time with the middle children, the Chamois, had begun a class in French literature for us older children. We met late afternoons and early evenings, either just before or after dinner.

We didn't have to attend the classes, but since there was little else for us to do, most of us did. We certainly didn't attend on account of Irene's teaching ability. She was very knowledgeable about and absorbed in French literature, but her teaching style was pedantic. She read long passages aloud, which she followed with her interpretation. Of course, it didn't help that we had neither books to read in advance nor a heated classroom. We sat around a long table in our winter coats. Irene's approach discouraged discussion. She responded to our attempts to discuss what she had read to us with dismissive mockery, saying, "If you had taken the time to listen . . ." or "If you had had the right preparation when you were younger. . . ."

On top of her strange teaching manner, Irene also looked funny. Her remarkably small, gray-haired head was out of proportion to her elongated body, and she was as unsmiling and humorless as her son, Alex. She had a difficult time getting the middle children to behave and pay attention, especially during the cold winter months when they were uncomfortable to begin with. Behind her back they referred to her as "Bleebla," in honor of a neighborhood cow. It didn't take long for that name to catch on with the older children as well.

One evening, she read us an essay by Molière and provided her interpretation. In response to our questions about French history, she told us about the French Revolution and how the uprising had been stimulated by the empty stomachs of the masses. When the class ended, I stayed to speak with her.

"Speaking of empty stomachs, what has happened to our fasting days?"

She looked surprised. My question had caught her off-guard. "There won't be any more fasting days," she said, her lips pursed tightly together.

"Why not?" I asked.

"I'm really not supposed to talk about it. But suffice it to say that our friends at the Swiss Red Cross didn't appreciate our sending their supplies to people in concentration camps. They told us their money should be used only for those of us here in Seyre. People in concentration camps should get support from their own organizations, whatever those might be."

"That doesn't seem right," I said. "We should be able to decide how much of our food we want to eat. The Swiss Red Cross doesn't have to spend additional money."

"Tell that to Maurice Dubois," she said angrily. "I told him proudly about your sacrifices, and he scolded me. I don't want to describe the details of our conversation, but he told me that if we want to continue to receive support from them, we'll have to play by their rules."

I suppose that was payment number two due to the Swiss Red Cross, following our Christmas payment. I told Irene's story to Ruth, and her response was decidedly pragmatic: "We have to decide which is more important, principle or food. For now, I think food is more important."

Oh, how terrible it is to be dependent on others for your very existence, especially when your benefactor is doing good things. One of the Swiss Red Cross's very important accomplishments late that winter was to help restore mail deliveries to us from our parents and relatives. I finally began receiving letters directly from Mutti. Her news was not very good — similar to what she had reported in the letters to Lilo — but at least each of us knew where the other was. Mutti had, since the February letter to Lilo, moved to an apartment in another part of Darmstadt. She didn't say much about it, preferring instead to write about the health and welfare of my grandmother, Oma Josephine, and Aunt Martha and Uncle Hermann.

Though Mutti said little about the status of Darmstadt's Jews, I had a terrible sense of impending doom based on the mailed news other children were receiving. I was almost afraid to open her letters. I had been feeling increasingly anxious and pessimistic since an incident that occurred one day at lunch. Just as I was opening a letter from Mutti, a scream pierced the room. A commotion arose around one of the children. I rushed over to see Ilse Wulff, the girl who was so sick on the train ride, lying unconscious. While Elka Frank rushed to find eau de cologne to revive her, Walter Strauss picked up the letter that lay next to her.

"Here is the problem," he said after scanning the letter. "Her mother writes that Ilse's father just died in China, and she is all alone and terrified that she'll soon die as well because conditions are so bad." Ilse was revived, but the message was clear to all of us: The war was beginning to claim our parents as victims, and things would only get worse.

Springtime

E ARLY IN February 1941, the Swiss Red Cross made available to us an old castle about seventy or eighty kilometers further south in France, not too far from the Pyrenees. It hadn't been inhabited for many years and was said to be in a dilapidated state. Rather than move all the children to live there at once, the administration decided to move most of the older boys and girls there so they could help in restoring the building. Ruth, Dela, and I were to remain in Seyre, together with four of the older boys and two adults, Elka Frank and Elias Haskelevich. We were in charge of all the Chamois and Mickeys. Alex spent most of his time at the castle, which had the intriguing name Château la Hille. He came to visit us about once a month and related the progress the boys were making. It all sounded so wonderful. They were constructing beds, one for each of us, along with tables and benches, and the girls were sewing sleeping bags and doing the cooking and laundering. The boys were also building a cistern, but it was apparently quite difficult to complete.

Life for the few of us left behind became much quieter and more enjoyable. Elka took care of the smaller children, assisted by one of us girls in the afternoons. The boys and Haskelevich took charge of procuring our food. That left Ruth, Dela, and me to do the laundry on the first two days of the week and cleaning and sewing on the other mornings.

During those months of late winter and early spring, I got to spend more time with Haskelevich. I found him fascinating because of his stories about his life in Russia and Vienna. Area farmers apparently were similarly charmed, because he was able to obtain foods that had been off-limits to Alex and the Swiss Red Cross, such as fresh milk, butter, eggs, and even wine. Sometimes he took me along on his visits to the farmers. He easily entered into any sort of conversation with them. He smoothly moved the discussion to the terms for exchange — how much of his tobacco in exchange for how many potatoes or how much maize. From these discussions, I learned many interesting things, like the best times to slaughter a pig, take a cow to a bull, harvest the corn — and who was keeping company with the rich farmer's wife up the hill when he was away at the market. On his occasional trips to the Swiss Red Cross offices in Toulouse, Haskelevich invariably returned with books like Tolstoy's *War and Peace,* Dostoevski's *Crime and Punishment,* and Victor Hugo's *Les Misérables.* One other thing I liked about Haskelevich was his closeness with Walter, whom he affectionately referred to as "my son."

There seemed to be an element of re-birth during these months of melting snow and the first scents of spring. As primitive as conditions were at Seyre, it was home, and Haskelevich was a father figure, certainly more caring and fun than Papa.

But I need to mention another very important event, because it would have huge ramifications for the lives of all of us as the Nazis' hold on Europe tightened. This important event was the arrival of our new authority figure from the Swiss Red Cross — Rösli Näf. I saw Rösli step from the passenger side of Maurice Dubois' Bugatti. It was right around Easter, and Elka Frank and I were cutting up half-rotten potatoes for the evening's dinner.

Rösli had a stern look on her fair face. Her blonde hair was pulled back in a bun. Her pale blue eyes seemed cold. Her body was solid, thanks in significant measure to her broad shoulders. And as Maurice marched her up and down the main street, she walked with a long stride, swinging her arms. She conveyed a sense of purposefulness and authority.

By the time Maurice finally brought Rösli into the kitchen and introduced her to us, I was feeling some apprehension. "I want you to meet Rösli Näf, who just joined me at the Swiss Red Cross. She is a very skilled nurse, who recently returned from working with Dr. Albert Schweitzer in Africa. She'll be able to provide much more assistance than I can."

She had a firm handshake and she wasted no time on pleasantries. "Those potatoes don't look very good," she observed, looking at the pot Elka and I had filled with the half-rotten potatoes I had helped peel. "And where are your green vegetables?"

"We haven't had green vegetables for quite a while," I said. "It's still early in the spring, and the farmers don't have green vegetables yet."

"Well, if you had started a garden early enough, we might have peas or green beans by now. Have any of you ever planted a garden?" she asked, looking in turn at Dela, Ruth, Elka, and me. We all shook our heads.

"We'll take care of that," she said, providing the first glimmer of a smile. She spoke deliberately, drawing a breath between phrases, as if she were considering each of her words with considerable care.

With that, Rösli and Maurice departed to visit the boys and girls who were preparing Château la Hille. Two days later she returned with luggage and some shovels. Almost immediately, it seemed, she had selected a small plot of land behind the main building and begun to dig up the grass and weeds to prepare the ground for planting. She recruited Dela and me, along with several of the younger children we supervised. "Here, turn over the dirt in this section," she said to me as she put a shovel into my hands. "And you, little ones, take the stones I've dug up and make a fence around our garden." There was no chitchat. Rösli was all business.

But that evening, after dinner, we saw Rösli's softer side. She sat with a group of us — Ruth, Dela, Walter, Elka, Irene, and me — and told us how events had led her to Seyre. In Zurich, she had studied to be a psychiatric nurse and, in 1934, just before she was ready to graduate, she had attended a lecture by Dr. Albert Schweitzer, the Swiss physician who had established a hospital in the Congo to care for African natives. His commitment and compassion so impressed her that she wrote him to apply for a position. She expected that years would pass before she would have the opportunity to work with him.

To her great surprise, Dr. Schweitzer, who had not yet left Switzerland, telephoned Rösli a few days later and offered her a nursing position. Upon graduation, Rösli headed for Africa, where she became the hospital's agricultural director with special responsibility for launching a productive garden. Fresh vegetables, a part of most European diets, were rare in that part of the world.

Irene was especially interested to learn Rösli's view of Dr. Schweitzer. Even then, many newspapers and magazines had run admiring articles about him. "He is as gentle, and patient, and giving as the articles suggest, at least with the patients. They are often noisy and bring many family members with them when they come to the hospital. They push, shove, and gesture wildly, especially when they don't understand what Dr.

Schweitzer is saying to them. But he never loses his temper. He just goes about his business and, in the end, whether or not they understand his explanations, they accept whatever medicine, inoculations, or surgery he prescribes.

"He works terribly hard. Sometimes he does surgery at nine or ten o'clock at night. He rarely finishes work before 11 P.M. Then, late at night, he plays Bach on his organ. Even when the music awakened me, I loved hearing him play through the tropical nights."

Rösli's garden was a big success with Dr. Schweitzer and the rest of his staff. But she had less patience with the natives than Dr. Schweitzer, and her lack of patience was a source of friction between the two. "I couldn't tolerate the behavior he tolerated," she said. "Most of the natives were not intelligent and their primitive habits upset me. They didn't bathe, so they smelled. They also lied a great deal. Sometimes, they would steal vegetables from the garden, and that, of course, upset me. But Dr. Schweitzer always had excuses for them. And whenever we caught vegetable thieves, Dr. Schweitzer simply told them they shouldn't steal again.

"Once, I caught a young man walking off with a lettuce and a melon. When I reprimanded him, he just grinned at me, and I was so enraged, I slapped him in the face. Dr. Schweitzer saw the confrontation and reprimanded me. We had a terrible argument about this. I saw that there was no changing Dr. Schweitzer. He was committed to his ways."

In the spring of 1939, Rösli took a leave of absence to return to Switzerland and when, that September, the war broke out, it was impossible for her to return to Africa. She had heard about the plight of young refugees like us in southern France and she'd offered her services to the Swiss Red Cross, which referred her to Maurice Dubois.

It didn't take me long to realize there were two sides to Rösli. She was a caring person who wanted to help the less fortunate. At the same time, however, her cold reserve allowed her to feel superior to those less fortunate. I quickly realized she regarded us with the same sort of condescension she had for the ignorant African natives.

Rösli stayed with us in Seyre for only brief periods, though, and our lives continued to be rather relaxed. Alex Frank returned every few weeks to report on the progress being made in restoring Château la Hille, about which there was a growing sense of anticipation in our group. A castle? It sounded too good to be true. Yet I was increasingly inclined to believe it, because on his visits Alex reported good progress and was genuinely pleased about moving there. Alex wasn't given over to exaggeration or false excitement. If he said it was nearly ready and that it was a big improvement over what we had, well, there was a good chance it was so.

Competition

A S SPRING BURST forth, Ruth became actively interested in one of the boys, Werner Rindsberg. He was a serious fellow with thick, dark eyebrows, a sharply angled face, and a penchant toward sarcastic humor. He intimidated me, but Ruth seemed to have fallen madly in love with him. They went for frequent walks and sat on the front steps of our barn in the evening, chatting endlessly about Palestine, possible war scenarios, religion, and the philosophies of Sartre and Moliére.

Apparently the springtime was affecting Dela, too. Suddenly she spent more and more of her free time in the kitchen. The focus of her attention? Walter Strauss. At age fifteen, Walter was not interested in girls per se. He would rather spend time with Haskelevich and could often be heard roaring at the adult's jokes.

But Dela was not to be put off so easily. To the amusement of everyone, Walter's shirts were now the most cleanly washed and neatly pressed, and one could gain entrance to the kitchen only by walking past Dela stationed at the entrance.

I may have laughed along with Haskelevich at Dela's transparent efforts with Walter, but at this juncture nothing that Dela was doing amused me. It ate at me. While Walter may not have been interested in girls, Dela was rapidly growing into a beautiful young woman. She always had a pretty face, but now her slight body was gradually filling in at all the right places. I, too, was maturing and filling out, but I would never have Dela's natural beauty.

ON SEVERAL OCCASIONS during the month of July, Haskelevich arranged for the seven of us — him, Walter, Werner, Elka, Ruth, Dela, and me — to join farmers in the vineyards to help them harvest their grapes and later in the evening to help them make their wine. What an event! You have to experience this primitive manufacturing process to fully grasp its many wonders — that the alcohol is, for example, self-sterilizing.

We hauled bushels of grapes onto a wooden platform erected in a farmer's backyard, emptied them, and then jumped full force on the grapes, shoes and all. Now we mostly wore wooden shoes from Holland, which the Swiss Red Cross obtained via donations, and they were perfect for crushing grapes. The grape juice collected in the trough surrounding the platform and dripped from two corners into pails placed underneath. We had great fun in our new jobs, especially because of our compensation — supper at one of the farmers' houses.

What feasts they served! Pork, duck, potatoes, tomatoes, green beans, and even mousse or cake for dessert. But aside from filling our stomachs, the most fascinating feature of the meal was its conclusion: the farmers skillfully throwing the meat bones over their shoulders to the dogs, who waited breathlessly through the entire meal for these tidbits. They then gnawed on them, and buried the bones in the sand floor of the dining area! Mutti would not have approved.

These wine-making events gave me two additional bonuses. First, we got to fill all the containers we could tote with wine. We couldn't carry enough to make the wine run like water as it had the previous summer, but our lunches back in Seyre were once again complete. More important, I got to spend time with Walter when we were both having a good time.

It was during our first wine-making exercise I felt . . . a chemistry, I guess is what you would call it, develop between us. Most of us were on the platform enjoying the pure pleasure of doing something we were normally prohibited from doing — stomping on fruit and making ourselves wet and sticky in the process. But Walter was hanging back, hesitating. Haskelevich was teasing him. "Hey Walter, afraid of a little grape juice?" Finally, I reached out and grabbed Walter's arm and pulled him onto the platform. He pretended to resist, but he didn't really. I think Walter appreciated my gesture of warmth and fun, because he wound up having the best time of any of us stomping on the grapes. I am amazed by my spontaneity that day, because it was so out of character.

The only negative part of that experience was the disapproving expression (Was it "sour grapes"?) I observed on Dela's face as the evening progressed. Yet overall, she remained friendly to me and I to her, though, as you might expect, it was not something we discussed. I wasn't sure what to think about this curious little threesome that developed, except that it was a new, and most interesting, phase of my life.

BY THE END of July, the preparations in our new living quarters at Château la Hille were complete. We made our journey, approximately seventy or eighty kilometers, on a beautiful sunny day. We took a train for the first part of the trip; it was about 3 P.M. when we began the two-hour walk from the train station to the castle. I noticed immediately that the terrain there was more hilly than Seyre.

Suddenly, like a glow emanating from some roadside woods, the castle appeared. It was truly an old medieval fortress, naturally a pale tan, but nearly yellow in the sun, and surrounded by a high stone wall. It had remnants of a draw-bridge and a tower neatly constructed at each of the four corners of the building.

From just off the road, we could hear the cascading waters of a hillside brook, and the smell of pine and willow trees perfumed the air. As we walked up the long lane leading from the road to the château, the castle seemed to grow majestically, making me feel very small and human. I felt I was not the only member of our ragged group who was wondering how long it would be before we met our fairy godmother and prince charming.

The château was like an idyllic self-contained village. Some of the children were bringing in firewood. Others were busy digging weeds in the courtyard, where a vegetable garden was full of lettuce, cabbage, green beans, carrots, and radishes. In a field off to one side of the château, boys shouted and laughed together as they played an aggressive game of soccer. Rösli was carrying a huge bucket of water from an outside well when she spotted the new arrivals. I was pleased to be the first one she greeted, and she welcomed me with more warmth and energy than I had ever before seen.

"Inge, I'm so glad you're all here. Our new community is now complete. Look over there, we have our vegetable garden, and yesterday we harvested our first carrots. All we have to do is get our pump working properly so we can connect it to pipes leading to the château. And then, imagine, we will have running water!"

She called to Alex Frank, "Alex, would you please show our newest arrivals to their rooms?"

It was a little sad for me to realize that, once again, Alex was being treated like a bellhop. Alex didn't miss the connection, either. When Rösli was out of earshot, he said with more than a little sarcasm, "Please, let me show you to your rooms."

Opening the heavy wooden door that led into a dark central hallway, he paused, his voice swelling with pride. "First, though, let me show you some of what we have prepared here." A short way down the hall, off to the right, he directed us into the kitchen where Frau Schlesinger presided, proud as a peacock in a fresh white apron. As she chopped green beans and carrots for dinner she told us, "Here you will begin to eat properly and learn to love vegetables." She smiled broadly, eyeing the younger ones who were making faces.

She certainly had reason to be proud. Once again, after so many months of making do in Seyre, she had a real kitchen. Pots and pans, old and battered, but pots and pans nonetheless, hung from hooks along the wall and from the ceiling. Our gray steel dishes and cups were lined up on newly-built shelves. To one side was a huge, black wood-burning stove. In addition to burners for six pots, it had a large oven underneath. And across the room stood a real sink from which Rösli hoped to see our first running water pour forth.

As we stood in awe, Frau Schlesinger motioned us through to the opposite side. She opened a door and proudly announced, "You must see the dining room where you'll be eating."

It really was another world. The dining room was huge — ballroom-size — with parquet floors, dark wood-paneled walls, and several glass chandeliers. And when Frau Schlesinger flicked a switch, the chandeliers lit the room. We had electricity! Three long picnic-like tables covered with red-checked oilcloths were the only incongruities in the otherwise elegant room.

From the dining room, Alex led us up a flight of stone stairs to the second floor. The numerous large rooms had long floor-to-ceiling windows, and their black shutters had been opened to let in wonderful fresh air. Two or three of the rooms had been set aside as school rooms with tables and chairs. Rösli had her own office with an adjoining bedroom. We even had the luxury of a real "infirmary." It contained two beds, and the shelves were stocked with cotton, white adhesive tape, salves, and thermometers.

To us road-weary newcomers, though, the bedrooms were the most astonishing luxuries: They had beds. Admittedly, the beds were crowded in, ten to fifteen per room, and they were nothing fancy — basic wooden structures or black iron cots covered with hand-made sleeping-bag-style sheets and blankets. Nonetheless, they were beds. And on each bed was a red-and-blue wool robe, imported from Switzerland.

I was thrilled to learn Rösli and Alex had reserved a smaller room, with only five beds, for the older girls. I was to share it with Ruth, Dela, Inge H., and Alix Grabkowicz, a good-humored girl I knew only vaguely. She was notable for being the most buxom of all the girls. To reach our room, we had to walk through a larger room, which had about fifteen beds, for girls a bit younger. For the first time, we older girls were enjoying some status because of our age. That night, for the first time in over a year, we slept on beds. A straw mattress had been placed on each, along with a sleeping bag made out of sheets.

Dinner in the huge dining room, where each of us had an assigned seat, was a special treat. Not that the food was anything special. We ate the familiar corn meal, spruced up with fresh string beans and carrots from our garden, but the surroundings made me feel as if I were dining in an expensive hotel. I sat between Ruth and Dela.

The next morning was quite memorable as well. A clanging bell awakened us at about 7 A.M. Out in the courtyard, with the warm early-summer sun rising over one of her shoulders, Rösli Näf was waiting to lead us in group exercises. She had us stand in rows and raise our arms as high as we could, instructing us to "touch the sky" and then, without bending our knees, to touch our toes. After jumping jacks, we sat on the ground and did stretches. Most of the older children followed her instructions willingly, but she had considerable difficulty keeping the attention of the younger children. "Please watch me," she admonished. "This will help harden your bodies so that you can do all the difficult work that is required here."

After about twenty minutes of exercises, she marched all the girls down to the brook to bathe. The boys were on their own for bathing, and so Alex directed them to another part of the brook. Rösli had scouted out areas where thick trees and bushes would protect our privacy from the prying eyes of the local farmers.

In a flash, Rösli had undressed and lowered herself into the water up to her shoulders. I moved to follow her but the moment I put one foot into the water, I stopped. It was frigid, and the riverbed was slippery and slimy. How had Rösli gotten in so quickly?

"I will never get into that water," Dela said to me after making the same discovery. The other girls were screeching and hugging themselves.

I, however, was determined to prove to Rösli that I was hearty. What's more, I was desperate to clean myself of the grime from the previous day's journey. I forced myself simply to drop into the deep water near Rösli. The cold was jarring and my feet went numb. Once I was accustomed to the cold, I was able to appreciate the beautiful peace amid the pine trees, and the water was refreshing.

The frigid morning bath set the tone for my first full day at la Hille. My skin tingled, and I was full of energy. When Rösli started to tell each of us what our work assignments would be, I asked her to let me work in the garden and smilingly she agreed. "We will be clearing a new area where we will plant potatoes and cucumbers," she told me.

I felt more energetic than I could remember as I worked side by side with Rösli, preparing the soil for a garden on the far side of the château, near the brook. With the help of several Chamois children, we dug out rocks and turned the cool, black earth. Rösli impressed us with how much she knew about gardening. When I unearthed some wriggling worms and didn't even try to conceal my revulsion, she explained to me why we needed them. "They help the earth, and make our vegetables grow bigger."

Rösli told us that by adding our own fertilizer of decomposed leaves and other organic material from near the stream we could make the earth even more productive. "When I was in Africa, we had huge amounts of compost everywhere. Here, we have to work harder to find it." The best compost turned out to be along the sides of the stream. So we made several trips to the water, where I dug compost and filled up our wheelbarrow.

At lunchtime, we had another pleasant surprise. Alex and Frau Schlesinger had had the brilliant idea of moving our dining tables outside so we could eat under the bright blue sky. There were scrambled eggs (made from powder sent from Switzerland) to go with our fresh vegetables. Even though bringing everything outside meant additional work for everyone, nobody thought to complain.

Paradise

Rösli CAREFULLY organized our daily schedule at our new home. A nearby water pump, hooked up to send water into the château, made our household tasks much easier. I regularly tended our huge garden, spending most afternoons digging soil, pushing carts full of fertilizer to the garden beds, or taking long walks into the woods to cut down just the right size wooden poles to support our growing bean plants.

My agricultural activities, together with my noisy Dutch wooden shoes, earned me the nickname "cheval," or horse. While I don't believe my new name had all the negative connotations associated with the old one, it was pejorative enough to keep me on edge during my initial months in our new home. In some strange way it symbolized all the stimulating, and often contradictory, forces at work in Château la Hille.

The sheer beauty of the place nearly always stirred at least some positive energy in me, even during the worst moments. Walking around and through it, I imagined myself a medieval baroness. Viewing the surrounding countryside with its rolling hills and splendid forests and farmland was like looking over van Gogh's shoulder. From rooms on the second floor, we could sometimes make out the snowy peaks of the Pyrenees dividing France from Spain and, as would become ever more apparent, separating us from freedom.

Physically, the overall quality of our lives improved quite a bit at Château la Hille. That improvement, however, exacerbated a more subtle, complex dimension that often left me feeling sad and lonely. All of which leads me back to the painful side of my nickname.

Even now in my crazed confessional frame of mind, I have difficulty adequately capturing the social and emotional sides of our lives. Because so many years have passed, I now realize each of us was affected by the isolation, social cliques, creative energy, conflicts, and, yes, romance, in different ways.

We were, by and large, the same people who lived together in Seyre, but our new location had considerable impact on how we interacted. In Seyre, though we were interlopers, we were, nevertheless, part of the village community, small as it was. Here at the castle, we were out in the country and totally isolated. Because we were Jews made more vulnerable with each passing day, we confined our wanderings to the few acres surrounding us. Of necessity, we made our own community entirely from scratch.

In Seyre, we had been able to work as a cohesive group. Certainly we had formed small groups of close friends with whom we spent much of our time, but our allegiance to those groups took a back seat to the common good. At Château la Hille, the luxury of having supplies from the Swiss Red Cross meant our immediate survival wasn't so clearly at stake and the individual groups became cliques that created rivalries, played out in all kinds of ways. Some were played out innocently in soccer games or running races in which the German children challenged the Austrian children. Some were played out physically as the older boys regularly challenged each other to carry the most firewood for the stove. One of the teen boys, Leo Grossmann, showed off by carrying two full buckets of water in his hands — and a third in his mouth between his teeth!

Strange as it might sound to teenagers today (including my own Julie, so preoccupied with music and dating), some of the rivalries were played out in purely intellectual pursuits. Several of the boys, Walter S. prime among them, possessed extraordinary mathematical ability. These boys would spend hours challenging each other with complicated mathematical problems to see who was most clever. Sometimes, in the after-dinner hours, others of us would gather around in the dining room as they posed their problems and scribbled their calculations and answers. While Walter S. and several other boys like Hans Garfunkel and Peter Salz were very good, the champion most often was Addie Nussbaum, the younger brother (by just a couple years) of Lotte Nussbaum, who had challenged Alex Frank about our Christmas celebration. Jacques Roth, the protector of little Manfred Manasse, wasn't much for math, so he created his own competitive niche by becoming engrossed in translating French literature into German, and German literature into French; needless to say, he didn't have to fight off many competitors in making a name for himself in this arena — the only other person interested in such pursuits was Ruth, and even she wasn't as fully absorbed as Jacques.

I was not terribly competitive, nor did I have a special talent like mathematics or linguistics, so I established my identity as a strong and hard worker who could keep up with the boys in such chores as hauling wood or compost. But achieving so much distinction as to be nicknamed "horse" reflected the disdain some of the other teenagers felt for me.

Complicating matters further was our relationship with the adults in charge of us. In the summer of 1941, the administration of our colony was officially a joint affair between Rösli Näf, our Swiss nurse, and Alex Frank. The key word is "officially," because co-existence between two such totally different, quirky, and controlling personalities like Rösli and Alex was probably untenable. I had noticed the tensions when I arrived at the château to see Rösli clearly ordering Alex around.

I had remained close with Ruth and Dela, and I had a few other good friends, like my new roommates, Alix (Lixie) Grabkowicz and Margo Kern, though as the cliques grew more strongly separate from one another, I felt ever more isolated. All my life I have preferred to remain in the background. At the château, there was more pressure associated with groups than ever before, and the key demarcation point was increasingly associated with Rösli and Alex and our perceived allegiances to one or the other.

I noticed that Inge H. had become friendly with a group of girls that included Frieda Steinberg — my confidant in Belgium when I was being rejected by Gustav — and Ilse Brunell, a pretty, vivacious, dark-haired teen who loved to sing. The three never excluded me explicitly, but it didn't take long for me to realize that whenever I tried to join their conversations, I wasn't wanted. They turned away from me, and their terse responses to my questions made it clear they considered me an intruder. I could see my friendship with Inge H. rapidly deteriorating.

Once, as I was walking away from the group after being snubbed, I heard one of the girls say, just loudly enough so I would be sure to hear, "She's probably going to tell Rösli how bad we are." Her remark, in addition to making me feel rejected, woke me up to how my openly close relationship with Rösli was creating problems. Because of Rösli's strict sense of order, some of the children perceived her as their enemy, and from this stray remark I knew I was considered her collaborator.

If I had been able to be objective, possibly I wouldn't have been so hurt, because I knew adolescent girls are often mean to each other. I also knew that, in certain respects, many of the children viewed me as a leader, or at least as someone fairly responsible. Rösli continued the youth council that Alex Frank had started. The council was comprised of five teens elected by all the children to represent us with the adults. Walter S. had been president of the council since its inception, and I was elected some months later, during our time in Seyre, and subsequently re-elected. Aside from bi-weekly meetings with Alex and Rösli, during which we learned about the important chores requiring attention over the next few weeks, the council didn't do that much.

At Château la Hille, any such formalities as governance increasingly played second fiddle to informal approaches. Part of the problem was that Rösli was much more popular with the boys than with the girls, and for a simple reason: She favored the boys over the girls. She got on very well with boys like Jacques Roth and Walter S. Girls like Ruth, Frieda, and Inge H. bridled against her authoritarian, and often rigid, style. One of her favorite, and more grating, sayings was, "To clean where it has been cleaned before is good. To clean where it has never been cleaned is best."

She was especially unsuited to handling sensitive personal problems. I still cringe when I remember the morning that summer when we assembled to do our calisthenics. Instead of leading the exercises, Rösli dragged one of the mattresses out into the yard. In the center of the mattress was a wet spot. Seven-year-old Annette, a cute, dark-eyed girl with long, black hair, stood cowering behind.

"Annette was a bad girl during the night," Rösli announced. "She wet her bed. This is the third time she has done that in the last two weeks. I thought if you all knew about it, you might encourage Annette to sleep through the night without wetting her bed."

I had the same uncomfortable feeling I had back in Seyre when the children put the sign on little Manfred Manasse. Public humiliation didn't seem appropriate. And this time, an adult — a psychiatric nurse, no less — was humiliating a child.

The teenage girls also thought she was cold and insensitive to their concerns about homesickness, boys, and "female" problems. One day when Dela was suffering from menstrual cramps, she went to Rösli. "She told me I should drink some hot water or tea and it would probably go away," Dela recounted. "When I asked her about my bleeding, she said I should just use some toilet paper and try to ignore it — I shouldn't let it interfere with my chores. I think that she didn't want to hear about it."

I had begun menstruating some months before, in Seyre, and Frau Schlesinger had been very reassuring that it was normal and inquiring into whether I had cramps. She even provided me with our equivalent of sanitary pads — specially cut rags that she made available to the girls as needed, and which we were then responsible for laundering.

Rösli, however, was too absorbed in administering to the practical details of our lives to bother herself with our personal problems. As if her insensitivity to the girls wasn't bad enough, Rösli also came across as insensitive to the one boy whom many of the girls swooned over: the enigmatic Walter Kamlet.

As I've mentioned, he was the resident intellectual. Although he was self-appointed to that post, he probably merited the title. He liked to keep to himself but was rarely alone because so often the others sought him out. Once we got to Château la Hille, the girls were attracted by his aura of mystery. He never made overtures to anyone else, not even to Walter S. It was as if the two Walters operated in different realms, on parallel tracks.

Walter K. knew so much more than the rest of us. And, often, with a sigh and slight shake of his head, he would let us know how frustrating it was for him to tolerate our ignorance. Once several of us — Ruth, Lotte Nussbaum, Margo Kern, and I — were having an after-dinner discussion that inevitably led us to the one question that tormented us: What was making Germany behave the way it was? Walter K. had been sitting nearby, just outside our group. Although he had appeared to be completely absorbed in his book, he suddenly joined our discussion.

"You know, if you look at the histories of Germany and Austria, it isn't really all that surprising." He then launched into an extensive and succinct history of Germany and the Austro-Hungarian empire. He told us about the succession of royalty, the nineteenth-century wars with France, and Germany's conduct during World War I and its aftermath. When he had completed his eight-minute monologue, we all sat in stunned silence, admiring his brilliance.

Unlike many of the other girls, I kept my distance from Walter K. I didn't want to risk being the object of his ridicule or having him correct me. I also didn't want to be drawn into the battle that was simmering between him and Rösli. Their conflict was becoming more public day by day as the summer wore on.

Rösli insisted that, during daylight hours, everyone should work on chores, helping in the gardens, cutting wood, or cleaning the château. "Idleness is our enemy," she often said. Each day, Rösli would post a list of our assignments. Walter K. not only objected to Rösli's demand for structure and discipline, but also he simply had no intention of stooping to working with his hands. He made it clear to everyone that he had higher things to think and read about.

So, each morning, Rösli and Walter K. ran through a ritualistic scenario. While the rest of us were already outside doing our chores, we'd hear Rösli's voice booming, "Where is Walter Kamlet?"

"I think I saw him in one of the classrooms," one of the children might answer. "He was drumming with his fingers." Every one of us was familiar with Walter's habit of playing an imaginary piano — wherever his fingers happened to be.

Hearing that, Rösli would turn on her heels and march into the château, emerging a few minutes later with a glum-faced Walter K. in tow. His sorrowful look made him appear even thinner and more gaunt than usual. "Everyone must do his share," Rösli would intone as she handed him a hoe or shovel.

Sullenly, Walter K. would move some dirt around. But after perhaps twenty minutes or half an hour, he would disappear. And the ritual would start over.

In Walter K.'s defense, he had real excuses that justified his avoiding manual labor. For one thing, he wasn't in good health. He hadn't come with us from Brussels. Instead, he had come to our group from the French detention camp of Gurs, where he had been held with other Jewish refugees after Germany attacked France. Because Walter K. was a year shy of eighteen — the age at which the French considered Jews to be eligible for deportation to German-run concentration camps — Alex Frank had been able to obtain his release. But Walter K. was already weak from a terrible cough, which Alex presumed to be tuberculosis.

So while Walter K., along with the girls, was rubbing salt into Rösli's wounds, I was very much the exception — a girl who openly got on well with Rösli. Alex may not have been especially attractive to most of the girls, but he was, by default, the preferred leader. After dinner on many evenings, he and Elka could be seen chatting and, I would guess, even commiserating with girls like Ruth, Dela, and Inge H.

My loyalties were torn. I respected both adults for the immense responsibility they bore, even if I didn't agree with their individual styles. So I tried to be the ultimate politician by attempting to stay friendly with both leaders.

On top of all the social pressures, the war and the worry about our parents always lurked in the background. Mutti tried to leave Germany via Spain, Portugal, Cuba, Mexico, even via Russia and Japan for the United States — at one point she actually had a visa to Cuba — but she was unable to obtain the necessary exit papers from German officials to leave the country. So she still lived with her mother, brother, and sister in Darmstadt. I usually heard from her on a monthly basis, primarily through the twenty-five-word Red Cross letters that we were able to exchange via Switzerland.

My uncertainty concerning my relationships with many of the girls magnified my insecurity. I worried constantly about the direction of the war and about Mutti's fate — two concerns that were inextricably linked. During that summer and fall of 1941, both gave me plenty to be pessimistic about. Hitler's triumphs were accumulating. He had weakened Britain with his bombing campaign against London, and now he was concentrating his wrath on Russia, mounting a huge invasion. I kept up on the events to a minimal extent thanks, in large measure, to Hans Garfunkel, one of the mathematicians. He was a small teenager who often got into arguments with others about obtuse trivial matters and was on the losing end of foot races and related contests, but he was probably our most voracious news hound. Somehow he came up with an old radio and, together with some of the other boys, got it going well enough that we were able to receive occasional BBC broadcasts.

So we used these reports to try to calculate, whether negatively or positively, what might be happening to our relatives. With news of the Germans bombing London, Ruth, who had been focusing her anxiety on her missing baby sister, Bronia, now started to fret about her mother, who was living in London. Ruth still had not informed her mother that she had been unable to find Bronia before leaving Brussels. Instead of telling her that the little girl was unaccounted for, Ruth had been writing elaborate letters describing not only how she and her sister Betty were doing, but also about Bronia's growth. She went into great detail about how well

Bronia was doing, how she was adapting and learning French. Adding to Ruth's torment, each of her mother's letters back opened with an inquiry or comment about Bronia.

Yet other news encouraged me. As absurd as Mutti's efforts to leave via Russia or Japan might seem, I knew they weren't a total pipe dream. Dela's parents, who had made it to Russia some months before Germany invaded, were subsisting in Siberia. What counted was that they were still alive and far from the fighting. It was much easier to travel elsewhere from Russia than it was to travel from Germany. And their hope of leaving Russia was not unreal. Dela's older sister, Gisele, was already in Palestine, and she was trying to make arrangements.

Dela and I sometimes lamented about how difficult it was to move people who, like Mutti and us, were trapped behind German lines. "I sometimes feel like a prisoner," Dela once said.

"You are right," I answered. "We are prisoners. Prisoners in a big, beautiful castle."

Adding insult to the injury of this situation was an event during the summer of 1941 involving Werner Rindsberg, Ruth's boyfriend. It turned out he had relatives in the United States, in Brooklyn, and somehow they had arranged for him to exit our group and make passage to America. One day he announced he had received permission to travel to the United States. He would leave shortly for Marseilles to obtain his visa from the American embassy and from there head to Spain and, finally, Portugal, where he would board a ship to the United States. And he wasn't alone. Another girl our age, Hanni Schlimmer, had similarly obtained permission to exit, apparently thanks to a diplomatic connection that her father still had in Germany. She would meet up with her parents in Spain and exit via Portugal. And a few very young children were also being sent to the United States, apparently with help from the Quakers' American Friends Service Committee.

The irony wasn't lost on me. I, too, had relatives in the United States, including my sister and, more recently, my father, not to mention our cousin in New York, Robert Joseph. Why weren't they pulling the same strings as Werner's and Hanni's relatives?

I wasn't the only one stuck in place. Hans Garfunkel had relatives in Chicago to whom he wrote repeatedly, pleading for help to get him out. I commiserated with him about the difficulties.

As angry as I was about my relatives' apparent impotence, it was increasingly, in my mind, more about my anger toward them and less about feeling sorry for myself. Because I must admit, if I am going to be entirely truthful, and I have committed myself to truth here, that I didn't have the same sense of despondency about being left behind once again — in fact, I felt some element of relief at not leaving. Something, or rather someone, was tugging at me to stay on at Château la Hille.

Romance

WALTER S. and I often spent time together in Haskelevich's presence, but we rarely said a word to each other. Haskelevich made jokes about how we were "the silent couple," and others sometimes joined in teasing us about how we kept our relationship so secret. Underneath it all was the growing expectation that Walter and I would become a couple. When would that happen? I had not the slightest idea.

Once we were at the château, Haskelevich's role in our colony seemed to shrink. His key skill — negotiating food deals with local farmers — was no longer in as much demand now that the Swiss Red Cross was in charge. So perhaps to compensate, he tried to invent chores for himself and to involve Walter and me in them. Thus, he might need to fetch some kind of tool or special supplies in the nearby village of Montegue and would ask Walter and me to accompany him and help haul back whatever it was. In the process of walking the six or seven kilometers each way and conversing, Haskelevich was always the focal point. I would speak to Haskelevich and Walter would speak to Haskelevich, but for whatever reason, Walter and I would not speak to each other. Talking actually became quite awkward as I gradually became aware of the dynamic at work. The longer it went on, the more self-conscious I was about trying to speak directly with Walter. It was as if Haskelevich were mediating, or rather controlling, the situation. Any effort on my part or Walter's to speak directly with the other would have seemed to be an attempt to rudely circumvent Haskelevich.

Then, in the evenings, when Walter, the other teens, and I were sitting around the dining room reading, Haskelevich might wander in, begin conversing with Walter, and then suddenly raise his voice, glancing over at me on the other side of the room, "So, Walter, why are you hesitating? A lovely girl is waiting for you." Of course, such antics served only to inhibit both of us, as they would any self-conscious teenagers. Haskelevich, in seemingly encouraging us, was actually trying to discourage us. Of course I didn't realize that at the time. I just saw him as a nuisance and an obstacle to the ever-more-powerful feelings I had for Walter.

The situation wasn't made easier by the fact that we both were often in groups, whether we were working, eating, or playing games. Walter, especially, was so popular people gravitated toward him, and so he never was alone. If we were bashful to begin with, it was easy to avoid individual contact by letting the group work like a cocoon, insulating us from the need for private interactions.

One thing working in our favor was that most of the girls and boys had paired off during this summer. Following the lead of Ruth and Werner, Alix Grabkowicz was with Edgar Chaim. Ilse Brunell had become friendly with Heinz Storosum, Jacques Roth with Margo Kern, and Lotte Nussbaum with Bertrand Elkan. Or at least it seemed as if everyone was pairing off. Perhaps, after being together for more than a year, the boys and girls were simply becoming more comfortable around each other and began to do what came naturally.

And yet there was an artificial, almost tense, air around the situation. The couples were restricted to taking walks around the few acres of the chateau grounds and spent their time discussing their families and the books they were reading.

Adding to the tension was Rösli's growing nervousness. One evening she called together the eighteen or twenty older girls, those aged fourteen and over, for a brief talk in her office that was similar in substance and tone to what Mademoiselle Lea had told us individually back in Seyre. Only at la Hille, the feeling among the girls was much more serious than it had been in Seyre, where we giggled and joked about the warnings.

She shut the door of her office and turned to us. In the past, we had noticed that whenever she had a planned speech, she spoke in sing-song tones. And so she did now. It was clear she had rehearsed her words quite carefully.

"You are all very mature people, and I don't have to lecture you about the importance of responsibility. You all know the serious circumstances of the world around us, and you understand why we are here. I feel that it is my duty, as the administrator here, to remind you that personal responsibility is more important than ever. Some of you have begun spending more time with boys. That is only natural at your age. However, it is also a matter of potential concern to me. If things were to get out of hand and one of you were to become pregnant, it could draw the attention of the authorities. That would certainly pose a great danger to our entire community. Therefore, you must show a great deal of personal discipline. I cannot exaggerate the importance of this."

Each of us remained silent. For many of the girls, this was the first time Rösli had earned their respect. We could see she really did have our best interests at heart. While most of us instinctively understood the importance of avoiding "a scandal," Rösli gave a useful voice to our concerns. She dismissed us without asking if we had questions.

ONE EVENING in July, as I was sitting in the dining room reading, Walter came up to me to ask whether I would like to take a walk with him. That meant just one thing.

As I walked out of the castle's main gate with Walter beside me, his hands characteristically clasped behind his back, the moment had at long last arrived. Yet I was at a loss for words. We walked in silence for about five minutes, with the crunching of leaves and sticks the only sound as dusk settled in.

Walter broke the silence, formally asking, "I would like very much if you would be my girlfriend. Do you agree?"

With just a moment of hesitation as I fruitlessly pondered some funny or comforting phrase, I simply said, "Yes." That was the extent of my conversation to that point.

We continued to walk in silence. Finally, I asked him if he had read *Crime and Punishment*, the book I was reading when he asked me to take a walk.

"No," he said. "But I've heard that it is quite a powerful story."

"It is," I replied. "It takes some time to get deeply into it enough to appreciate it fully though."

"Well, I would like to read it after you are through," he said.

"I'll pass it along to you," I answered.

That was our entire exchange, and crazy as it sounds, I knew even then, I would always remember it. We returned to the castle after walking about twenty minutes, and the quizzical looks on faces told me that our silent approach confused many people who watched us leave and return.

Walter said good-night to me in the dining room and disappeared. I sat down and pretended to read, thinking I had to give the impression of being nonchalant. Only I knew the turmoil within me!

Why can't I just say I was floating? We had only taken a walk, hadn't even held hands, but it was as if we had kissed passionately. I felt exhilarated, I think, because those moments were so long in coming and then because so much was compressed into just a few minutes. I had finally confirmed that my feelings about Walter weren't just idle fantasies. He had asked me to be his girlfriend.

It was almost time to go to bed when the first reverberations began. Haskelevich, who left the dining room shortly after Walter, returned and stopped at my table. "Is it true that you are going to go with Walter from now on?"

I answered, "Yes," for the second time that evening and was vaguely aware Haskelevich was quite upset.

I should have been angry with Haskelevich. Hadn't he been the one ostensibly encouraging Walter and me to get together? But I couldn't be too upset with him. Haskelevich was a wonderful man in so many ways and had been so supportive and uplifting during my darkest moments in Seyre. I only sensed then what I fully appreciate now — he felt like a father to Walter and me. Now that Walter and I had found each other, we were showing our independence. The implication for Haskelevich was clear: We would have less need for his supervision and guidance.

And then there was the matter of Dela. Later on in bed, Ruth, who slept to one side of me, inquired with great concern if everything were all right. Dela, who had her bed to the left, pretended to be asleep. I was so preoccupied with how I would say "Good morning" to Walter that I gave little thought to the fact I may have double-crossed Dela.

Since the wine-making, Dela had eased up on her obvious flirtation with Walter. But clearly, she still liked him a lot — I could see it in the bright smile and eager voice with which she greeted him whenever their paths crossed. He was always polite to her, but never more. It was obvious, at least to me, that as attractive as she was, Dela was Walter's intellectual inferior. I should have been concerned with how this latest turn of events would affect my relationship with Dela and others. I worried, instead, that Walter's asking me to be his girlfriend was maybe, somehow, a mistake. Once he saw my loner tendencies, my inability to make conversation, my despondency, my looks, he would come to his senses and move on.

Celebrities

M Y INVOLVEMENT with Walter really did create an entirely new set of challenges — a certain living-up-to prestige is the best way I can express it. Although I was respected by the administration and by some of the children, I did not have anything approaching Walter's stature, nor did I possess the versatility of his charming personality. Walter personified reliability — mediating, tolerant, good natured, and empathetic. Though only sixteen, he regarded me as someone for whom he had to assume responsibility.

I don't mean Walter selected a girlfriend as he might a shirt or bicycle — only that Walter was like the president, or maybe prince, of our colony. He possessed a combination of leadership skills, maturity, and charm truly remarkable for someone so young. The younger boys idolized Walter for his storehouse of knowledge, his ability to make games and fun out of learning math and science, and his willingness to teach them chess or how to carve wooden figurines. Yet his maturity didn't diminish him in the eyes of the older boys. He had a charisma that drew them to him. Rarely was Walter alone. He always had an entourage with him wherever he went.

Also, disputes among the children were more often than not submitted to Walter's consideration. Often the boys argued about the outcome of foot races. Hans Garfunkel and Addie Nussbaum, two of our mathematicians, loved to run fifty-meter and hundred-meter races. We frequently heard their arguments: "I was first!" "No, it was a tie!" and so on. Invariably, they called on Walter to make the determination, and his word was always final.

All the boys wanted to be close to him. Like most of us, he had a small circle of close friends and a wider circle of casual acquaintances. But his casual friends loved to brag, "I'm good friends with Walter. I'll ask him what he thinks." And as Walter matured, more and more girls began looking approvingly at him. Dela was merely the first.

With all that was at stake, and with all the choices he had, Walter selected me. In the context of the château, the prince had plucked me from the crowd to be his princess. Being chosen by him was not to be taken lightly.

To my relief, the next morning's rituals passed quietly. Walter, coming up from the river with a group of boys, met Ruth and me going down to the riverside for our morning wash. "Good mornings" were exchanged in passing and an enormous load was lifted from my mind.

I did sense over that first day a very real change in my social standing. By late that morning, everyone knew about Walter and me. Nothing was explicitly stated, but some people treated me differently. Haskelevich kept his distance from me while Inge H. and some of the other girls suddenly came closer.

Equally impressive, many of the boys who previously had been indifferent to me now treated me as an old friend. One in particular was Jacques Roth. All of his involvement in translating French and German literature had made him increasingly distant and standoffish towards me. He worshipped Walter, so now it was as if Jacques's arrogance had been wiped away and, in his view, made us the best of friends. When I asked him what he was currently translating, he went into extensive detail about a segment of a Joseph Conrad story he was working on.

That evening, after supper, Walter came to sit next to me to read. We spoke very little. During the next two weeks we spent most evenings going out for walks. It was a relief to leave the castle, since we could more easily talk with no one straining to listen. Walter enjoyed these walks. We mostly discussed our family situations. As bad as mine was, Walter's was worse. Both his parents still lived in Germany without any foreign relatives or any chance to leave. His brother, Siegfried, who was twenty-one years old, was still at Gurs, a refugee camp in southern France, and although Walter had spoken to Red Cross officials, they were unable to help him because he was over the officially protected age limit of eighteen years.

We were like a celebrity couple, with everyone trying to catch snippets of our conversation. It was uncomfortable for me, introvert that I was. Yet Walter took little notice. He was more accustomed to others watching him and monitoring his movements and conversations.

As time went on, I learned more about Walter's family background. His mother was an artist who had trained in Paris and, according to Walter, was quite accomplished, having had her work exhibited in art shows and galleries around Germany. His father was a lawyer. I thought of Mutti's admonition to me in our last conversation aboard the train to Cologne; certainly Walter's family would have met her standards. Her only objection might have been that Walter had had a totally secular upbringing — he had no recollection of ever going to a synagogue. But for Mutti, that would have been a minor drawback.

Walter's parents were a more openly loving couple than mine. I determined this from his reaction, or lack of reaction, to my hesitant and meandering description of Mutti and Papa — the Uruguay affair, Papa's business failings, Mutti's reluctance to push our American relatives. He didn't comprehend the tension these issues created, or if he did, he said little. I took it to mean such craziness was foreign in his family. His parents' main failing, from what I could tell, was that they were even more naive about Hitler than my parents, since they apparently took no action to get anyone in the family out of Germany prior to putting Walter on a train to Brussels in early 1939. Yet even in this respect, Walter was not the least bit angry or embittered. I refrained from expressing my amazement at his parents' poor judgment and did not let my resentment about my own parents poison our atmosphere.

In those early days, our relationship had a stiffness that was difficult to break through. One especially lovely evening, Walter took me up a nearby hill to watch the sunset. The willow trees were completely still. The hills around us gave off a soft pink glow. The beauty of the landscape and Walter's presence weighed heavily on me. I just wanted to chatter about how wonderful it was to be away from the group, but I felt inhibited, for we had not yet reached the stage where we just chatted and joked. Our conversations were formal and serious. I was thinking to myself, "How long will I be able to go on this way?" I don't know whether Walter sensed my thoughts, but he did not spend the next two evenings with me. I was perturbed but also realized how much I was looking forward to spending time with him.

I wanted to be carefree, as carefree as the young couples I saw strolling arm in arm down Avenue Louise in Brussels, or as Loulou was with her boyfriend. I wanted Walter to be as charming and easygoing with me as he was in groups. I wanted to laugh with him and to hold hands. To hug and kiss him.

I was trapped by my own ineptitude, by my fear Walter was on his way to discovering "the real me." I wished I could find a way to re-create my spontaneous wine-making overture. And Walter? As charismatic as he was in front of his constituency, he was clearly ill at ease alone with a girl.

I wanted to discuss so many things with Walter — how I felt about some of the girls, the politics around Rösli and Alex, Haskelevich's behavior, and all the assorted things that were tearing at me in one way or another. But I couldn't be sure these subjects were "acceptable" topics for us, at least at this point in our relationship. Also inhibiting me, I believe now, was my sense that I shouldn't become a burden to him. In his leadership role, Walter actually had a great deal of responsibility. To the extent that he was confident and relaxed, so were other children. If he became distracted or despondent, perhaps this would quickly be communicated among all the children. I coped with this concern by remaining quiet and distant.

I was tremendously relieved to see him head in my direction the third evening. Without hesitating, I got up and, seeing Walter's happy smile, I knew everything would be all right.

I ran up a hill and taunted Walter, "Bet you can't catch me!" And when he caught up to me at the top, I grabbed his hand and led him running down the other side, picking up speed from the incline. We laughed breathlessly like silly children, but we didn't cross the line Rösli had set.

Walter's return most certainly boosted my ego. I hadn't been successful in breaking apart the bond between us.

The one bond that did break, though, was with Haskelevich. Some time in late August, he approached me. "It's come time for me to move on." He spoke very casually. He said his decision was because of Rösli's administration. "Things have just changed too much, become too formal." He planned to go live with an area farm family, which shouldn't have been much of a problem for him to arrange, given his farming expertise and natural charm.

I couldn't help but think that Rösli was only part of the problem. The other part was that Walter and I had grown up too much.

MY SIXTEENTH BIRTHDAY was a couple of weeks later. Walter, waiting for me in front of the dining room before breakfast, somewhat awkwardly handed me a present. The four-color silver pencil and a self-made wooden pen and pencil case were very pretty, but how much more I treasured his photo, which he had inscribed for me ("To Inge, with much fondness, Yours, Walter")!

That was September 19, 1941. My "Sweet Sixteen" couldn't have been any sweeter. This was likely the happiest day of my life. There was no other way to describe it. No other day since has come as close to the sense of total joy and fulfillment that I felt, after rushing through breakfast and finding a spot alone in a study room, as I slowly, very slowly, opened the white tissue paper wrapping and fingered the special gift. By pushing down on one or another of the buttons along the side of the silver pencil, I could make it write in red, blue, green, or black. He must have purchased it in Montegue, though I couldn't imagine where, since it was such a tiny village, or perhaps he had Haskelevich acquire it in another town. Walter had come through for me in a totally unexpected and grand style. And all the other children and adults knew it, and seemed for once to share my happiness. Oh, what I would give to live that day again. And how I wish I still had that inscribed photo. I believe it was lost in the confusion of later events.

Melodies

LATE DURING that summer of 1941, we discovered that Walter Kamlet's finger strumming wasn't just an act. He really did have a talent that justified his avoidance of manual labor. It all became apparent on a Sunday afternoon when a small, decrepit moving truck pulled up to the château. Amid much fanfare, an old piano was unloaded. It was the gift of Alex Frank's mother, Irene, who had long idolized Walter K., probably for his classical old-world talents. She had committed herself to locating a piano to relieve the maestro of his frustration at not having a musical outlet. For weeks she scoured the countryside, and finally discovered the little-used instrument in the house of a village some kilometers away, and arranged to rent it for a token amount.

Walter K.'s disposition changed the moment the piano appeared. Rösli insisted the piano be placed in the dining room, so everyone could have access to it. But everyone considered it Walter K.'s. That afternoon, and nearly every morning and afternoon thereafter, our château was a concert stage, and we all worked to the strains of classical music wafting over the fields around us. I never got enough of listening to him practicing the "Spring" Sonata by Beethoven, Minuets by Mozart, and Schubert lieder. It was so peaceful to hear the music of the old composers floating out to me in the garden.

Love has a way of attuning one to the higher things in life. So it was with our daily lives, or at least my daily life, and the music that eventually became a part of our strange existence. Even Rösli was charmed. No longer did she hound Walter to perform regular chores. She was satisfied that Walter was earning his keep.

Shortly after the piano arrived, we saw our musical options expand even further. A second musically-talented member of our group was Heinz Storosum; he played the violin. Heinz was nearly the opposite of Walter: short, cheerful, personable, and not especially intellectual. At first, Walter could not stomach Heinz. He complained that Heinz's playing was "empty, soulless, and pompous." But the rest of us were impressed with the beautiful sounds Heinz coaxed from the battered violin Rösli had obtained for him via the Swiss Red Cross office in Toulouse.

In the interests of the larger group's cultural good, Rösli encouraged the two to adapt to one another's style. She reduced their daily work load, making them responsible for just one small bit of joint manual labor: to lead our single goat to a meadow each afternoon and, on the way, collect grass and weeds for our rabbit. The two maestros spent most of their time together discussing music, and over a period of several weeks, a certain level of mutual respect arose between them.

I knew things were going well between them when, that fall, I began hearing them play Beethoven's "Spring" Sonata for piano and violin. Not long after my birthday, I discovered why they were rehearsing it. The older children and members of the staff were invited one evening to Irene Frank's large bedroom. The piano had been moved to her room at Walter K.'s request, and with Irene's enthusiastic backing, so it doubled as a musical practice area. That day, in celebration of Irene's fifty-third birthday, Walter K. and Heinz performed the "Spring" Sonata, along with several other classics, together and solo.

We all sat quietly and in growing awe. They played flawlessly and with such great feeling it was as if we had been transported to a professional concert. But their beautiful musical performances also triggered memories of my old life in Darmstadt. I was overwhelmed by visions of Mutti. I could picture her sitting in our formal living room on winter Sunday afternoons, listening to classical music on our phonograph as she knitted us wool shawls and blankets. Oh, how I wished I could have just one such afternoon with her again. At Château la Hille, the mail service was inconsistent, and weeks could go by during which I might not receive even a single piece of mail from anyone. The few letters that did make it to me in addition to the Red Cross notes were her terse updates about the health of relatives. "Aunt Bertha has bronchitis again. I try to make sure she drinks plenty of tea."

For a very brief period that summer, she saw some rays of hope, as Mutti wrote in one letter:

Dearest Inge,

Today at last there is some good news. Papa and Robert Joseph have arranged for me to travel to Cuba. I understand I have a visa. They have made arrangements with Hamburg-American Line for me to travel from Portugal. Now I have to complete the process of obtaining exit papers from Germany. That is not an easy matter, as you might imagine. I must complete everything before August 1, when my Cuban visa expires.

Aunt Martha is feeling well again after her flu. The warm weather helped her recover. I am sewing her a summer dress. Oma Josephine also sends her regards. I also have some ironing to do, for which I am paid.

I hope you have enough clothes. You must be growing. Do your clothes still fit? Can I send you anything to wear?

Now I must go. I want to fill out the new exit forms. I will let you know about the date of my leaving.

> *Love and kisses,*
> Mutti

Mutti might exit Germany and I was in love. Life had taken a favorable turn.

But August 1 came and went, and Mutti didn't receive her exit papers. The visa to Cuba expired. In the months after that, Mutti included just a few snippets about the frustrations of emigration. "For a possible visa to Russia, I was told to come back in a month," she wrote in one letter late that summer. Her reticence to communicate suggested there was little positive news to report. She wanted to spare me the miserable details of her increasingly depressing life.

OUR LIVES at Château la Hille took on ever more structure. At Rösli's behest, various Swiss personnel arrived to teach and to supervise the younger children. But Rösli's moods were maddening. She could be insensitive and gruff one moment and positively brilliant the next. One of her best moves during that fall of 1941 was to arrange for Eugene Lyrer to come from Switzerland to be our teacher. Until then our education had been a volunteer effort. Irene Frank had focused on teaching the middle children

French, enduring their giggles and whispers. Walter S. taught the younger children mathematics and science. Walter K. taught the middle children history. In the evenings, Irene taught French and literature to any older children who had energy after a full day of chores. But for everyone, there was little consistency and planning behind it all.

Herr Lyrer arrived at Château la Hille that September. Walking up the dirt road with two of the boys who had gone to pick him up at the Foix train station, he carried a small overnight bag. Next to him, one of the boys balanced a wheelbarrow that held his second piece of luggage — a huge wicker suitcase. Herr Lyrer was a middle-aged man, about thirty-five or forty years old, who looked like a caricature of a professor. A short man in a rumpled wool suit with white shirt and tie, Herr Lyrer had piercing gray eyes, a jagged nose, dark bushy eyebrows and mustache, and graying black hair behind a receding hairline. Almost the instant he arrived, he opened the wicker suitcase to reveal it jammed full of such classics as *Treasure Island*, *War and Peace*, and Dante's *Inferno*. He had traveled all the way from Switzerland and most of his luggage consisted of books!

Herr Lyrer was a scholar and a teacher. In addition to establishing a library in one of the study rooms we used — his thirty or so books roughly doubled the size of our existing collection — he also instituted a formal schedule of classes for all the children. He taught history, mathematics, and German shorthand. Although he asked Irene Frank to continue teaching French to the younger children, he took over teaching duties from the two Walters.

For the older children, his presence meant the opportunity to renew regular afternoon classes. In the evenings, he read to us. I know it sounds strange — sixteen- and seventeen-year-olds listening to an adult read them stories — but most of us loved Herr Lyrer's deep voice resonating with *Trials and Tribulations from the Death Ship Caravan*.

Many weekends, Herr Lyrer traveled to Toulouse, and we awaited his return with anticipation. He invariably came back with a rucksack full of books he had acquired — probably with his own money, because the Swiss Red Cross funds were exclusively devoted to obtaining ever-more-scarce food supplies. We all raced to the library, hoping to be first to borrow one of the new books. Because Ruth had been named the official librarian, I usually had no trouble getting one or another of the new books. I remember how exciting it was to be the first to read *Moby Dick*. Each of us savored the few hours we were allowed to escape into those volumes.

Even though it had been Rösli who had invited Herr Lyrer to the château, the two of them didn't get along very well. Having few intellectual interests of her own, Rösli had little patience for other people's reading for pleasure. As far as she was concerned, our chores had to rank first and foremost in our lives. Consequently, she forbade recreational reading during our work hours of 8 A.M. to 4 P.M.

We all wanted additional reading time, so Ruth eventually came up with a solution. She had the idea that we should get up early in the morning — at the first light of dawn, around 6 A.M. — to do our reading. Not only did we get extra time for reading, but Ruth obtained the satisfaction of getting around one of Rösli's edicts.

Another pleasant outgrowth of Herr Lyrer's presence was the encouragement we received to perform skits and plays. Edith Goldapper and Ilse Brunell, two talented girls, loved to organize these events. They usually encouraged wide participation among the older children and in their enthusiasm managed to create excitement about the productions among everyone, young children and adults alike. We staged most of our performances in the dining room or outside in the courtyard to audiences comprised of the younger and middle children and eight or ten adult staff members.

Edith, whom we called "Omi," played the piano well enough to sometimes accompany Walter K. Pretty Ilse's silky brown hair flowed over her shoulders and, with her smooth soprano voice, everyone was appreciative when she joined Walter K. and Heinz as a soloist in their concerts. Boys especially liked her, and she enjoyed flirting, but Heinz had been her boyfriend for a while.

Together

WALTER S. CONTINUED informally teaching arithmetic to the younger ones because it came so naturally to him. He was very good in mathematics and he enjoyed teaching. He even secured a physics book and studied from it each evening while I was reading, or trying to make sense out of, a business and bookkeeping text that Alex had given me.

In retrospect, maybe that was what drew Walter and me together: We were opposites. While I was very pessimistic about our future, Walter was ever the optimist. He didn't just talk about the future — he planned for it. He studied from that physics book because he envisioned himself becoming a physicist. Though in Germany he was raised in a non-religious home, he had in Brussels become curious about Judaism and actually signed up to learn Hebrew (unlike me, who was forced by Gustav to take weekly Hebrew lessons). His Hebrew teacher turned out to be a Zionist, and Walter was fully taken with romantic ideas of emigrating to Palestine. So his vision was to be a physicist in the Jewish state of Palestine. I was (and still am) very cynical about Palestine/Israel. I couldn't imagine Jews living any more happily together than they did living as part of a larger culture, such as Germany.

"You know, in Palestine, we will be building a homeland from almost nothing," he said a number of times. "We will not only grow our own food, but we will have the world's best scientists and artists." He didn't say it, but I knew he saw himself as one of those top scientists.

What most struck me was his use of the word "we," as in *he and I*. I nearly held my breath as he spoke about "us" in this idealistic future. I realized as he talked on about Palestine I didn't care where I lived, as long as I was with him. So I began talking about the wonderful things we would do in Palestine — building a home and growing wonderful fruits and vegetables. Wasn't it the land of milk and honey?

I studied bookkeeping in the same spirit. I had little interest in numbers, but that book communicated my commitment to a future life together. Actually, I increasingly found myself interested in nursing as I watched Rösli tend to children in our small sick room. But there was no book to study about nursing, so I stayed with bookkeeping.

WITH RELIEF I learned the news of America's entry into the war on December 7, 1941. Southern France had come to feel more and more the pressure exercised by the German occupation in the north, with food in ever shorter supply. We were still able to hear the English news broadcasts from London, and the news of steady German advances in Russia made us fear the worst. We reasoned that the entry of the United States of America into the war might finally supply the Allies with the added strength they so badly needed. But would it be in time to do us any good?

It certainly wouldn't help Mutti's efforts to leave Germany for the United States. While that option seemed ever more distant, even without war, the fact the United States was now officially fighting Germany seemed to reduce Mutti's ever-dwindling options even more. But for the first time in what seemed forever, we saw a glimmer of hope that the tide of the war could change.

In terms of my day-to-day living, I tried to stay wrapped up in my chores and classes, and it seemed as if most of the other children did as well. I enjoyed trooping out on cold mornings with Walter, Jacques, Alex, Lixie, and others to gather and chop wood in the nearby forests and then haul it back in a wheelbarrow. Irene Frank continued to teach French literature. She tried hard to engage us in Victor Hugo's *Les Misérables* — all ten volumes. Most of us had no interest in it, but Ruth and Jacques loved slogging through the literary French, and together they studied the strange French spellings and pronunciations.

What increasingly occupied our attention that December was readying the entertainment for the upcoming Christmas celebration. Last year's debate about whether we should celebrate Christmas was merely a distant memory, as were our own Jewish holidays. The prospect of celebrating Christmas energized us as much as it did our Swiss Red Cross supervisors.

Walter K. and Heinz spent endless hours practicing the Mozart and Schubert pieces they were planning to play for us. They weren't great friends but had come to respect each other's musical abilities.

Edith Goldapper and Ilse Brunell meticulously planned a presentation of one of Molière's comedies, "The Precious Damsels." They attempted to recruit me to play the part of Cathos, the niece of a well-to-do bourgeois. I declined, telling them I'd rather contribute behind-the-scenes help, building background scenery. Because the entire play takes place in an elegant Parisian house, all we had to do was stage the play in our dining room, adding some painted sheets to suggest different rooms for different scenes.

Once I heard the performers rehearsing their lines, I was even more relieved I had declined a role. At one point, Cathos asks Magdelon: "As for me, Uncle, all I can tell you is that I find marriage a very shocking performance. How can one endure the idea of sleeping beside a man who is absolutely nude?" That was only one of a number of suggestive lines, and I could only imagine how quickly my face would flush red. I also wondered how Rösli would react.

Rösli was totally absorbed in worrying about the holiday meal. Almost every day, she mounted her rickety bicycle and pedaled her way to one of the nearby villages and towns — Montegue, Pailhès, or Foix — trying to use our ration cards to secure such staples as flour, sugar, and butter. Most days, she was only marginally successful, thanks to the German pressure to the north. Then, she had to figure how to squirrel away such long-lasting items as flour and sugar, all the while encouraging Frau Schlesinger to use up more perishable goods like butter and eggs by baking cookies that could be stored.

I looked forward to the Christmas celebration for the good food and camaraderie, but I also felt more than a little apprehension. Christmastime in each of the previous three years had signaled difficult times ahead: Three years earlier, in 1938, it preceded by only a couple of weeks my departure from Darmstadt. In 1939, probably the best of the three years, I was living with war clouds hanging over us at the Home Général Bernheim, and last year in Seyre it was the last pleasant event before months of miserable winter conditions.

All of us were feeling the same anxieties, but we very much wanted to enjoy the celebration that Christmas Eve. Rösli had thought of and obtained nearly everything, even beautiful glass balls, shiny silver paper, and wood-carved angels to decorate the tree; that evening she surprised us all when she produced sugar candy to hang on the tree. "I saved it for tonight because I didn't want anyone to be tempted to eat it in advance," she explained. Together with the candle holders from the last year, the tree sparkled. As if all that wasn't enough to overwhelm us, Rösli gave each of us a small chocolate bar she had wrapped with a small paper bag of cookies.

Dinner was extraordinary. Frau Schlesinger had prepared delicious cold chicken, sandwiches, several kinds of potato salad, and bean salad. Dessert was a Gugelhupf, along with a wonderful sweet bread pudding. Frau Schlesinger was in an especially good mood because Alex Frank had arranged for her husband, Ernste, to be designated an "essential" gardener, making him exempt from deportation. She, Ernste, and their son, Pauli were glowing with happiness. We had invited several farmers along with their wives and children, and watching them all, I couldn't help but feel envious of their being together. Like all the other children, I would have given anything to be reunited with my family. After dinner, everyone gathered for the performance of "The Precious Damsels," which had the adult staff members laughing knowingly among themselves. Rösli blushed whenever the lines were a bit risqué.

Not surprisingly, the highlight of the evening was when Walter K. and Heinz performed. Walter played Beethoven's "Waldstein" Sonata and Grieg's "Ghost" Concerto, and then he and Heinz played several Bach and Beethoven pieces. They capped off the evening by playing "O Tannenbaum" and "Silent Night."

I went to bed with a warm, if somewhat longing, feeling. *Bittersüss* (bittersweet).

Control

As ANTICIPATED, winter brought with it a certain number of problems. The most immediate one was clothing. Many of us had outgrown the coats we brought with us and the warm clothing the Swiss Red Cross sent the previous winter. However, we received a shipment of wool from Switzerland, and our most important needs were taken care of as soon as we finished knitting gloves and sweaters for everyone in January.

More urgently, many of us now developed carbuncles, which, according to a local doctor, were caused by lack of vitamins. The disappearance of fruits and vegetables from our diets had caught up with us once again. And once again, my skin bore the brunt of the scourge. I suffered terribly, though it wasn't as awful as it had been the previous winter. At least this time the sores were confined mostly to my legs. We treated them with Eau de Javel — chlorine solution. They were slow in healing, and new ones popped up the minute one of us breathed a sigh of relief.

But the worst of our post-Christmas difficulties were "people" problems. Most seriously, the Alex-Rösli situation came to a head. It had been simmering for months.

During the summer and fall of 1941, Rösli continued to expand her own role and reduce Alex's. In effect, she had been turning their joint administration duties into a one-person operation. For a time, Alex had assumed responsibility for structural and building matters. He had completed the well and installed the piping that led into the house. He also made sure the boys chopped enough wood each day for the stove.

Once the water was running and the boys had established a regular routine for obtaining wood, Alex had less and less to do. In a vain attempt to hold onto vestiges of his co-directorship, sometimes he created new responsibilities for himself. One fall day, for example, Alex assigned six of the older boys to a project replacing rotted beams in an abandoned barn a few hundred yards from the château. It turned out he hadn't informed Rösli, and she had assigned the same boys to help harvest potatoes from one of our gardens. When she found the boys in the barn and learned what had happened, Rösli was livid. From outside the barn, I overheard the confrontation.

"Alex, you must inform me when you want to make work assignments," Rösli demanded.

"I am in charge of structural projects," Alex replied. "I needed to get the barn fixed before the winter snow comes. You must let me get these matters completed."

"And we need to get the potatoes harvested before they rot. From now on, I must insist on approving any projects you want to do," Rösli said.

Alex turned and walked away. He looked very dejected, as though supplanted by Rösli. He had saved us in our hour of greatest need and deserved to be treated with more respect. But because the Swiss Red Cross controlled the purse strings, he had little leverage.

Moreover, Alex had to think about more than just himself. He had his wife and mother to worry about, too. They weren't abstract worries. Elka's health continued to deteriorate. At one point she was sent to a hospital in Foix, but she returned after a few days because conditions there were so bad — understaffing from the war made her leery of whatever care she had received.

If Alex weren't needed, and the Swiss didn't like him, might they force him and his family to leave? Where could they go? France and the rest of Europe had become a jungle for Jews. Irene Frank sometimes referred to Rösli disparagingly as "The Valkyrie" in her conversations with Alex. Walter K. explained to me that "valkyrie," usually used as a negative term, were mythological women who sent men to their deaths in battle.

Alex's departure, when it came that January 1942, wasn't just a surprise but a shock. He announced to the older children he was leaving the château to work at a nearby farm. Elka and Irene would stay on at the château. As he prepared to leave, rumors swirled about concerning the "trigger" behind Alex's departure. The most oft-repeated rumor had it that Rösli had accused him of taking food — and had obtained his agreement to leave in exchange for continuing to harbor his wife and mother. There was another more disturbing rumor — that Rösli had accused him of being sexually involved with one of the girls. I never saw any indication Alex would have abused his position by committing either of the two rumored offenses.

The worst of our post-Christmas trauma was to come just a few weeks after Alex's departure, at least for me. It stemmed from the friction between Rösli and Ruth, which also had become worse over time. Ruth not only continued to mature physically — her once-solid torso had become much more curvaceous — but also emotionally as she became increasingly independent and resistant to authority. She especially resented taking orders she considered silly or inappropriate.

Ruth found most offensive Rösli's practice of grading each of us on how well we made our beds and how neatly we kept our little "cubby" area of shelves where we stored our clothing. Outside each bedroom, Rösli posted a list that tracked our scores from her daily inspections. So much attention to trivial and insignificant matters grated on Ruth, particularly after we read Vichy's propaganda sheets reporting German military advances around Europe. We knew the news reports were slanted to enhance Germany's achievements; nevertheless, we could tell that even with the exaggeration stripped away, the truth was very grim.

Exasperated one day after reading one of the Vichy news sheets, Ruth complained, "Here we have thousands of people dying every day and this woman is worried about how we fold our blankets or tuck in our sleeping bags."

I thought Ruth was holding Rösli responsible for too much. "What do you want Rösli to do about Hitler?" I asked. "She has her hands full taking care of all of us."

"She could be using the time and energy she spends on inspecting our beds to put aside supplies for the war effort, or mobilizing relief agencies," Ruth argued.

A few days after our conversation, I returned from an early-morning wood-chopping expedition to hear Ruth shouting at Rösli on the château's second floor: "The world is going up in flames! We are sick with worry about our parents, and you treat us like retarded children!" She was holding one of Rösli's lists of our neatness scores, and her dark brown eyes were livid with anger.

"Regardless of what is happening in the outside world, we must have order here," Rösli answered. "Please put the list back up. We cannot be responsible for the craziness of the world."

Ruth threw the list to the floor as she ran down the stairs and out the front door. When she returned late that afternoon, she was smiling. "I have found a solution," she told me. "The Schmutz family has hired me to care for their small children. I can live with them on their farm. I won't have to endure this stupidity any longer."

"Will we see you again?"

"Yes, on weekends," she said. "They live a two-hour walk from here, but I will return on weekends to see Betty, you, and my other friends."

I couldn't share Ruth's happiness. I would be left without my best friend.

ABOVE: *Inge's parents, Clara Neu and Julius Joseph (center), were married in March 1919. Inge's Oma Josephine is seated to the right of Julius, and Opa Hermann and his wife are seated to the left of Clara. Cousin Gustav Wurzweiler is seated to the far left of Clara.*

LEFT: *Inge's Mutti and Papa in approximately 1920.*

RIGHT: *The Joseph family in the 1920s: Papa and Mutti with young Inge (right) her older sister, Lilo (left) (the family's live-in maid is to the left of Papa).*

BELOW: *Julius Joseph (right) at his animal-fat rendering factory in approximately 1930.*

Inge (left) posed with her older sister, Lilo (center), and their mother for this photo just before Lilo left Germany in spring 1938. Her father was in jail at this time.

Inge's journey from her home in Darmstadt, Germany, in January 1939, through Belgium and France, including her first attempt to escape into Switzerland in January 1943 and her second, successful escape in October 1943.

LEFT: *Inge (top center) with Lotte Nussbaum (left) and Edith Goldapper (right) and younger children they helped care for, taken in Brussels, 1939 or 1940.*

BELOW: *At Château la Hille in the south of France, which Inge called "an idyllic self-contained village," the Swiss Red Cross protected her and other German Jewish children from the Nazis.*

ABOVE: *Daily life at la Hille included outdoor meals.*
(Photo from the United States Holocaust Memorial Museum, courtesy Sebastian Steiger.)

BELOW: *A dormitory at la Hille.*

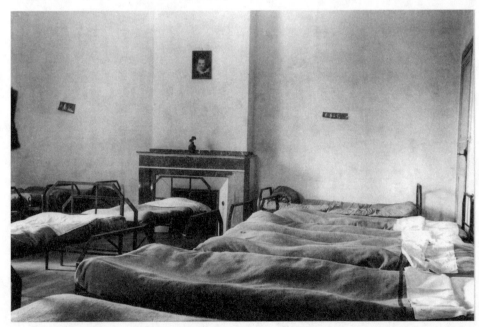

Daily chores at la Hille in-cluded carrying water and tending the potato garden.
(Photos from the United States Holocaust Memorial Museum, courtesy Sebastian Steiger.)

ABOVE: *There was also time for play at la Hille.*
(Photo from the United States Holocaust Memorial Museum, courtesy Sebastian Steiger.)

BELOW: *Elka and Alex Frank administered the Home Général Bernheim in Brussels, the group home to which Inge was taken by her cousin Gustav. When Brussels was attacked by the Germans, the Franks helped the children escape by train to southern France, where the Swiss Red Cross came to their aid. This picture was probably taken in Brussels in 1939.*

ABOVE: *Maurice Dubois of the Swiss Red Cross talks with a boy outside the château.*

BELOW: *Glora Schlesinger and Rösli Näf (right), the Swiss Red Cross nurse who directed Château la Hille.*

Inge with Walter Strauss (left) and Elias Haskelevich (center), probably taken in 1941. After the war, Inge mused, "Then there is the photo of Walter and me. Each time I view it, it is as if I must shield my eyes from the sun."

ABOVE: *Edith Goldapper,*
who organized plays, and
Walter Kamlet, the pianist.
(Photo from the United States Holocaust
Memorial Museum, courtesy Walter Reed.)

RIGHT: *Ruth Schütz (left), who had*
aved Inge from jumping from a win-
dow at the children's home in
Brussels, with Inge at Château
la Hille around 1942.

LEFT: Inge Helft w[...]
group with Inge Jos[...]
Strauss that attemp[...]
Switzerland.

BELOW: Three of In[...]
Hille (left to right): [...]
who was also in the [...]
tempt an escape, Elk[...]
Brunell.

ABOVE: *Walter Strauss (top center) and Inge (top right), with Hans Garfunkel, one of the mathematicians (bottom left), and other friends at Château la Hille around 1942.*

RIGHT: *Manfred Vos, who made the first escape attempt along with Inge and Walter.*

BELOW: *Seeing Henri Vos, Manfred's eight-year-old brother, "was like seeing a miniature Manfred, every single day" after the failed escape attempt.*

The postcard that Walter sent Inge in March 1943, shortly after his arrest, reads in part, "I have not been at peace as much as at present, now that I managed to decide to stay." Inge concluded that he had decided not to attempt an escape.

ABOVE: *Inge, at left, with other girls at Château la Hille in the summer of 1943, several months after Walter was arrested and before Inge made her solo escape in late August.*

BELOW: *The forged identification card that Inge used in traveling through France under the name "Irene Jerome" in the fall of 1943.*

The only known photograph of all the la Hille children together, in Seyre, 1940. Inge is in the center of the second row from the back, with her arms around Edith Goldapper (left) and Alix Grabkowitz, with Ruth Schütz to the right of Alix.

After the war, Inge settled in Chicago to study nursing and make her career. Here she is visiting her father, who lived in New York City, sometime in the late 1940s or early 1950s.

ABOVE: Inge married Frank Bleier in the late 1950s. Here they are with their daughter Julie at a family wedding in 1977.

LEFT: Inge Joseph Bleier in about 1980.

RIGHT: *Rösli Näf, the Swiss Red Cross nurse who directed the children's home at Château la Hille, at her home in February 1995.*

BELOW: *Inge's nephew David Gumpert visiting Château la Hille in 1994.*

Laundry

THAT SPRING, about ten of us decided to resume our practice of denying ourselves in order to help those in camps. We realized from letters trickling in how much better off we were than most refugees at that time. We had a little routine where we hid the slice of bread we were served in the morning and again for lunch and handed the slices over to Walter S., who stuffed them in his pockets. Because he was seated close to the dining room door, he was able to vanish after the meal was finished to take the bread up to one of the towers of the castle. During warm weather we spread them out and let them dry in the sun; otherwise, I toasted them over the fire we used for boiling the laundry. The latter was more complicated, because my activities were in full view of everyone. I am still amazed the administration did not notice anything amiss. Sometimes we collected the dried fruit we received for dessert to add to the packages. We sent packages out about every ten days to Walter's and another boy's brothers, still in Gurs, the French camp in southern France. Walter, who went daily to the nearest village for the mail and errands, was in a key position to send the packages. The letters of thanks that we received from the two older boys strengthened our willpower.

It's strange now to think that in our barebones existence at the château we were, relative to other Jews in Nazi-controlled territory, living in the lap of luxury. Yet, we never had quite enough to eat — to the extent children argued about whether one or another received a larger slice of bread in the morning. Once, when Ruth's younger sister, Betty, spilled some precious milk on the table at dinner, she actually licked it up, like a cat, to keep from

wasting it. It was especially difficult for the teenagers, since we were growing and always hungry; yet we were expected by the Swiss, and by each
other, to sacrifice food to help the younger children among us.

Our additional efforts on behalf of the refugees helped solidify the
bond between Walter and me. Both of us received satisfaction, once again,
from doing something positive for those who didn't share our compara-
tive comforts. If we were young during the 1960s, we might have joined
the Peace Corps.

Moreover, because we were working behind the backs of Rösli and the
other adults, it was as if we were co-conspirators. We had daily decisions
to make and tasks to perform — whether to store the bread in the tower or
toast it over the fire, when to wrap the packages, where to hide them prior
to Walter's taking them to Montegue. It was what I imagined married life
to be like.

The daily planning and tasks brought me and the others closer.
Though no one ever said anything, I benefited from the perception that I
wasn't totally loyal to Rösli, that I was willing to betray her for something
more important than the arbitrary rules of the Swiss Red Cross.

These activities also partially masked my recurring feelings of loneliness, especially during holidays. Easter, a day that triggered so much anti-
Semitism throughout history, was one of my favorite holidays. In Germany, it was a secular celebration. On Easter Sunday, Mutti and Papa
would hide colored eggs and pieces of chocolate under cabinets and in
closets around the house before Lilo and I got up. We scurried around our
large house trying to be the first to find the best treats.

Shortly after Easter of 1942, I wrote this letter to Lilo in Chicago:

April 20, 1942

My Dear Lotti:

I hope that you and Lutz are well and that you are settled in
comfortably. I have not had mail from you for a long time. Your
last letter was dated November 23. I don't understand why I have
no letters from you and Papa. All the other children have had
mail. I heard from Mutti last in January. Please write to Papa that
he can send letters for Mutti to me, and I hope to hear from you
soon.

How did you spend Easter? I suppose you both were free for a few days. Do you still work in the same office, my little Lotti? It is difficult for me to realize that you are married. I remember you as a sassy little kid when we last saw each other.

Here at Château la Hille there were none of our famous hunts for candy and eggs. We now have four days of Easter vacation. We had many visitors, and on two days we were allowed to do whatever we wanted — going for a walk, ping pong, etc. For the second free day, a planned excursion had to be canceled because of bad weather. We had a good concert last night and there was dancing until 10:30 P.M. You would have enjoyed it, but I don't care for it.

Do you still read a great deal? We have quite a few good books and I still love to read. What do you hear from Hilde and Walter? From Robert, Selma, and the others? Have you been lately in New York to see Papa?

Next week we will resume our lessons and the structure of our days will be different. We have several gardens and fields where we grow potatoes and vegetables. These will sustain us for the summer and later.

I hope you answer soon and that I will get your mail. Please let me know whether there might be a possibility to bring Mutti to you.

> *Love,*
> *Inge*

This letter was returned to me some weeks later, stamped with "no forwarding address." We were now completely out of contact, again.

Interestingly, I did not mention Walter in my note. At the concert I didn't have much contact with him. It was difficult for me to be with him in group settings because everyone wanted to be with him and he was naturally friendly. As much as I hated to admit it, I felt he was too friendly, too accommodating. What were these boys doing for Walter? In that respect, my feelings echoed Mutti's reactions to Papa and his employees. Both Walter and Papa were nice to the point of neglecting the most important people in their lives.

Besides, I wanted Lilo to feel guilty about not writing to me. If I told her about my wonderful boyfriend, how guilty would she feel? And yet I didn't want to worry her about the growing uncertainty of my future. After all, no path was making itself apparent for an exit from Château la Hille, and even I didn't want to think too much about that.

AND AGAIN it was June and July. I spent most of my time gardening, and this year it offered extra enjoyment. We had started a small garden in the castle yard itself, about twelve garden beds, where I grew cucumbers, carrots, radishes, and tomatoes. It kept me busy each afternoon, although it was much smaller than our regular garden, which was off to the side of the castle. Because this summer was very dry, I was not allowed to use water from the pump for watering the plants; instead, I had to fetch it from the river.

The more involved I stayed in our day-to-day chores, the less I thought about the passage of time and our growing uncertainty.

Inside our community, not only did vegetables continue to sprout forth, but so did love. Dela's growing involvement with Manfred Kamlet, Walter K.'s younger brother, was a big relief. Manfred was totally different from his brother. He looked a lot like Walter K., but was actually a friendly fellow and not nearly as intellectual.

Speaking of Walter K., one of the more interesting relationships that evolved was between him and Inge Helft, the indulged, dark-eyed, olive-skinned girl. She was very much turning into the intellectual who loved to discuss such ideas as whether or not God exists and the relevance of existentialism to our lives. She also liked to write poetry. Apparently her level of discussion and poetry were up to Walter K.'s approval, for we often saw the two of them perched on one or another of the hilltops when Walter S. and I took our after-dinner walks.

But as wonderfully peaceful as our existence appeared on the surface, lunchtimes provided the most vivid reminders of the deteriorating state of the world outside our walls. Our mid-day meal became increasingly tense because that's when our mail arrived, delivered by a French postman on a bicycle. Increasingly, one or another of the children received bad news from a relative or had letters addressed to parents returned with the notice, "Gone without leaving a forwarding address."

One day, Edith Goldapper received a letter telling her that her parents had been deported. "My father fought for Germany in World War I!" she screamed frantically. "He lost the sight in one of his eyes. Now they try to kill him! Why? What did he do?" There was no comfort for her or anyone else who received such horrible letters; the rest of us knew one day it would be our turn.

WALTER WAS, as always, more optimistic than I. He continued to make plans for our future, including minute details. Late one evening, as we returned from an errand on a nearby farm, we crossed the bridge over the brook where our laundry equipment was located. Because it was pitch dark, Walter had taken hold of my hand, and as we passed the makeshift laundry, he squeezed it and said, "After the war is over and as soon as we are settled, I will buy you the best washing machine there is." In spite of my happiness about his vision of a life together, I could no more imagine the end of things than I could dream of one day possessing a modern washing machine!

Instinct

A S TIME MARCHED on in 1942, a stark reality haunted all the older children: While French law still protected Jewish children until they reached age eighteen, we were all getting older, inching toward that awful milestone when we could be rounded up and sent to a concentration camp. I was looking toward my seventeenth birthday that coming September. And then the countdown would begin. What would I do when I turned eighteen?

As if to underline my concern, we received ever-more-frequent visits at the château from Lieutenant Danielle, a French police official. Every few weeks he arrived, wearing a blue uniform and rimmed cap, in his unmarked car. We watched as he spoke with Rösli, appearing pleasant but distant and officious.

I could sense a certain tension between the two. He wanted her to give him written lists detailing the names and birth dates of all the children. He was always curious about the occasional new arrivals. Rösli resisted providing him with information in writing, all the while trying to keep their relationship relaxed and casual. "You know, Lieutenant," I heard her telling him more than once, "I can simply tell you what you need to know."

She was hesitating and he was increasingly aggressive. Rösli wanted to protect us, and Lieutenant Danielle wanted his officers to be able to get their hands on us before we vanished into the countryside.

Already some of the teens approaching eighteen had started to slip away. Werner Epstein, a husky fellow who loved to help Frau Schlesinger in the kitchen, had departed the previous fall, a few weeks prior to his eighteenth birthday on December 14. One day he simply was no longer with us. Word circulated among us that, hoping to remain anonymous long enough to outlast the war, he had gone to work for a sympathetic farming family.

As the summer dragged on, I increasingly had visions of a German-controlled Europe. But I could not conceive how I would figure into such a world. I had heard about concentration camps. But being sixteen years old had been my protective shield. As of August 1942, no one under the age of eighteen had been arrested.

As ANXIOUS and crazy as I often become, I do have an instinct for danger. The anxiety of which I spoke wasn't just something I alone dreamed up, based on Lieutenant Danielle's visits.

Hans Garfunkel shared my anxiety. In fact, his instinct may have been even more finely honed as he caught snatches of increasingly scary BBC reports. Jews were being rounded up in various parts of France, including Paris. He couldn't determine, however, if the French were still respecting the rights of children, if the roundups were distinguishing between those under and over age eighteen.

One evening in mid-August, as Walter and I walked on a hill near the château, he told me Hans was so distressed over the radio reports he was hearing that he had begun hiding food in the nearby woods and tried to convince Walter and two other boys to begin sleeping there at night. One of the other boys agreed with Hans, but Walter and the fourth boy were opposed.

"Hans is a worrier even in the best of times," Walter said. "I told them that the police won't bother children out in the country. What sort of interest could they have in rounding us up? Hans's proposal seems so desperate, and we have no cause for desperate measures at this point in time. Besides, look at my brother. How much better off are we with the Swiss Red Cross protecting us?"

The force of Walter's arguments, and of his personality, convinced the boys to abandon Hans's plans and they remained in the château. I wanted so much to believe Walter, but I was having trouble. "You know, maybe Hans isn't so crazy, for once," I said. "What would be wrong with the older ones among us sleeping in the woods at night? The weather is warm. We would get some practice for avoiding the French and the Germans, because surely, at some point, we will need to hide from them."

Walter looked at me, skepticism written all over his innocent, boyish face. "Now you're becoming as hysterical as Hans. Do you want to get everyone in a panic? And upset Rösli and the others from the Swiss Red Cross, as if we don't trust their ability to protect us?"

I backed off. I wished I had just a fraction of Walter's positive outlook, if only to mute my own anxiety. As August progressed, though, I began to doubt his wisdom. Sometime around August 15 or 20, Lieutenant Danielle showed up and ordered Rösli to provide him with the list he was seeking. I don't know exactly what he said — probably something about new regulations or perhaps a direct threat — but I saw her hand him some papers.

Then on August 24 a young Jewish girl from Paris, about eleven or twelve years old, joined our group. She had somehow been smuggled to us by her parents, and she told a harrowing story of Parisian Jews, surprised in their homes, being rounded up by French police.

"Did they arrest children and teenagers as well?" I asked, afraid to hear her answer.

She looked surprised. "Yes, they took entire families, everyone, even the youngest children and infants."

A wave of nausea trembled through my body, reminding me of the morning in Brussels more than two years ago when Frau Schlesinger informed us the Germans were attacking. Our protective shield was quickly crumbling. We would discover just how completely on the next day, August 25.

Regrouping

I AWOKE with a start in the early-morning darkness that August 25. I had been dreaming about being in Darmstadt with Mutti. In my dream a deep horn — not a car horn — was sounding. Here in real life, I realized the horn had come from the darkness outside our room. As I thought the question — what would trucks or buses be doing in the middle of the night at this remote castle in the southern French countryside? — my gut told me the answer.

I strained to listen for other sounds outside the room. Hearing nothing, I got up and tiptoed on the cold stone floor to one of the two long, narrow windows, unlatched the glass, drew the window toward me, and pushed open a heavy, wooden shutter against a strong, humid wind. Trees were silhouetted against the first light of dawn in the sky. It must have been 4:30. As I stuck my head out the window, I heard a man's voice directly below, speaking in French. "Why do we arrest children?" he asked. A second male voice answered, "Those are our orders."

As I brought my head back in, I heard the unmistakable sound of Hans Garfunkel's voice coming from another part of the château. "Mademoiselle Näf! Mademoiselle Näf! The gendarmes are here, Mademoiselle Näf!"

"It is the police, and they're right outside our window," I announced to my roommates, just stirring from their sleep. "We have to try to find a way out!" But even as they struggled in their confusion to comprehend what was happening, something told me it was too late. My suddenly dry mouth kept me from saying more.

I rushed out of our room and into the larger adjoining room, carefully negotiating my way through the long dormitory with eight iron beds on either side occupied by mostly younger girls. Out in the hall I stepped carefully to avoid the porcelain urns, placed outside the dorms for use as emergency toilets so we didn't have to use the outhouses at night, and headed for the stairs.

One floor below, at the foot of the stairs, a dim hall light was on and I saw Rösli, dressed in her navy blue, wool bathrobe with her blonde hair hanging loose, talking to a khaki-uniformed policeman with a silver-braided, black-rimmed cap. "You are not allowed here," she stated firmly in her breathless speaking style. "This house is under the authority . . . of the Swiss Red Cross. . . . The one hundred children here . . . are under our authority . . . and as the director . . . I cannot allow you in."

"We have our orders," the policeman, equally firm, replied. I spotted a clipboard with papers in his hand. "Some of the older children must come with us," he said, nodding to the papers, apparently containing a list. He handed the clipboard to Rösli. As she scanned the list, about a dozen policemen swarmed around her toward the stairs. They were in full battle dress with blue uniforms, black tunics, revolvers on their waists, shin-high black boots, and black-rimmed hats with silver braids; they were ready to mount the stairs.

"Please let me go up to my room and dress first," Rösli requested.

"We don't have time for that," the khaki-uniformed commander replied, shaking his head.

"Then at least let me get the children up so they aren't awakened by strange policemen at their beds."

Again, the policeman shook his head. "You can go with my men if you would like. But we must ensure security." The policemen parted ranks to allow Rösli to lead them up the stairs to the dormitories.

Back in my room, now dimly lit from an overhead bulb, I smelled smoke. Lixie Grabkowicz had started a small fire in the room's large fireplace and was heaping letters and photos into it. "What are you doing?" I asked.

"I don't want the police to find anything about my parents. Who knows what they will do to them?"

I briefly considered following suit, but I couldn't bear the thought of throwing away my letters and photos of Mutti, even if it meant the Germans would get hold of them. Instead, I quickly began dressing in one of the red cotton jumpers supplied by the Swiss Red Cross and worn by nearly all la Hille girls during the warm season. In the midst of my panic, I noticed the dress had become a bit short.

Margo and Dela were whispering something about trying to escape into the woods. "It's too late," I announced. "There are dozens of police and they are completely on their guard. We might be able to try running away later, but right now we are prisoners." The clunk-clunk of boots on the stone stairs leading up to the bedrooms was an exclamation point to my argument.

Rösli entered our dormitory and told us tersely, "Our château is surrounded by gendarmes. They are stationed in front of each door and we must do as they say. Please get yourselves dressed as quickly as you can, begin packing some things for going away, and come down to the courtyard. The police have asked us to cooperate."

Rösli kept her words to a minimum to avoid weeping. As she and the policemen walked back through the adjoining dormitory occupied by the younger girls, I saw two gendarmes posted at the doorway. Were we expected to get dressed under their watchful eyes? Looking out the second-floor bedroom window, I made out the moving black figures of men in the field below.

I focused on gathering socks, underwear, and berets. Would I be away so long that I should bring my heavy, blue sweater? Should I wear my comfortable but irreplaceable leather shoes or clip-clop in my Dutch wooden shoes? No, wooden shoes might be okay for doing laundry in the nearby brook and tending the vegetable garden in the courtyard, but not for running away. What about letters, family photos, the Sherlock Holmes stories I was reading?

I couldn't concentrate, and it wasn't just the shock of the police raid. I felt anger welling up. If I had just listened to my instincts and to Hans Garfunkel, instead of to Walter S., I wouldn't be in this situation. If Walter were more savvy about the world and less naive. . . . For the first time in a long time, I thought about Gustav. I had never heard a word from him after Brussels, though I knew from Mutti and Lilo's letters he had made it to the United States.

No, I wouldn't take any warm clothing along. That would be giving in to the notion I might never return to Château la Hille. But I would take photos of Mutti, Papa, and Lilo. And some paper to write letters on.

I was about to ask Dela what she was taking, because she was always very organized and practical about such matters, until I saw how seriously absorbed she was in packing. Indeed, no conversation went on among any of us as we organized our clothing from our shelves and boxes under our beds and used the outhouses immediately in back of the château. As I pulled on a pair of thin, white socks and tied the worn, black laces of my precious, brown, leather shoes, it hit me. The language! We were being ordered around by uniformed men speaking soothing French. Whenever I dreamt about my last days in Germany or imagined being rounded up, the orders were being barked out in harsh German from German soldiers or police.

The sounds of boots on stone floors resounded throughout the huge château. While there was no way to change the course of events, I summoned my courage to seek one concession from the two policemen standing in the doorway. "Please, can everyone dress alone?" I asked. The men ignored me, and a leering smile spread across the face of one young policeman.

I was a little ahead of everyone else in dressing and packing, and so I surveyed the situation. Maybe, just maybe, while the policemen were preoccupied with making sure everyone was dressing and packing, there might be an opportunity to slip out the front door. I walked past the two gendarmes, who seemed not to notice me, and stepped quickly down the stone stairs leading to the ground floor. As I crept through the dimly-lit hallway leading to the château's front entrance, I heard the sound of crying just outside a half-opened door.

It was Rösli, sobbing and pleading with the commanding officer. "Please tell me where you are taking the children. That's all I ask."

"I don't have that information," responded the commander.

"You must know something," Rösli sobbed. "You aren't just going to drive around in circles with these children. Please, just one bit of information."

The commander finally hesitated. His voice lowered, barely audible on the other side of the partially open door. "I will tell you one thing," he said to Rösli. "Take the valuables, the gold and watches, from the children before they leave."

Rösli stopped crying mid-breath and gasped. A nauseous feeling overcame me. We were going to be taken to a concentration camp. I had heard stories about how guards at the camps collected jewelry, cash, and other valuables from Jews when they arrived.

When I emerged from the hallway leading from the kitchen to the château's courtyard, Rösli had her hand over her mouth. The commander was walking away from her through the large courtyard. There was no running away. My initial impression had been correct — police were everywhere. In addition to the thirty or forty still inside the château, a dozen uniformed men, guarding the two arched entrances leading from the courtyard, milled around.

A high point of each day had been seeing the courtyard and its eight-foot-high, beige stone walls with elegant round turrets at each corner. Always so romantically medieval and French, the structures now seemed dark and forbidding in the early-dawn light.

Before long, all the teens were in the courtyard along with a few curious younger children. The children were silent and attentive, even the irrepressible Pierre Bergman, a small, dark-haired eleven-year-old who always argued with adults and talked with his friends. To make matters worse, the policemen were taking no care to avoid trampling the carrots, cucumbers, and tomatoes in our newest vegetable garden. Where we were going, I knew, the vegetable garden would make no difference.

I kept my eyes on the tall, slender commander in beige and the clipboard he held in his right hand. When it was clear all the teens and adults were assembled, he announced: "By order of national authorities, we are undertaking a regrouping of refugees in this area. I want those whose names I call to go back into the château and assemble in the large room on the first floor. I will begin the roll.

"Inge Berlin.
"Ilse Brunell.
"Edith Goldapper.
"Alix Grabkowicz.
"Inge Helft.
"Ruth Herz.
"Adele Hochberger."

I was fascinated by the clash between the French pronunciation and the German names, as the commander invariably placed the emphasis on the wrong syllable. Thus, Edith Goldapper became "Edith GoldapPER" and Adele Hochberger became "Adele HochberGER."

"Inge JOSEPH."

At hearing my name, I walked back into the château, my legs stiff and heavy. I tried to focus on what additional items to pack, in hopes the terrible churning in my stomach would subside.

I heard the names called outside.

"Margot Kern.
"Helga Klein.
"Rita Leistner.
"Lotte Nussbaum.
"Ilse Rosenblatt.
"Ruth Schütz.
"Edith Moser.
"Inge Schragenheim.
"Irma Seelenfreund.
"Frieda Steinberg.
"Ilse Wulff."

I wasn't sure whether the commander noticed Ruth wasn't there or if he knew she was living with a farm family. We all avoided eye contact as we silently filed into the dining room.

Outside the dining room, in the courtyard, it was the boys' turn.

"Charles Blumenfeld.
"Henri Brunell.
"Emile Dortort.
"Bertrand Elkan.
"Werner Epstein.
"Hans Garfunkel.
"Manfred Kamlet.
"Walter Kamlet."

Walter Kamlet, six feet tall and razor thin, looked, with his wavy brown hair uncombed, especially awkward. He quickly glanced at Inge Helft. I couldn't be sure if the police knew Werner Epstein was no longer among us. The roll continued:

"Kurt Klein.
"Pierre Landesman.

"Leon Lewin.
"Kurt Moser.
"Adolphe Nussbaum.
"Jacques Roth.
"Pierre Salz.
"Heinz Storosum.
"Walter Strauss."

As Walter walked in, heads turned. The ever-present smile on Walter's face was gone now, and his dark, raccoon-like eyes receded into his face, making his pug nose more prominent. He scanned the assembled group until his eyes met mine. He gave me the weakest of smiles, more a clenching of his lips, and walked over to where Jacques Roth stood. The two whispered to each other.

"Norbert Stückler.
"Manfred Vos.
"Luzian Wolfgang."

At the end of the list, the commander hesitated and then called out two more names: "Glora Schlesinger and Ernste Schlesinger." Our cook now looked more somber than I had ever seen her. Her balding, good-natured husband, Ernste, held her hand.

Outside in the courtyard, I heard a child crying. It was probably Pauli, the Schlesingers' nine-year-old son. I had always envied the chunky boy, the only one of the children to have his parents with him. He had never flaunted his good fortune but somehow seemed smug in his security. Now, he had the unenviable privilege of watching his parents taken from him.

As I looked around at the thirty-seven teens and two adults gathered in the château's ornate dining room, I remembered Walter giving me my sixteenth birthday gift there. My seventeenth birthday was three weeks away. My mind churned along with my stomach. People in concentration camps often died. How did it happen? Did they starve? Were they beaten? Or shot?

Rösli walked in ahead of the French commander, who addressed the group: "You are allowed to go to your rooms in groups of three and pack only as many things as will fit into a rucksack or small suitcase. Do not bring anything sharp like scissors or knives or pencils. If you cooperate, everything will go smoothly."

Then Rösli added: "The Swiss Red Cross will do all that it can to help you. In the meantime, cooperate with these men. Also, please don't take any watches, jewelry, or other valuables with you. Place these things into an envelope with your name on it and give it to me before you leave."

I sensed this last comment, seemingly an afterthought, went by most everyone, distracted and confused as they were by all that was going on. I would have to unpack my pen and pencil. Inside the dorms, each girl was focused on the same task: pulling together final photos and letters, along with underwear, socks, and a blouse or two.

When everyone was back in the dining room, four of the under-sixteens silently handed out a thick slice of French bread, a can of condensed milk, and two bars of chocolate to every other child, to be shared by two. One of the policemen standing alongside whispered loudly to his partner, "See, you worried about arresting children. Your kids don't get Swiss chocolate."

Rösli also had insisted that while we packed we should be allowed a quick breakfast of bread and a bowl of warm milk. Apparently satisfied that security would not be compromised, the commander relented. We ate in silence. I forced the bread into my dry mouth and washed it down with the milk from one of the gray tin cups.

Then we were herded out into the courtyard. By now, all the younger children had gathered as well. The commanding officer went through the roll again and, as he did, some of the younger children began crying.

As the names were called, we were told to line up in twos. By this time, the police realized both Ruth and Werner Epstein were missing, and they conferred among themselves as to whether other police had already picked them up at the farmers' houses. Two policemen inspected each of our suitcases and rucksacks and removed anything with a point, such as pencils and scissors. Finally, we were lined up in two columns with police in front, along the side, and in the rear.

The police lieutenant walked up to Rösli and formally thanked her "for your cooperation." Rösli's face contorted and for a moment she looked like she might spit on the lieutenant. "You received my cooperation only in the interest of the children's safety. If I had known what you had planned, I would have helped the children run away in advance. I never thought I would see the behavior of France come to this, to arresting children."

The lieutenant stared at her, surprised, and turned away without a word. He then directed us to walk through the château's ornate entranceway and onto the waiting bus. With armed police on all sides and the high castle walls nearby, I felt suddenly small and powerless as I walked, with Dela, onto the long driveway toward the dirt road leading from the château toward the highway. Several neighboring farm families — the Schmutzes and the Didieus — stood near the road. I spotted the skinny fourteen-year-old, Gaston Didieu, standing next to his short-haired mother, who was wiping tears from her eyes. Gaston had often joined in our soccer, tag, and other games.

An old, black police van with hard, wooden seats waited for us. "Where do you think they are taking us?" Dela asked as we sat down. I resisted the temptation to remind her we'd left our valuables behind.

"I don't know, but I can't imagine it is anything good," I responded.

"I wonder how long this bread and chocolate is supposed to last us," Dela said. That was Dela, thinking about the basics.

I wanted to share my latest observation: In all the instructions and reading of names, never once had the French police used the word "Jew" or been seriously insulting. Leave it to the French to give a touch of dignity to the process of rounding up Jews and even allow a departure meal.

Soon the bus was bumping along the quarter mile from the château to the main road. This was the first time I had been in a motorized vehicle in more than two years — since our last bus ride through Brussels to the train station. I could barely turn my head to view the three-story Château la Hille, its jagged wall, round turrets, and remains of a moat dating from the 1300s. As the rising sun shone through the trees and onto the tan stones, the château looked truly majestic.

Waiting

AFTER HOURS in the bus, we arrived at Camp le Vernet. It was huge, with endless rows of barracks, surrounded by messy coils of barbed wire, topped off by watchtowers at each corner. The boys were led to one building and the girls to another. We were ordered to strip, and an attendant searched us for money and jewelry. Rösli held our few valuables, and they really were few. Our worldly possessions were limited to what we wore and the few clothes in our rucksacks. When one girl objected to a silk scarf being confiscated, the female guard retorted: "Where you're going, you won't need anything like this."

We each received a small piece of cardboard with a number written on it and a string to attach it around our necks. Then we were assigned to our barracks.

I was struck by how the reality of the concentration camp matched what I had imagined. The fences enclosed row upon row of long buildings, some constructed of wood and others of metal and tar paper — all in various states of disrepair. Le Vernet occupied about fifty acres and held a couple thousand inmates.

Inside our barracks, contiguous wooden bunks of two levels held about thirty people; thus, each building held about sixty people. A single light bulb provided a dim light in each of these structures, which had slats along the sides but no real windows to let in light. When we were assigned to our barracks, each of us was issued a wool blanket with a warning to treat it carefully because we wouldn't be given another. This blanket was our only cushion on the hard wood bunks. I was glad it was still summer and warm outside; the unheated barracks and single blanket would have done little good against the winter cold.

I was detached from the reality of my new home — almost as if I was an observer on a tour. It was as if I half-expected Rösli or some other responsible adult to step forward and say, "Okay children, now you know what a concentration camp is like. Let's gather our things and prepare to return to the château." By that evening, though, as I stood in line for the thin soup called "dinner," I knew this was for real.

THE NEXT DAY, I noticed many Spanish prisoners. They marched by our wire enclosure, heavily guarded, carrying shovels over their shoulders. From the other refugees in our block we learned le Vernet was one of the smaller but harsher French concentration camps. Worse even than Dachau in Germany, some of the prisoners claimed. At Dachau, it was said, the prisoners were murdered, while at le Vernet, they died of starvation and disease. For those who survived, le Vernet was used as a sorting station for deportation to concentration camps in the east.

Shortly after we arrived, I spotted Ruth, whom I recognized by her short, brown hair and animated gestures while talking with another inmate. She had been arrested at the farm where she was working and brought to the camp a few days before we arrived, so she knew the routines and at least some of the gossip. She was especially glad to see familiar faces, and of course I was thrilled to see her.

The camp had been a men-only camp, but one section, which we were in, had recently been set aside for Jewish women and children. We eventually learned Camp le Vernet had a total of three main sections — one for various non-Jewish, male political prisoners and Spanish partisans in the civil war in Spain, one for Jewish men, and ours for Jewish women and children. It was still known by its original designation as a "camp de repression," a place especially set aside for political extremists. Only recently had the Nazis begun sending Jews there because of the need for additional places to hold all those being rounded up.

Each day, dozens more arrivals poured into the camp. In some cases, mothers arrived with very young children. And as they did, our barracks became increasingly crowded. By the third night, about eighty women crowded into the bunks with us, meaning we could sleep only on our sides and shift position only if everyone moved in unison. Not surprisingly, we slept in the same position all night.

In all the movement of people around us lay the truly terrifying implications — once the camp was full, people would be moved out, since le Vernet was a way-station on the way east, presumably back to Germany or to Poland. It was too awful to contemplate — le Vernet as the first stop in a circle back to Germany. Even more awful to contemplate were the many rumors that conditions in some of the German and Polish camps were far worse than what we were experiencing. We were hungry as it was. I hated to think of being more hungry with winter coming upon us.

So it was in those barracks, late at night, in the dim light of a single bulb that stayed always lit, I whiffed my first scent of death. No one was actually dying. We had arrived too recently to be badly affected by the primitive conditions. It was in the low conversations among the women and the crying of their children — all wondering what came next and all expecting the worst.

FOLLOWING ROLL CALL in the morning, we were left to our own devices. We really had nothing to do, so we walked up and down in the space between the barracks and the wire fence. The French guards viewed us with suspicion, their sternness calculated to break down our initiative and self-esteem. The monotony was broken only by the distribution of food, primarily ersatzcoffee, vegetable soup, and, at times, some bread. We tried to organize some games and to sit together and sing, but by the time the third and fourth days came along, our enthusiasm for these pastimes had worn dangerously thin. Because we had to leave behind our paper, pens, scissors, and pocketknives, we couldn't write to our families.

What would I have written to Mutti or Papa? I could have told them we were dry and fed. But not about other things, like obtaining eating utensils. We were issued a blanket but that was all. Everything else was up to us. Ruth alerted us we would need to somehow come up with a cup, plate, and spoon if we wanted to eat and these items were available only at a premium. She had fashioned something from an empty can. Several of us went scavenging through some garbage containers outside the kitchen area and found some cans of our own.

Then we faced the basic matter of keeping ourselves clean. Water ran only two hours a day, usually in the morning. So hundreds of people competed for the few water spouts that ran into huge wooden sinks, actually troughs. Having a large bowl or similar utensil made this whole bathing process more doable, but that was easier said than done. As with the eating utensils, each of us had to fashion something if we wanted to wash ourselves and any of our clothes. Dela and I shared a large can I foraged for in the garbage when we found our eating utensils. When it came to the higher matters of life, like privacy when washing, the only solution was to take our water into a barracks building where we didn't have to wash under the eyes of guards.

After a few days, I fell easily into the prisoner routine. We lined up in the morning for the interminable roll call of prisoners — sometimes repeated two or three times — stood in line again for breakfast, washed ourselves, shuffled around for a few hours until lunch, and then shuffled around again.

Small occurrences took on much greater significance in these circumstances. Because it was late summer, we encountered some good fortune on the food front. French farmers were in the midst of harvesting fruits and vegetables, most of it designated for shipment north to supply the Germans. But some of what they had wasn't considered suitable for shipment north, or for sale, so they dumped their "rejects" at le Vernet. Of course, for us, the vats of nearly-rotten peaches, berries, watermelons, and green beans were a huge treat. The only problem was eating so much ripe fruit and raw vegetables upset our empty stomachs and made us run to the outhouses — trenches with primitive wooden structures over them.

Two other important events occurred. The first was more important to me than to anyone else. On our initial evening at the camp, a middle-aged woman poked her head into our barrack and asked, "Is there an Inge Joseph here?" Startled, and expecting some kind of bad news, I rushed to her.

"A Walter Strauss wants you to try to meet him tomorrow morning at about ten o'clock," she said. She then explained where I should try to find him, at a point in the barbed wire fencing separating us from the Jewish men's area. I neglected to ask this woman how she got the message, but I surmised afterwards that most likely Walter had approached a man as he was talking to this woman and asked that the message be relayed. As time went on, I realized such messages were regularly carried around to new arrivals so that families and friends could try to re-establish communication. And other boy-girl couples among our group similarly made contact this way.

Walter's and my fingers overlapped as we held onto the barbed wire fencing separating us, and as they did, a well of emotion moved up from my stomach and into my chest and throat, catching in my voice. I suppressed the urge to cry. We spoke quietly and quickly as every so often, "for security," guards would shoo away people speaking through the fence.

Walter was still shaken from the ordeal of the arrest. He reported that most of the boys were very discouraged. Walter Kamlet was especially depressed. "There are all sorts of rumors going around about where we might be sent," he said. "Most of the speculation is about Poland where, we are told, the biggest and worst camps are located."

"Hopefully, the Swiss Red Cross will be able to help us," I responded. "I am sure Rösli is doing all she can."

"She didn't keep us from being arrested or from being taken away," he said. "I just wish I had listened to Hans and begun sleeping in the woods."

The second and more important event occurred two days later, on our fourth day at le Vernet. We had just finished our breakfast of bread and brown water when suddenly a commotion arose near the camp's main entrance. Guards were running and raised voices were coming from a small crowd moving from the entrance into the camp.

As other inmates and I edged toward the ruckus, I heard several of the guards yelling at each other. "Who let this woman in!? What is she doing here!?"

Then I heard a woman's voice announcing, loudly but calmly, "Please, I have business here." Rösli!

The small crowd of guards gradually gave way, and I could see her waving her Red Cross identification papers and chatting pleasantly with one of the guards who spoke to her in Swiss German. She continued walking slowly, as the guards moved with her, toward the commander's office. They clearly were at a loss about how to handle the situation, since it was quite unusual for someone to be trying to force her way into our compound. The commander had heard the commotion, too, and was walking toward Rösli.

"I am with the Swiss Red Cross based here in France, and we have been caring for a number of children in Montegue," I heard her tell the commander. "You arrested thirty-nine of these children and two of our adult staff. These are my children, and I have come to take them back."

I didn't hear exactly what the commander said, but he obviously told her we weren't about to be released. Before we knew it, Rösli was a resident of the camp as well, staying in a building reserved for the French Red Cross.

Her arrival had turned our entire situation completely upside down, from hopelessness to exultation. But the optimism was short-lived. When Rösli called us in to the stark Red Cross hut for a meeting to explain the situation, it was clear we were far from leaving the camp. She used lots of euphemisms about "the hospitality of the camp commander" and "the consideration everyone has shown me" — I presume because she didn't want to offend anyone while negotiations were ongoing — but the only concession she had won was being allowed to stay at the camp temporarily while Maurice Dubois worked to get us out before deportations expected in two days. He was in Vichy, the capital of the puppet French government, and he was trying to convince officials there to help us. In any event, Rösli kept our meeting brief, probably to avoid questions she couldn't or didn't want to answer.

ON THE AFTERNOON of the fifth day, the rumor spread that four blocs, ours among them, would be leaving the following morning. That evening, guards instructed us to pack and be ready to leave by early morning. I had been telling Walter the Swiss Red Cross would be able to get us out of the camp before we came up for deportation. But now that we had received our orders, I had given up hope myself. Rösli told us she continued to await a decision from officials in Vichy to whom Maurice Dubois had appealed for our liberation. Would it be granted and would it arrive in time?

Rösli was fairly calm, given the circumstances, and I found this encouraging. Maybe it was that her hair was no longer flying in all directions and was back in a bun. She didn't tell us much about the specifics of what was happening with Dubois such as whether he was making progress, when he might know something, or what his chances of success were. In an impromptu discussion outside our barracks late the afternoon of the fifth day, she talked with a few of the girls about how she came to us at le Vernet.

She had spent the rest of the day after we were arrested simply trying to reorganize things at the château because all her help — the Schlesingers and the older children — were gone, and she still had sixty other children to care for. As luck would have it, several Swiss Red Cross officials from Toulouse arrived to visit the next day, so they took over for Rösli while she headed out to Foix, the equivalent of the county seat, about fifty kilometers away. She rode her bicycle most of the way and took a bus the rest of the way.

She wandered from government bureau to government bureau seeking information about us. Finally, a sympathetic bureaucrat whispered "le Vernet," and she was able to piece together bits of information leading her to our exact location, about sixty kilometers away from Foix. She also heard the same rumors we did, that deportations were imminent and that time was of the essence. While she had the information, she didn't have authorization to enter the camp, and the French bureaucrat who could give her that authorization was away. So after returning to la Hille, she headed for le Vernet the next morning without authorization. Unfortunately, her bicycle got a flat tire on the way to the train station, so she hitched a ride with a milkman for part of the way and invested all her remaining cash in a taxi for the last thirty kilometers.

Once she arrived at the camp, the guards didn't want to let her in, so she just kept walking and talking. They were about to throw her out when one of the guards intervened. It turned out he had spent time in Switzerland and spoke Rösli's Swiss German dialect (which was very difficult for those of us from Germany to understand). He agreed to bring her to the camp's commander, who in turn agreed to put her up in the hut reserved for French Red Cross representatives.

Word had gradually spread around our bloc of mothers and children that a Swiss Red Cross representative was in the camp — and was trying to help gain the release of us teens. That night, after the guards told us to pack up, Rösli was besieged by mothers with young children begging for help. I could see the line in front of her hut just before the guards scattered them. The few who had been able to speak with Rösli returned dejected; she had told them she was prohibited by Swiss Red Cross rules from helping anyone except the teenagers under her care.

ON THE SIXTH MORNING, everyone was unceremoniously awoken at 6 A.M. Nobody paid much attention to the distribution of coffee and bread. I grew ever more tense. I tried to force a smile, but it was almost painful. What was it going to be like? By 8 A.M. everyone was lined up in front of their barracks. Approximately three hundred people made up our bloc, all young, many of them brothers and sisters. Then names were being called and the detainees walked to the camp's front gate. Men and women were separated once again into two groups. Many did not dare even to look at each other.

By 8:30 A.M., everyone whose name had been called was lined up in front of the camp's open gate. About one hundred meters away a train of cattle cars stood with their wide doors rolled open. In front of two barracks, only two small groups remained — the boys and girls of our group. None of our names had been called. Not a word was said. What did it mean?

The men and women lined up by the camp's gate were ordered to move. They were led directly to the waiting freight train. We could see streams of people from other parts of the camp heading the same way. The guards yelled orders in harsh voices. "Straight ahead! No talking! Just do as you are told!"

The guards beat men trying to join their wives and children. Older men and women fainted, and the guards gave them injections of some kind of stimulant so they could go on the train. One man who had slit his wrists was thrown onto the train, bleeding profusely. Women tried to shove little children into our group, but the guards pushed them on mercilessly. The guards' harsh voices mingled with the cries and moans of the refugees.

The doors of the cattle cars slammed shut. We were still standing in front of our barracks, silent witnesses to the turmoil in front of us. I saw Rösli walk out to the train, moving as if in slow motion from car to car, collecting cards, letters, and packages, presumably to be sent on to relatives.

After Rösli had collected all the items and was walking back toward the camp, a man's voice bellowed out from one of the cattle cars, "Tell them in Switzerland how they treat men who have fought for France.... Long live Switzerland!"

Slowly, so slowly, my anxiety began to dissipate. While it might have been obvious to some of my friends, it was just dawning on me that we hadn't been selected for special punishment, but rather for special, privileged treatment. We had been left off the death train.

Ten minutes later, the train had vanished, and within a few minutes the commander came to our barracks. He announced we were to wait for Rösli and return to the Red Cross home that day. After a perfunctory "Merci, Monsieur" from us, we were left alone. We grouped our rucksacks together and sat down on them. Everyone was silent. The departure we had just witnessed suppressed any exclamation of joy.

Later during the day, we were checked out and returned by train with Rösli to Château la Hille. The story of our salvation emerged during our train ride and shortly after we returned in several conversations other children and I had with Rösli. Just as Rösli had taken matters into her own hands to gain access to le Vernet, so Maurice Dubois had taken matters into his hands to gain access to key authorities in Vichy. When he arrived at the capital of occupied France, he learned the appropriate Swiss embassy official who might have approached French security officials was out of town. The Swiss official wouldn't be back in time to deal with our situation, even assuming he would have been inclined to help us in the first place. As the clock ticked and Rösli telephoned with her increasingly desperate messages about the approaching deportation, Maurice decided to approach France's chief of security on his own. Somehow he arranged a meeting, and during the session he portrayed himself as a Swiss official having much more authority than he really had.

It turned out Switzerland was providing shelter and other assistance to hundreds of non-Jewish French children who were refugees in various parts of France. "You must help us save the Château la Hille children," Dubois told the chief of security.

The official refused. "What makes your children any different than the thousands of other foreign nationals we are holding? Everyone is covered by the same laws!" he arrogantly replied, about to end the meeting and order Dubois to leave.

Dubois then resorted to the only tactic he could think of: a threat. "If you don't release the children under Swiss Red Cross authority, I will retaliate by ordering Switzerland to suspend all its considerable aid to French children. Then you will have even more refugees than you can handle, and these will be French."

The French official hesitated and then grudgingly agreed, changing our status to "non-deportable." But he warned Dubois that this was a "special circumstance," and that Dubois shouldn't come to him if we were arrested again. Dubois then telephoned news of his victory to Rösli the night before our scheduled deportation. Rösli quickly calculated it would be counterproductive to tell us in advance of our changed status, out of fear that word would quickly spread through the camp and in the pandemonium annoy the French enough to rescind our release. Having seen the loading of refugees onto the boxcars, I knew Rösli's concerns were justified.

While Dubois had achieved an important accomplishment — after all, it wasn't too often Jews were freed from concentration camps — it wasn't a complete victory. While he was busy negotiating with French officials in Vichy, his wife, Eleanor, was pleading with Swiss immigration officials in Bern to allow us entry to Switzerland. She had succeeded in obtaining permission from French officials for us to receive exit visas, but Swiss officials adamantly refused to provide us with entrance visas to Switzerland.

At the train station, we received an enormous welcome from the younger children, who had come to greet us. Slowly our turn of fortune began to sink into our minds.

Two events following our return remain in my mind. Immediately after we returned to Château la Hille and were unpacking our belongings and going through mail, Inge H. let out a shriek. For once, it wasn't a shriek of horror but of joy. She had received word of the impossible: a visa to the United States. Apparently her mother in England and relatives in the United States had been able to engineer this amazing feat. However, she would soon discover that the hope was just a mirage, since there was no way for her to obtain exit documents from France or ship passage at that point in 1942, the height of the war.

Then two days later we all learned just how lucky we had been. Hans Garfunkel picked up a BBC broadcast containing "unconfirmed reports" that deportees on a freight train from southern France had been killed — it wasn't clear how — before reaching a designated concentration camp.

Onions

WE FELL BACK into the routine of our lives at the château. But a new undercurrent of reflection, speculation, and anxiety intruded. We knew what happened in August could easily repeat itself. There were fewer soccer games and foot races. No complaints about Rösli and her leadership style. Fewer after-dinner boy-girl walks.

Most of us were less inclined to be in groups and more inclined to remain alone. That usually didn't bother me so much, since I often liked to be alone. But during this period, I didn't welcome the solitude, since I so often felt like crying. The château, as beautiful as ever on the crisp fall days of September and October, was cold and lonely.

As much as Rösli tried to maintain her proper official air, I knew she was very frightened by the le Vernet affair. The most vivid evidence I had was her treatment of Ilse Brunell, the vivacious brunette with the beautiful singing voice. While she and I weren't close friends, we had enough contact and friends in common that I came to learn quite a few details of her post-le Vernet ordeal.

For reasons known only to Rösli, she selected Ilse to be Château la Hille's spy. Rösli arranged employment for Ilse as a clerk in a Foix government office, working for a woman who drew up deportation lists and living in the woman's home. During the week, Ilse would live at this woman's house in the town of Foix and every few weekends she would return to la Hille. If she learned anything about possible roundups or arrests, she would alert Rösli. "You are our security against deportation," Rösli told her.

Under the circumstances, the arrangement made sense, but it didn't work for Ilse. On her occasional weekends back at la Hille, Ilse spilled out her guts about the assignment. She wasn't being fed enough. She was being overworked. While she didn't say it, I sensed that most of all she hated the pressure she was under to be on the lookout for crucial information. What if she missed something important? Was she then responsible for us being arrested? It was a lot of pressure for a seventeen-year-old, and I was glad it wasn't me.

Another reverberation from le Vernet was that Walter became less available, and when he did meet me, he was increasingly distant, preoccupied. Was it something I had done or not done? While that was my instinctive first question, something told me it had nothing to do with me. When we did talk, he was entirely focused, obsessed with how we might escape.

"Some of the boys are talking about going to live with farmers, but I am concerned with us splitting up. I worry the farmers will be more afraid to help us because of the deteriorating security situation," he said at one point. "I also don't want to give up what little protection the Swiss Red Cross affords us."

Walter seemed like a chess player who is boxed in and sees the potential for check-mate a few moves down the road. He tried desperately to figure a way out of the predicament, but couldn't, at least for the moment.

I'M NOT SURE where the idea came from, but some days after our return to the château, Eugene Lyrer, our teacher, and Ernste Schlesinger, Frau Schlesinger's handyman husband, together with Walter S., Jacques, Addie, and others of our group, began busily building our "Zwiebelkeller," or onion cellar. This was a large attic room off Herr Lyrer's room on the château's second floor. Its gray, wooden rafters had been used to hang onions to dry.

Herr Lyrer's room was entirely wood-paneled, except for two doors — one leading into his room and the other leading into the onion cellar. The men and boys decided to cover the door leading to the onion cellar with exactly the same paneling as the walls, and they engineered an ingenious sliding door, only about two feet high, at the bottom. Whether this was Walter's idea or not, he latched onto it with fervor. Simply building it lifted his spirits, and I am convinced that his carving and carpentry skills helped make the hiding place amazingly deceptive. From the outside, it was impossible to tell that it had once been a door or that there was now a sliding panel.

The onion cellar became our new hiding place. We now used this room as our sleeping quarters, the girls on one side and the boys on the other. Should police arrive during the day, two rings of our bell would tell us to hide in the onion cellar.

To enter and leave the cellar, we had to lie on our abdomens and slide through the small opening. Once we were inside, Herr Lyrer closed the opening from the outside. We could not leave until we heard a prearranged knock in the morning.

At first, sleeping in the cellar seemed like an adventure. It was a little like the sleepovers that Julie used to have with her friends when they were young teenagers, with quiet giggling and whispering.

But the novelty wore off very quickly, after just a night or two. For one thing, we couldn't speak in normal tones, since we never knew if police might be hanging around outside the château without anyone being aware. For another, the place was musty and smelled of onions. Even though it was no longer used for storing onions, that smell would always be there, and it penetrated the pores of my skin. But the worst part of sleeping in the onion cellar became apparent on the second night. Just as I started to doze off, I heard a barely audible scratching sound. It took a few seconds to realize I was hearing an animal prowling around. At the same instant, I heard a girl's loud whisper, probably Dela: "Oh, my God. It's a mouse."

One of the boys whispered back, equally loudly, "Just cover your head. They won't bother you." So we did that — we covered our heads and listened to the mice scurry about.

AS WINTER APPROACHED, several of my friends received news that parents, brothers, and sisters had been deported. The worst, for me, was when Walter learned his brother had been deported from the Gurs camp in France and his parents from Germany. Though the events occurred a few weeks apart, Walter received the letters on the same gray November day. I knew from watching Walter read his mail that he had received bad news. I suspect we had all fallen into the habit of watching each other read our mail, hoping against hope it wouldn't be more bad news while suspecting it would be. Walter said nothing after reading his letters and quietly receded from the dining room, much as he had when we were hiding bread and dried fruit.

I didn't know what to do or say. I decided to wait a bit before searching him out, so he could be alone. After lunch, I found him where I expected, on one of the hills where we often walked together. I didn't say a word — just sat next to him.

"Siegfried [his brother] has been sent to Poland," he said after some minutes. "My parents wrote from a train, but presumably they are in Poland as well."

"I'm sorry," I said. "Do you have addresses, so we can send some things?"

My question brightened Walter a bit, as if he had forgotten there was a little something he could do. "Siegfried has an address. I guess my parents will, too, before long."

We held hands as we walked back to the château.

But our day of sadness wasn't yet complete. As we walked, we heard the rumbling of trucks on the country road that ran near the château. This wasn't one of the occasional trucks plodding by but a convoy of German army vehicles. There must have been twelve to twenty troop carriers, jeeps, tanks, and flatbeds with artillery on top. What stopped my heart wasn't the immense size of the weapons nor the sight of soldiers in helmets and battle fatigues, but the small red-and-black Nazi flags flapping on several of the trucks. I hadn't seen the Nazi flags since I left Germany nearly four years earlier, and their stark colors and swastika emblem vividly reminded me that the Nazis were in full force. The convoy didn't even hesitate as it roared past the turnoff to la Hille, so the soldiers weren't looking for us, but the message was clear: The Germans were occupying southern France and would be our new neighbors.

Meetings

S OMETIME IN EARLY December I received a cryptic twenty-five-word
message that came through the Red Cross in Switzerland from Mutti
— who was in a concentration camp, Piaski, located in Poland. She asked
me to notify Papa to send food and clothing. I forwarded the message to
Papa in the United States.

The fact that so many of my friends had had the same experience
didn't make it any easier for me. All I could think was that Mutti had endured my experience of a few months earlier — waiting near a train track
for her name to be called, staring into the dark emptiness of a box car.

To make matters worse, from the substance of her message she appeared to have gone alone, sent separately from her mother, brother, and
sister. And winter was upon us. She had one blanket, if she were lucky. She
was sleeping in a dilapidated, drafty barracks on a hard, wooden platform.
Warm, brown water for breakfast. Watery soup for lunch and dinner, if
they even served lunch and dinner. And unlike me, she had no Swiss Red
Cross working on her behalf.

I wished I didn't know so well what she was experiencing. I wished I
could naively hope she was in a place where she was being decently fed
and clothed. The only feeling I've had since then that even begins to capture my feelings of that December day has been when I've been on nursing
duty as a mother is dying during childbirth. It is a rare event doctors don't
like to discuss. But it still happens, and when it is progressing, the doctors
and nurses do everything they can to turn things around. We turn up the
oxygen, try to isolate the sources of internal bleeding, inject a heart stimu-

lant, prepare the tracheotomy, and so on and so forth; yet, no matter what we do, the situation continues to deteriorate. It is as if we are caught beneath an avalanche of snow or mud. The event assumes an air of inevitability defying our every effort to prevent it.

Under these circumstances Christmas 1942 arrived. During the week of December 24, Rösli held a meeting with the older boys and girls. She told us that there was a chance for us to cross the French border into Switzerland from another Swiss Red Cross home located near Annemasse, a French town on the border that was within walking distance of Geneva.

Christmas that year was an after-thought. Rösli had already dispensed most of our favors during our arrest in August, and the ever-tightening supplies made it impossible for her to put aside new treats — there just wasn't enough to eat day-to-day. This must have been painful to Rösli and other Swiss Red Cross representatives, since Christmas was so very important to them. But Rösli was preoccupied with our pending escape.

The meeting with Rösli was only for those of us who had been taken to le Vernet — she and the other Swiss Red Cross officials had decided that the younger children were relatively safe. I couldn't help but be taken with the sea change in Rösli's demeanor. Here was a woman who, not long before, had opposed sending food to refugees in concentration camps because it violated bureaucratic rules. Now she explained her calculations for our escape to Switzerland. She said it could work over the next two or three weeks because the upcoming Christmas and New Year's holidays meant border guards and police were less likely to be on full alert.

"As you all know, the security situation has become ever more difficult," Rösli stated in our first meeting in her spartan office. "I have concluded that the Swiss Red Cross can no longer offer you adequate protection, so your very safety here is in jeopardy. For those of you who are willing to take the risk, I believe it is possible for you to escape. I have made some arrangements with others who are willing to help along the way. However, you must know that any escape attempts are very risky. If you are caught, you could be killed. You must also know that I have taken this on personally, and the Swiss Red Cross knows nothing about it. So if anyone isn't interested in doing this, please tell me now or privately after this meeting."

The room was completely silent.

After that initial meeting during the week before Christmas, we had two more meetings — briefings and rehearsals for our escape attempt.

What I recall most vividly were Rösli's instructions about what we should do if we were stopped by police at any time on our way to the French-Swiss border.

"You are each to be given a Swiss French name. You will say that you are from the Geneva area of Switzerland, that you were walking in the woods during the holidays and must have become lost. You neglected to bring any identification because in Switzerland you do not always need to carry identification — you did not know how important it is in France. You must act as if you do not understand German and respond only to French questions."

We were to depart in groups of four or five, the composition of which was to be determined by Rösli. We would be awakened during the night, receive our instructions, and leave in the early morning darkness. Each of us packed a rucksack before going to sleep without knowing for sure who would leave when. When we awakened Christmas morning, four of our group were not among us. There was to be a three-day interval between departures. The second group of four boys and girls left December 28, and those of us remaining went to bed each night wondering when our turn would come.

We felt a mixture of excitement and fear. The excitement began to outweigh the fear when we learned the first group successfully made it to Switzerland. It became positively spine-tingling when we learned the second group had also escaped. Eight of our group were now free in Switzerland. I couldn't wait for my turn. Any fear I had had evaporated with the knowledge success was within our grasp.

AROUND TWO O'CLOCK on the morning of January 5, I felt a light tap on my shoulder. Rösli motioned me to take my clothes and follow her to the onion cellar's exit. After I crawled out into Herr Lyrer's room, I saw four of the other boys and girls waiting already. With a sense of relief, I noticed Walter S. was one of the two boys; Manfred Vos, a boy I didn't know very well, was the other. Dela and Inge H. were the two girls.

We each received a package of jelly sandwiches and dried fruit wrapped in newspaper and the following instructions: We were to leave within the hour by foot to a train station in Foix, to catch the 6 A.M. train for Toulouse. Under no circumstances were we to leave from the station of Pailhès, only half the distance of Foix, because we were known by too many people there. We were to wait in the Toulouse station for the train to

Annemasse, which departed at 5 P.M. As much as possible, we should stay separate from each other and mingle with other people waiting in the train station. At 3 P.M., an employee of the Swiss Red Cross in Toulouse, who knew us, was going to hand Walter five tickets to Annemasse. From Annemasse, we were to walk to a Swiss Red Cross home. We would be given further instructions there.

It was about 3:30 A.M. when we departed Château la Hille. The night was extremely cold, and the country road to Foix was covered with ice. Fortunately, no traffic approached as we walked one behind the other along the side of the road, often holding onto each other to keep from falling.

At some point during our walk through the wintry blackness, Walter and I found we had put some distance between ourselves and the other three. We stopped to wait for them to catch up, and as we stood together, Walter seemed, for the first time in weeks, more relaxed and self-assured.

"I arranged it so that you would be part of my group," he said.

"I assumed as much," I replied, watching my breath in the moonlit darkness.

"I worry a little about the others in our group. Ruth was supposed to be with us, but she wasn't feeling well, so she asked not to come for fear of slowing us down."

I knew well what Walter was referring to. Ruth would have been great because she was cool under pressure and a fighter. Dela could be very childish in a stressful situation. More than two years had passed, but I still remembered Inge H.'s immature behavior during our flight from Brussels when she insisted on bringing more clothing than was appropriate.

Manfred Vos was nearly unknown to me. He was so quiet, unassuming — and short — as to be nearly invisible. He was more of a loner than I. I knew he either had just turned or was about to turn eighteen years old, and thus, he was a year or so older than Walter and I; his family was from Cologne, and his father had been a shoemaker. He had a talent for sewing and had become our prime tailor, mending socks and pants. Beyond that, I don't believe I ever had an extended conversation with him, nor, I would venture, did Walter.

We fell down because of iciness on the road, but also because we were so excited and nervous to be getting our turn. It was a turn at life, at hope. Yet somewhere in my gut, anger gnawed at me. I was anxious about three of the people I was traveling with. I should have had something to say about whom I would be risking my life with. But I knew what Rösli had done. She had selected two of her most responsible teens — Walter and me — and teamed us up with three of the weaker ones so we could support them. But was that fair to Walter and me? We never got to ask that question. And I would learn only later what a terrible disservice had been done.

Chess

WE CAUGHT our 6 A.M. train, which was very crowded and traveled uneventfully to Toulouse, arriving about 10 A.M. We immediately separated, with the understanding we would meet at 4:30 P.M. at the track of our departing train.

The hours of that day seemed as if they would never pass. I spent most of my time in the corner of one of the waiting rooms, reading discarded newspapers near a newsstand. The station was a huge, cavernous structure built from gray stone — actually quite striking from the outside, like something from medieval times, complete with turrets along the sides. Despite its size, it was terribly crowded, mainly with soldiers, both French and German.

Occasionally the five of us passed each other, but we did not even glance at one another. Only once was I approached — by a slender, black-haired French soldier who looked about my age. He shyly asked me if I lived in Toulouse. "Oui," I said as I moved quickly away, taking up a place at a newsstand where I read the headlines announcing German invasions and advances around Europe and Russia. Never before nor since have I counted the seconds, minutes, and hours as tensely as on January 5, 1943, in the Toulouse station.

Finally, we boarded the train. All five of us were able to sit in one compartment. Our plan was to take turns walking the corridor every hour in order to see whether passengers were being checked for "cartes d'identités" (identification cards), which we did not carry. As foreigners, we would have required special traveling permission, but this was seldom granted, and especially not if the destination was the Swiss border! Our plan in the event of an identity check was to hide in the toilet of an already-checked car.

The train ride to Annemasse lasted about seventeen hours. We were dead tired but dared not sleep, for fear of a dreaded identity check. More than anything, I wanted to let myself doze off. The five of us were settled alone in our compartment, Dela, Inge H., and me on one side and Walter and Manfred on the other. There was room for three other people in our compartment, but thus far we had it all to ourselves. The door was closed, and the gently swaying train headed east at full speed through the blackness of the French night.

It was unfeasible for all five of us to sleep at once. At least two, and probably three of us, had to be awake at all times, making sure we weren't caught off-guard by a police inspection. "Maybe we could take turns dozing," I said to Walter. "Two or three of us should always be awake. If we are careful, we can do it."

"Oh, how much I would love to sleep," Dela broke in. "I'll even sleep less if you let me go first. And I'll wake you each up so gently, you won't mind that you've been awakened."

Dela was already showing her childish side. She was always first in line for special treats, like extra food or clothes. Her sparkling blue eyes with their long lashes and her girlish way of sugar-coating her selfishness somehow made her demands endearing to others. And she was usually rewarded for her efforts.

Not this time, though. Walter wasn't biting. Rather, he was frowning, first at Dela and then more intensely at me, probably for initiating the suggestion. His full, dark eyebrows came together. "Inge, I don't think it's a good idea," he said to me. "We need to stay alert and ready to move at any time."

We couldn't even doze a little on an uncomfortable train! All in the name of a scheme to elude the police. How could five of us possibly sneak past the police to another car and then all cram into a toilet? Walter was in charge, I told myself, and we couldn't argue at this moment.

Meanwhile, we had other worries. The compartment next to us was occupied by German soldiers. As the evening progressed, the laughing and shouting that came from that compartment grew ever louder. They had clearly been drinking and, before long, were roaming the corridors. The train became crowded, and three strangers intruded themselves into our compartment; we had no choice but to remain in our seats and not speak.

We almost gasped in unison when one of the German soldiers entered our compartment. He looked at Walter and Manfred, sitting together, and asked in German, "Spielen Sie Schach?" (Do you play chess?). The boys stared, flabbergasted, at him, which he took for not comprehending German. He left, only to return with a chessboard. I don't know what possessed Walter, but he nodded that, yes, he played. Walter's relaxed smile suggested he had been waiting for just this moment. The soldier beamed and motioned Walter to follow him to the next compartment.

The noisy yelling continued for several hours and, as we occasionally took turns walking by their compartment, we saw four German soldiers playing cards and gesticulating loudly, while Walter and the soldier who had come into our compartment silently played a concentrated game of chess next to the window.

Walter was an excellent chess player, and I worried whether he would have enough sense to let the soldier win. Walter returned about midnight and, shortly after, in Lyon, the Germans left the train, much to our relief. Walter then explained his strategy. He figured that by playing with the German, he would keep him busy and divert the group's attention from us. Walter won the first game, but as I had hoped, let the German win the next two games.

The rest of our trip, about another ten hours, passed uneventfully. As if in reward for having weathered our experience with the soldiers, Walter even allowed us to doze off individually for half-hour periods, while the other four of us stayed awake.

The crisp, cold air that greeted us as we emerged from the train at the small, wooden ticket station at Annemasse was a wonderful contrast to the stale, smoke-laced air of the train compartment. Much to our relief, the French soldiers around the station weren't checking identification papers. It was still the New Year's holiday, and perhaps they were thinking more about that than security.

Only one road led away from the station, so we simply began walking down it, single file, as when we left the château. We walked toward the French Red Cross home that Rösli had directed us to find. It was about fifteen kilometers away, in the country, about a two-and-a-half-hour trip on foot.

I was giddy with relief. We had eluded the German soldiers on the train and the French police at the Annemasse station. We were only a few kilometers from Switzerland. Though we were still in France, the farm-houses and A-frame buildings here were built out of dark, wood logs, rather than the stone and concrete of the Château la Hille area.

The others must have felt the same excitement. Dela, who was imme-diately behind me, began laughing and singing one of the silly songs we often sang at la Hille.

And the shark, he has teeth
and he has them in his face.
But in his stomach he has cod liver oil,
but the cod liver oil you cannot see . . .

We had been walking about an hour when a motorcycle with two German soldiers, one driving and the other riding in an attached carrier, drove up to us and, without a word, turned back on the road. Within five minutes, the motorcycle repeated this exercise. My heart was in my mouth. We didn't know what was going on, but wished we did not have our rucksacks with us. Walter felt we were attracting their attention — that they thought we were smuggling wine or food to someone in the area.

Each time we breathed a sigh of relief, more trouble cropped up. In retrospect, I think that was the first sign of serious trouble affecting our escape plans.

Finally, we arrived at the Swiss Red Cross home, a large, wooden house, where about fifty French children, non-Jewish refugees, were housed. They were off on an excursion, so the house was empty. A middle-aged woman, Anne Marie, received us and led us right away to the dining room where she told us to remain. She gave us the first food we had eaten since finishing our sandwiches the day before — some piping hot vegetable soup, French bread, and soft Camembert cheese. We were fam-ished and the food tasted wonderful.

She was anxious to know whether anyone saw us approaching the home. When we told her about the Germans on the motorcycle, she be-came concerned. I worried that she would decide to delay our escape, but she continued to speak as if everything were going according to schedule. At ten o'clock that evening, she told us, Jose would meet us and take us for the three-kilometer walk to the border. She also told us the two preceding groups of boys and girls had arrived safely in Switzerland, confirming our earlier reports. She hoped to have all the older children there within the next few weeks.

She left us alone, but we were so excited we couldn't sleep. "I can't wait to get to Switzerland," said Dela. "Maybe then I can get David [her baby brother] out of that awful Brussels orphanage, before the Germans get him."

Inge H. had even bolder hopes. "Once we're in Switzerland, I'll be able to arrange to get to England and finally see my mother. She worries so much about me. Nothing would make her happier."

I kept my wish to myself. I knew it was too far-fetched to think I might be able to extricate Mutti and my aunt, uncle, and grandmother from their concentration camps. Walter was silent as well, probably for the same reason. Manfred's silence suggested his family was in similarly dire straits.

When I finally put my head down on my rucksack, I dozed. I had a vision of being with Mutti. She was like her old self, before Papa's arrest — her radiant smile lit up her soft, brown eyes and her pretty face was tilted to one side. She wore a white silk shawl over an elegant, black velvet dress, like the dresses she wore when she went to the opera with Papa. She was stroking my cheek, pulling a blanket up over me.

When Walter gently shook me, it was dark — the only light in the room came from two candles on the dining room table. "It is time," he said. "Jose is here. We must get ourselves ready quickly."

Snow

ANNE MARIE STOOD over a map on the dining room table. She showed us the route we were to take to get to the border, about four kilometers away. Jose would guide us on this part of the trip. He was a member of the French Underground and had done this many times.

Anne Marie picked up a second map to show us the route from the border to Geneva, only about fifteen kilometers into Switzerland. Then she told us the name and address of the people we needed to find in Geneva. She made us memorize this information, since she didn't want us to have anything in writing. She didn't say why, but we knew — in case we were caught, she didn't want to expose those people to danger.

As we were going over the information, Jose noiselessly slipped into the room. He was a wiry, olive-skinned man with curly black hair. He looked to be in his early twenties and appeared preoccupied. When Anne Marie had finished with the maps, he took over and told us that "things will have to be changed a bit." He didn't make eye contact with any of us. The problem, as he explained it, was that it had begun snowing during the late afternoon hours, and the snow had continued to fall steadily.

"So I will not walk with you all the way to the border. Otherwise, my foot tracks might be followed back into France. I will go with you through the woods, until you reach a field. There you will be only a short walk from the border. You will reach the fence, crawl under, and you will be in Switzerland. Then all you have to do is go straight ahead and on your left you will find the road to Geneva. I don't expect any problems because it is still the New Year's holiday week and the border will not be heavily guarded."

"What do we do if we get lost?" Inge H. asked.

"You will not get lost," Jose answered.

Despite his words, Jose's nervousness made me nervous, also. If the border was lightly guarded, why was he afraid his footprints might be followed? Since it was snowing heavily, wouldn't his footprints be quickly covered over? It didn't feel comfortable that we were being encouraged to cross the border when someone from the French Underground, very familiar with the terrain, was afraid to accompany us. If it wasn't safe for him, why was it safe for us?

Coming on top of the incident with the German soldiers on the motorcycle the previous day, Jose's change in plans had definitely deflated my hope. "Should we perhaps wait another day?" I asked Anne Marie weakly. She shook her head no. Anne Marie probably wanted to get us out of her house as quickly as possible.

I tried to take comfort from the fact that Walter seemed calm and reassured. "In Geneva, we will look at washing machines," he joked as we walked away from the Swiss Red Cross home.

WE HAD WALKED for about fifteen minutes when Jose motioned for us to begin crossing a field. He was taking his leave. No words were spoken. We walked in single file, bent forward as much as possible. First Walter, then me, Dela, Inge H., and Manfred. It was pitch dark and snowing heavily, but we knew the frontier was guarded on both sides and spotlights could shine on us at any moment.

Within ten minutes, we arrived at the barbed wire. Walter pulled the lowest strand up for me to burrow through the shin-deep snow and over to what we hoped was Switzerland. I pulled it up for Dela, and Dela held it for Inge H., who held it for Manfred, who then held it for Walter. Walter smiled ever so slightly at the sight of me covered like a snowman as he moved back to the head of the line. It was so easy. We continued to walk silently. We had to find the road leading to Geneva without being observed.

After walking for about ten minutes through bushes and fields, we suddenly faced more barbed wire. What was this fence doing here? We stopped and debated in loud whispers whether or not we should pass it. Walter hesitated, but he was gradually persuaded by my argument that if we didn't cross it, we would have to retrace our steps, and that would lead us back into France. I reasoned that the first fence had been erected by the

French and this second one by the Swiss, with the land in between being a no-man's land. Everyone else was persuaded as well, so we passed under this fence in the same manner as the first, with each of us pulling up the bottom wire for the other.

I kept hoping Walter would tell us we were at the road to Geneva. But no road appeared. Instead, within just a few minutes of walking, we confronted a third barbed wire fence. Were we in France or Switzerland? There was no explanation possible for this third barrier. Should we or shouldn't we cross? It was snowing ever more heavily, and we could see nothing clearly in the distance.

We stood and looked at each other. Something in my gut told me we should cross under this fence as well. What was the alternative? We needed to continue going forward. I was confident that we had walked as instructed, in nearly a straight line toward Switzerland. But I didn't feel quite as confident as I had at the second fence, because I couldn't come up with a logical explanation of why the third one would be here. Possibly, in the heavy snow we had somehow circled back to the second fence and were now walking back toward France, even though I doubted it. Walter was clearly thrown by this unexpected obstacle and argued against continuing. He speculated we had wandered off the prescribed path. "We may have come back to the second fence," he said, capturing my unspoken fear.

My heart was pounding. We were still in the open and extremely exposed. At any moment, a spotlight might shine on us, or soldiers might begin shooting. Anger welled up. Why hadn't Jose stayed with us? It was snowing so heavily that any of his footprints would have been quickly covered. Why hadn't he at least warned us of this possibility?

Inge H. was sobbing quietly. Just as I feared, she was unable to handle the pressure, much as when we fled from Brussels to France.

Now Dela piped up. "Please, just make a decision. My feet are freezing." Dela always was either too hot or too cold, too wet or too dry.

Dela looked at Walter for a decision. Inge H. and Manfred had shifted their gazes toward him as well.

Walter returned the gazes, looking over each of us individually with his furrowed brow and penetrating, brown eyes. The wet snow had plastered strands of his straight, black hair to his forehead. I could almost hear the calculations going through his mind.

"I think we should begin walking up this way, along the fence and toward the woods," Walter said, pointing in the direction of some trees off to the side. "At least we won't be as easy to see as we are out in the open here."

No! No! No! my mind shouted. But my mouth kept silent.

I knew exactly what was going on in Walter's mind. He was worried — not about himself, but about us. That was Walter's way. His way was fine when we were deciding how to parcel out food or organize a group activity at Château la Hille, but here, in a time of crisis, his nature clouded his judgment — encouraging him to hesitate in a situation requiring instinct, decisiveness, and, yes, a sense of self-preservation.

Now, Walter was trying somehow to find a middle road, as it were, in a situation where compromise was impossible. Our only choice was to go forward or go back. Yet he wanted additional time to evaluate this unanticipated third fence. I decided not to object. The last thing I wanted was open dissension between Walter and me in front of the other three. I also knew that to argue with him in this situation would do no good. He had such a strong sense of responsibility he would stick to his viewpoint. Since he was the leader of our group, his view would hold sway with the others, no matter what I thought.

Exploration

A FTER WALKING for about a half hour along the fence toward the trees, we suddenly noticed a light ahead of us. Now we had another decision to make: Should we approach it? But how could we make a choice, not knowing whether we were in France or Switzerland? Finally, after some discussion, we devised a plan: Walter would go ahead, closer to the house, to try to determine where we were. The rest of us would wait for him in order not to arouse suspicion. If he didn't return in a reasonable amount of time, we were to return to the third fence, if we could find it, and continue on. I wanted to give Walter a hug and a kiss. But I restrained myself. "Please be careful, Walter," I said.

Walter disappeared into the darkness. At least half an hour went by. We were drenched by wet snow, and still Walter had not returned. The light continued to shine brightly ahead of us. Had Walter lost his way?

The queasiness in my stomach had turned into a painful cramp. Our whole plan was unraveling before my eyes. With Walter gone, I knew I had to take charge. I needed to make a decision about what to do next. I sensed Walter was almost certainly in trouble. If he were all right, he would have managed to return or to send word to us. As much as I yearned to help him, I thought it best to follow his advice — and our footsteps — back to the point at the third fence where we had decided against crossing. Once there, I explained to the others, we would proceed under the fence.

Nothing doing. Dela and Inge H. wanted to follow in Walter's steps to the cabin. "I am wet and frozen," Dela said. "At least at the house, we'll be able to warm up. Maybe the owners have taken Walter to the Swiss police for help." Her eyes were glistening from the snow and her tears. Her wet, black hair hung limply. Inge H., who was still crying, nodded her agreement with Dela. Manfred said he thought we shouldn't just leave Walter, and besides, he was wet and frozen as well.

I was in the same state but willing to endure more cold and snow. There was too much at stake. Again I wished I had attempted this border crossing with just Walter, or even alone. Without the others along, I knew I could have persuaded Walter to go under the third fence. If there had to have been an additional person, I wished it had been Ruth.

As much as I had been through with Dela — first in Brussels and later in France, when we had competed for Walter's attention but still remained friends — I had had it with her. She was too much of a child for this kind of situation. And for all Inge H.'s high-sounding philosophizing with Walter Kamlet, she was also a baby. Her wealthy parents had always indulged her every wish, and now I was reaping the bitter harvest. And Manfred? He was spineless and stupid.

I hated being in groups, even if we were just chatting or playing games. I had never liked trying to persuade people to go along with my way of doing things. That was probably because, too often, I was unsuccessful. I'd just as soon rely on my own instincts, act alone, and not have to worry about others who might break down under the pressure. I started to argue again for heading back to the fence, but Dela interrupted: "Are you going to just leave Walter?"

"That's what he told us to do," I said firmly.

"Yes, maybe that's what he said. But that's not what you do. You don't just abandon your closest friend." She emphasized "closest friend."

Inge H.'s sobbing became more intense.

Clearly, I could not control the group's rapidly deteriorating emotional and physical condition. I thought briefly about leaving the group and going alone back to the fence, but I quickly dismissed the idea. I had the responsibility for the group — the responsibility foisted on me by Rösli. We had no choice but to go after Walter. Once again, I was going against my instincts. Why didn't I just insist they come with me, challenge them to follow me?

As we approached the light, we saw it came from a small house that looked as if it belonged to a farmer. I certainly hoped so. We approached the front door. I was about to knock, when a harsh voice called out from the side: "Halt!" This must be the Swiss farmer, I hoped, and together we turned toward the figure emerging from the side of the house.

Too late! In a flash, I recognized the German army uniform. More soldiers were pouring out the side door.

I felt the way a deer or bear must feel when she catches sight of the hunters with their rifles pointed and realizes, too late, what is about to happen. But we were even more stupid than animals. What fools we had been not to draw the proper conclusion! No, what a fool I had been! I sensed this would happen, yet I let the others, whom I knew to be fools, convince me otherwise. I felt my heart pounding as if it were going to burst my chest; but also I felt unrestrained anger — at myself, at Dela and Inge H., at Manfred, and at Walter.

As the soldiers crowded around us, things seemed to move in slow motion. They shouted questions at us but I could not comprehend what they were saying. There was too much to register and, in the midst of all the upheaval, my mind was instinctively calculating, like that of a mink caught in a fur hunter's trap, some way, some opening, out.

Commander

W E DID NOT answer any of the soldiers' questions in German but explained to them, in French, that we lived near Geneva and had lost our way in the dark and snow. I tried to do most of the talking because my French was best, but one of the soldiers who spoke French directed questions at the others as well. It didn't help that Inge H. was wiping away tears as she answered in stumbling French.

They discussed among themselves in German the probability that we were trying to cross the border. One of them reasoned we probably belonged to the same gang as the boy who had been arrested and taken by the French border guards when they shifted guard duty twenty minutes earlier, at midnight. They were almost certainly talking about Walter, I surmised. The French and German soldiers apparently alternated frontier guard duty. Walter arrived at the house while the French were there, probably the only positive glimmer in this entire episode. It was the special luck of us four to knock on the door when the Germans were in charge. The soldiers decided to take us to their commanding officer.

They ordered us to follow one German soldier while a second walked behind us. As we trudged silently, single-file through the snow, I suddenly remembered that the glasses I carried in my ski pants pocket were in a case with the name and address of an optometrist in Darmstadt. I needed to get rid of that case before it destroyed my credibility about being French Swiss. Luckily, the case had two parts made of hard cardboard, one of which slid over the other. I crumbled the shorter one, which carried the name, and let it drop next to me. The soldier behind me did not notice in the dark.

After walking ten or fifteen minutes, we arrived at a building at least three times the size of the farmhouse where we were arrested. It looked like a small hotel. Now it appeared to be the German border headquarters, because three or four German soldiers were standing guard in front.

The front door opened and we entered what appeared to have been the lobby of a hotel or the sitting area of a restaurant. We were told to stand there and wait for the commanding officer to receive us.

My heartbeat speeded up again. The commander was sure to be experienced at interrogating people trying to cross the border.

I was unable to forget that my previous two encounters with the enemy — the Brussels invasion and the le Vernet affair — were primarily the result of being in the wrong place at the wrong time and not the direct result of any decisions I made. This third time I had no one to blame but myself. I might have blamed Walter, but I understood his way of thinking, how he let his sense of responsibility cloud his judgment.

As I looked around the smoky room with border officials seated at desks and armed guards posted outside, I couldn't see any way out of the situation except possibly, somehow, to talk our way out of it.

After about ten minutes, we were led in to meet the commanding officer. Husky and rather imposingly dressed in a brown uniform, he sat behind a huge desk. With his slick, brown hair combed straight back and heavy jowls, he looked like the kind of man who might be a bartender at a beer hall. But his eyes held a serious, almost devious, look. Just behind him, on either side, were a bright red Nazi flag and a smaller red-, blue-, and white-striped French flag. He barely glanced up at us from some papers. He inquired tersely about who we were and where we were from. When we indicated we didn't understand German, he repeated himself in broken French. I did most of the talking and stuck to our original story. He sent us out without comment and, after a few minutes, each of us was called in separately.

In all the jumbled thoughts and feelings of the moment, I tried hard to remain completely focused on what was going on around me, particularly what was being said. I had to make sure I had my story straight. The commanding officer would try to trick us, intimidate us, or set us up against each other. This time, I was going to trust my instincts.

But what about the others? I knew I couldn't depend on them. But I could do nothing to control them, either. And all the while, the question kept swirling about, and swirls about even now: What was I doing there?

After about a fifteen-minute interlude, we were interrogated again, this time individually. I pretended not to understand German. I answered only questions spoken in French. I kept my answers simple, so I could remember them. But the going was getting tougher. As he interviewed me the second time, the commander paid less attention to his papers and more to me. Both his tone and his words were thickly arrogant.

"You know, you aren't a very pretty girl. That large nose of yours makes you look like a Jew. Now tell me the truth. Who are you and where were you going tonight?"

I stuck with my story. I was Isabel Genelle, and I lived between Geneva and Lausanne. My father, Jean, was a woodsman, and my mother, Claire, took care of my siblings and me.

His fat face turned an angry red as I completed my story for the third time, and his voice grew louder and louder as he tried to trap me with incriminating questions. He asked me several questions in French and, without warning, switched to German.

"How could someone who knows her way around get lost near the border? . . . What did you say your parents' names were? . . . What road leads from Geneva to Lausanne? . . ." I recognized his German dialect was from the Mannheim-Ludwigshafen region — not far from my home in Darmstadt. My cousin Gustav had lived there before he went to Belgium.

Once again I was dismissed, as if I were a pesky dog. Each of the others was called in. Divide and conquer — that was the Germans' approach. I realized now what a desperate strategy Rösli's idea of posing as French Swiss teens would turn out to be. While my French was excellent and Dela's was passable, Inge H. and Manfred knew precious little. Indeed, Inge H., with her Saxonian dialect, even had trouble with certain German pronunciations. Many of the children made fun of the way she mispronounced ordinary German words.

After about an hour, the four of us were reunited. Even though we obviously couldn't converse about the situation, I sensed everyone had maintained our cover story. We sat in the lobby area waiting to be interrogated for a third time. Manfred was called again, only this time the soldiers led him to a different part of the building. What was going on? I suspected more serious intimidation was close at hand. Sure enough, a few minutes later I heard muffled screams followed by banging on walls.

I hoped against hope I wasn't hearing what I was hearing, and I didn't want to look into the eyes of Dela and Inge H. to find out whether they were hearing the same horrible sounds. Inge H. had regained her composure. She and Dela were afraid enough as it was, and I thought a wrong look from me could set off tears from one or the other.

Then Dela and Inge H. were called separately into the commander's office for about fifteen minutes each. Both exited wiping tears from their eyes and avoiding mine as the guards led them past me to another part of the building.

Sentence

B Y THE THIRD TIME he cross-examined me, the commander was smiling smugly.

"So, you are Inge Joseph from Darmstadt," he said in German. "Not far from my home."

I could feel my heart pounding heavily once again.

He said nothing, waiting for my reaction.

I said nothing.

He picked up a piece of paper. "And your friends are Adele Hochberger from Berlin, Inge Helft from Murzen, and Manfred Vos from Cologne. You are Jews, and you were trying to escape to Switzerland. You have come from Château la Hille near the Pyrenees. You have been helped by the Swiss Red Cross, a Miss Rösli Näf? This is a very serious matter, I'm sure you realize."

Obviously, Manfred had broken down, and Dela and Inge H. had followed suit.

I responded in French that I didn't know what he was saying. He repeated the information in French. I told him it was false. I was Isabel Genelle from Switzerland. He became furious and began shouting. "Why do you continue to lie? I know why. You lie because you are a Jew! That's what Jews do. They lie!"

I was astonished — not so much by the insults and invective, but by his persistence. If he knew the truth, why did he have to get me to admit it? Here he was a grown man, a commanding officer, and I was this poor, miserable teenager, a caged animal. The whole matter seemed to have come down to a personal struggle between the two of us. He was determined to intimidate me into confirming his statements. But for reasons I still can't quite fathom — something instinctive, once again, I suspect — I wasn't going to give him that pleasure. A strange stubbornness had enveloped me, as if the tiniest chance I had at survival depended on maintaining the fiction of being Isabel Genelle.

Almost as quickly as he had flown into a rage, he appeared to calm himself and said quietly, in German, "This is your last chance. You can co-operate and go back with your friends. If not. . . ."

I hesitated. He was offering me nothing — maybe a few more days or weeks to live — but it seemed so tempting. I could be done with the terrible pressure, the abuse that probably wasn't even yet near its climax. I could be reunited with Dela and we could share our feelings of terror.

The silence stretched on. He continued to stare at me.

Finally, I answered in French, "I don't understand what you are saying." I waited for the dam of anger to burst.

He shouted in broken French, "In the morning at seven o'clock I have you shot if you don't answer the truth. Answer now!"

My story remained the same. I was not going to change one inch of it. For the first time since we had left the château, I was completely calm. If this was the way it was going to be — well, I was going to face it. No German was going to get the satisfaction of breaking me down. Especially not a barbarian like the one facing me. His open hatred for me was completely matched by mine for him.

Then the commander's voice quieted a bit, as if he were once again trying to calm himself, and he began speaking in French.

"One more time, tell me where you live."

"Between Geneva and Lausanne, in the country."

"Where are your papers?"

"I left them at home."

"*Warum?*"

"S'il vous plait?"

"What were you doing by the border?"

"We were out walking after celebrating the New Year with friends. It was a beautiful night with the snow, and we decided to go walking."

Now he glared at me, and again his voice rose in anger. "That is a lie! You are a group of dirty Jews from Germany, and you were trying to escape from France to Switzerland."

"That isn't true. I am Isabel Genelle, and I am from Switzerland. You must release us so we can return to our homes."

"So," he said firmly, slamming his fist on his desk, "this morning at seven, you will go before a firing squad."

I was surprised by the suddenness, and finality, of the decision, but I was still at peace. I sensed that my growing tranquility in the face of his growing anger befuddled him. He ordered a soldier to lead me away and not let me speak with my three friends. I gathered they were together again in another part of the building.

As I SAT ALONE on a hard desk chair, the very real prospect of impending death wasn't nearly as frightening as it had been when it was merely an abstraction. Now that I knew how and when my death would come, I was not at all terrified.

But I did wonder.... How would it feel when the bullets penetrated my body? Would there be a great deal of pain? How long would it take for death to come? What would happen after that? I tried to push those thoughts from my mind. I had to pay close attention to what was happening around me.

It was dark and a single candle burned on one of the tables. An old cuckoo clock in one corner ticked off the minutes. A soldier guarded each door, and I heard the even steps of others marching in front of the house.

I sat there for at least two hours, I judged by the tick-tocking of the cuckoo clock. I was worried about Château la Hille. Would the Germans now go there and arrest the other boys and girls? If so, it would be due to our terrible mistake in missing the border and approaching the wrong house. We were certainly showing poor gratitude to the Swiss Red Cross by involving its name in this mess.

If I died, at least I wouldn't have to face the consequences of my stupidity at that third fence. I wouldn't have to deal with the adults who had inadvertently let us down — Jose, Anne Marie, Rösli. But most importantly, I wouldn't know about the other children who would die because of my incompetence.

Falling

I HAD A STRONG urge to go to the bathroom. I didn't want to speak German or assume the soldier standing near me spoke French, so I just stood up. He immediately stepped forward. I told him in French what I wanted and he led me down a narrow hall to a bathroom. He handed me a candle as I entered. I did not lock the room, somehow sensing a prisoner was not entitled to that much privacy.

Immediately, I noticed a large window behind the toilet. I stepped on the seat and tried to pull it open. It was stuck. I pulled harder. With a grumble, it opened. I'm not sure how loud the noise was, but in the silence of the night and the circumstances of my situation, it seemed like a loud bang, as if it must have been too loud to go unnoticed.

First, I decided to take care of my immediate business. Then I listened at the door but heard nothing in the vicinity. So I stepped onto the toilet seat, and then the window sill, . . . and then jumped.

I seemed to be falling and falling. When I landed and fell to one side, a bed of snow cushioned my fall. How was it that I went down so far although I had jumped from the first floor? The moment I got up, I realized I had dropped down another level, to the basement steps.

I dashed up the stairs, straight across a yard, and had just crossed the road when I heard shouting and commotion. I could not run fast enough to get away. When I heard the howling of dogs, I made up my mind. Down into a ditch I went, deep into the snow, pressing myself as close to the ground as possible. I swept snow over myself and then lay face down on the ground. For the first time all night, the snow was my ally.

The soldiers and dogs trampled the road next to me. One of the dogs practically ran over my legs. Angry voices shouted and debated — "Which way did she go?" "Who let her out?" "She must be somewhere close by!"

The calm I felt earlier had evaporated, replaced by pure terror. If they caught me, they would surely beat and torture me before killing me. It seemed I lay there for an eternity. But after some minutes, the voices and howling moved away from me. They were hunting in another direction. I continued to lie still for a long time.

Even though I hadn't yet succeeded in getting away, I began to worry: Would the soldiers take out their frustration about my escape on my friends? Should I be trying to do something on their behalf? But what could I do, since I wasn't entirely out of this myself?

I had a slim chance while it was dark, but only if I could get away quickly to the Red Cross home. They needed to be warned that the Germans knew we had come from Château la Hille. Jose had to know that his escape route was under scrutiny. And there was the matter of Walter having been arrested by the French.

I started running across the fields. Dawn was breaking through, and good luck was with me for a second time this early morning, because I recognized the road we had come from only the day before on our way from the Annemasse train station to the Red Cross home. I could see the house on a hill. I believe I ran faster than I ever had before and, within minutes, I reached the home and began pounding on the door to be let in. A surprised-looking boy, maybe twelve or thirteen, answered but hesitated to admit me, making believe he didn't know whom I was asking for.

"It is very important that I speak with Anne Marie," I panted.

Anne Marie appeared, took one look at me, and pushed me ahead of her up to a library. I began to spill out my story as I walked up the stairs. By the time I sat down on a hard chair in the library, I had just about completed my account. Without hesitating, Anne Marie mapped out her priorities. She would first telegraph Rösli, using a code they had previously agreed on among themselves. She would also telephone the Swiss Red Cross office in Toulouse and tell them about Dela, Inge H., and Manfred. As far as Walter was concerned, she would inquire at the police station in Annemasse. Finally, she would warn Jose not to guide anyone along our route for a while.

As level-headed as Anne Marie was, she was also clearly disconcerted. She obviously had never envisioned such a serious outcome. As she completed her recitation of the list of steps she needed to take, she looked at me, wet and disheveled.

"You must leave here immediately. The Germans will undoubtedly come looking for you and will question us about whether we have seen you." She took me to a front window and pointed me in the same direction as the previous evening, back down the road that paralleled the Swiss border and led off into the woods toward the barbed wire. "Try again to cross, now, before it is fully light."

I knew she was trying to do her best under emergency circumstances when she directed me out of the Red Cross home. But I had a gnawing feeling in my gut, much as I had had the previous night. I felt she was rejecting me, trying to get me to disappear, or, worse yet, trying to throw me back into captivity with my friends. I might have felt better if she had directed me to the home of a friend where I might have rested a bit. As she bid me farewell yet again at the front door, I imagined questions I was sure were in her mind: "Why are you the only one of the five who left here yesterday to have escaped? . . . How could you leave your friends with the Germans? . . . Have you created a worse situation for your friends by angering the Germans by your escape?"

It was 7 A.M. on January 7, 1943, when I left Anne Marie. I walked straight ahead, down the hill, and past some woods. As I walked, I shivered with cold and fright. My clothes were completely drenched.

At the bottom of the hill, I veered off across the field and toward the woods. I was halfway across the field when I saw a man on a small road ahead. I scurried back to the woods. It had stopped snowing at last, and snow nearly to my knees covered the ground.

I continued walking through the woods and entered a clearing about twenty minutes later. Suddenly, I heard men's voices, and moments later, I saw two soldiers less than one hundred meters away. I turned back, trying to make as little noise as possible.

Clearly, there was no hope for me to cross the border this day. Too many people were searching the area. I had stopped being anxious, perhaps because I knew I was done trying to cross, or maybe because I was dead tired. All I wanted to do was sit down and rest, but I dared not, for I would probably fall asleep. So I kept on walking. But where could I go? Anxiety and emptiness overwhelmed me, but something kept pushing my legs on. I simply could not have come this far only to fail for lack of some kind of temporary shelter.

Then an idea flashed into my mind. I could hide in a French baby clinic in Annemasse for a couple of days. The director was a French Swiss woman who once spent a week at Château la Hille. This thought gave me hope.

But if the baby clinic turned out to be a dead end, what would I do? Maybe try to find shelter in a church. It was still early in the day. I couldn't imagine that many people would be praying. But I was so tired, I couldn't do much more thinking.

I picked up my pace and saw, to my relief, few people out on the streets at that early hour. Still, I was fearful because my wet, dirty appearance made me stand out. I lowered my head as I reached the main section of Annemasse. I asked an elderly woman walking toward me for directions to the clinic. She pointed me on my way, a few streets further. I explained to the teenage girl who answered the door that I must see the director because it was important. The director, a matronly-looking woman probably in her forties, arrived within a few seconds with an anxious look on her thin face.

"I am Inge Joseph. I am from Château la Hille. I met you there several months ago when you visited. I need a place to stay for a day or two before I go on my way again."

She said nothing as she scanned me up and down, but the look in her clear, blue eyes told me she understood something was terribly wrong. She took my arm and drew me into the home.

"What is wrong?" she asked after shutting the door.

She listened quietly as I once again relayed the events of the last twenty-four hours. She asked a few questions and then led me to a small bedroom. She told me to lie down and rest.

With much difficulty I peeled off my wet clothes. My wool sweater smelled awful. The skin on my arms and legs was wrinkled from the moisture. The bed was so wonderfully clean and dry! I fell into a deep sleep.

IT WAS DARK when I awoke. A red wool robe had been carefully placed over the wooden chair next to the bed. Out in the corridor, I met the director, who led me into her sitting room, a combination office and den. A second woman, Madame Barrow, was already there. It turned out she was the director of the Swiss Red Cross home where Anne Marie worked and from where we had begun our ill-fated escape attempt the previous evening.

Madame Barrow was a petite, charming woman who spoke in a high-pitched voice. She was a take-charge person. Both women had wasted little time while I was sleeping. Madame Barrow had already been to the Annemasse police station and had actually spoken to Walter. She learned he would be taken to a nearby prison the next morning and in about five days, he would appear in court. She was certain he would be set free at that time.

Because it was a weekend, she hadn't spoken to the Swiss Red Cross Toulouse office. That would happen in the morning. However, she reasoned the Toulouse office could probably not interfere on behalf of Dela, Inge H., and Manfred unless the Germans were to approach the Swiss Red Cross. She doubted that would happen.

I didn't know what to do with this stunning news — the likely survival of my Walter, the likely demise of my other three friends. They told me two German soldiers had appeared at the Swiss Red Cross home near Annemasse around midmorning and inquired whether those at the house had seen a girl bearing my description. They left when Anne Marie told them she hadn't, and nothing further had happened. Seeing the look on my face, both ladies assured me I was safe at the clinic and could stay there for the time being. They had clean, dry clothes for me. The next morning we would make another effort to get me over the border.

Early the next morning, I followed the niece of the clinic's director, a woman in her mid-twenties, during her regular morning outing with her six-month-old daughter. The plan was that when she nodded her head, I would take the road to the left, leading directly into Switzerland. If a soldier was stationed at the crossing, I was to keep following her instead.

Sure enough, a soldier was there, and I followed the niece back to the clinic. In the afternoon, Madame Barrow told me she had spoken with Toulouse and was told I should return with her to the Swiss Red Cross home outside Annemasse and then cross the border from there as soon as possible. Contrary to her original assumption, the Swiss Red Cross would question the German authorities in Annemasse about my three friends. The Red Cross would prefer, though, I not be within a few kilometers of the German headquarters when this was going on, since any evidence of further Swiss Red Cross complicity would certainly complicate matters.

So now I had new hope. It was such a slim thread, though, hoping Dela, Inge H., and Manfred might be rescued. I lolled around the baby clinic, watching expectant mothers come for examinations and depart and appreciating the warmth and dry clothing. I felt like a terrible burden on my wonderful hosts. They were putting their lives at risk for my sake, much more than I had ever done for others.

But beyond all of that, beyond uncertainty and doubt, I felt terribly frustrated. Why was it so difficult for me to extricate myself? It seemed the harder I tried and hoped and pushed, the more deeply into trouble I fell.

Lights

O N THE EVENING of January 8, at about eleven o'clock, I left the Red Cross home again, taking the same route the five of us had traveled with such high hopes three nights earlier. I left with an older man, Maurice, who would be my guide. I pleaded with him to accompany me all the way to the mystery road leading to Geneva. He assured me he would.

As I left, I thought about how much I owed to Anne Marie and Madame Barrow. As we walked, Maurice explained how we had become confused three nights earlier. Blinded by the snow, we had not crossed the field straight ahead, but had veered off course and reached the Swiss border about three hundred feet to the right of where we were supposed to cross. At that point, the border no longer ran straight but looped in and out between French and Swiss property. Thus, we had entered Switzerland by passing the barbed wire the first time, but then we had reentered France when we crossed the second fence. When we decided not to cross the third fence, we made a fateful mistake because we remained in France instead of crossing back into Switzerland. The confirmation that my instinct had been correct was of little comfort now.

As bad as conditions had been three nights earlier, they were favorable this evening. There was little snow in the woods. It was clear and not very cold. Maurice walked with me up to the first barbed wire fence and pointed to the left. There, fifty feet away, was the road leading to Geneva. How obvious it all appeared now. He began walking back toward France, waved, and motioned to me to keep going. I crossed the fence the same way I had three nights earlier, got onto the road, and began walking.

I walked and walked. It seemed I had been walking for about two hours. I did not encounter anyone. Occasionally, I saw the lights of a house. Following the road was so simple. Why, oh why, did we have to miss the way three days ago?

As I closed in on my goal, the enormity of our calamity began to sink in. Right now, all five of us should have been humming our silly little songs, hitting snow off evergreen branches, sliding on the ice patches. Instead, three would most likely be walking only to their deaths.

Although I was alone, I was not much afraid. I had only the uneasy feeling one experiences when walking in any dark, unknown place. Before long, I was on the outskirts of Geneva. The street lights shone brightly — something I hadn't seen in years because of the enforced blackouts in France. Then I glimpsed the expansive waterfront of Lake Geneva and the reflections of the lights dancing on the black water.

EVERYTHING OCCURRED so quickly. A shadowy figure ahead of me was yelling something. I didn't understand his words. I assumed, or rather hoped, he was speaking to someone else. I continued to walk. The voice became louder and harsher. It was meant for me.

As the figure came closer, I saw it was a Swiss soldier. He looked me over and said, reproachfully, "I was about to shoot because you kept on advancing." He questioned me about who I was and where I came from. I was relieved to be able to tell the truth.

I had to accompany him to a police station, where several officers asked me a lot of questions about where I came from, my family situation, when I was born, and the like. They filled in forms as I answered. They told me I would have to wait until they telephoned the central station. I sat alone on a wooden bench and wondered where in Switzerland I would be sent — to a jail, a detention camp of some sort, or to my contacts from the Swiss Red Cross? Any of those options would have been fine with me. After a while a policeman returned and explained a horrible fourth option I had never considered — being returned to France. A new law, effective since January 1, mandated that no person sixteen or older who entered Switzerland illegally was permitted to stay in the country if found within a certain radius.

I pleaded with them. I told them I had friends in Switzerland who would take care of me. It was no use. This was the law, and as long as a report has been made, they could not make an exception. A soldier drove me, sobbing, in a Jeep back toward the border.

Why didn't I know the full provisions of that new Swiss law? I understood that I needed to be sixteen or younger to enter, so when the border police asked my date of birth, I said September 19, 1926, instead of 1925, to make my age appear to be sixteen instead of seventeen. I could just as easily have said "1927." Did Rösli not know about the law's provisions? Did she warn us about it? Did I somehow get confused during the terrible ordeal of the previous three days? I never raised the question with anyone afterward, and no one from the Swiss Red Cross ever said anything to me about what I should, or should not, have known. Perhaps they were being considerate of my feelings.

The soldier who was driving me back to the border felt sorry for me. He stopped the Jeep in front of a small farmhouse and told me he would ask his wife to fix me something to eat. I definitely didn't want to accept food from him to salve his guilt. I told him I wasn't hungry, but he insisted and woke up his wife.

We sat at a round, wooden table in their small farm kitchen as he told her my story and how I was to be returned to France. She asked him to let me remain with them to help with the house and children. He hesitated. Clearly, he was considering giving in to his wife's suggestion. "Please," she said.

I sat there silently, hoping against hope. The silence hung there as hours seemed to pass.

"No," he sighed finally. "Too many forms have been filled out. We will be discovered. I must carry out my orders."

Much as I would have liked to have eaten the soup his wife had heated, I tersely refused.

I was going around in circles, always landing back in France. Why did I bother to escape the Nazi border guards? Why did I desert my friends? Maybe that was the message. . . . I should have stayed with them, and now I was being punished. God wasn't going to give me freedom if they didn't get freedom. I didn't feel this way so strongly then, but I most certainly feel it now.

The obedient soldier drove me back to the border, lifted up the barbed wire, and I climbed through. I did not notice the French soldier behind me until I was about five steps back into France. He arrested me for illegally passing the frontier and not carrying identification papers or a permit to travel. As if any Jew would willingly try to sneak across from Switzerland to France! At least he was pleasant about it.

He drove me to a small police station, gave me a cup of coffee, and told me not to worry — I would be free within a few days because I was under eighteen years of age. In Switzerland, my age doomed me, but here in France it helped. My only problem: free to do what?

I spent the rest of the night cramped on a small, wooden bench, dozing. At 8 A.M. I was taken to the police station in Annemasse and, after a few more hours of sitting, I was ordered to join a group of about twenty people assembled in front of the station who were to be taken by bus to the nearby prison in Annecy. We were all handcuffed to one another in a human chain before being loaded onto the van. If only Mutti and Papa could see their little daughter now — stepping onto a prison van in handcuffs. This confining situation produced the inevitable result among our group — slow-footed shuffling, averted eyes, gallows humor. "Perhaps this is how they escort foreign guests to a French banquet," joked a middle-aged Austrian man in a tattered overcoat.

From the conversation in the van, I learned that these people, like me, were all non-French — of German, Austrian, Belgian, or Dutch origin — who had attempted to cross the border into Switzerland. None of us were criminals. But as we sat in the van, handcuffed to each other, the hope of escaping a Nazi concentration camp diminished by the minute as we drew closer to the French prison.

As I sat there, one of a group of refugees, I wanted more than anything for Mutti to know I had escaped so she could face her death in peace. On this van, though, the last vestiges of hope were evaporating as the bus slowed in front of the stone-walled prison. I was one of the masses of refugees, just like Mutti.

At the prison entrance something strange happened — a guard who was checking us in singled me out from the group. Because I was under eighteen, I was destined for a different location. A policeman took me to a local station, a shuttered stucco building that, from the outside, looked much like other simple houses. Inside, however, it had six jail cells in the back. Like the officer who arrested me coming back into France, this slender dark-haired man was very kind. When he brought me into one of the cells and realized how cold it was for the second week of January, he arranged for me to sit right next to the stove in the front. Only during the night did I have to be in a cell, and even here he gave me an extra blanket to cover myself on the straw-filled mattress. Still, I was quite cold.

Each morning, a second policeman brought me coffee and rolls. For lunch, one or the other came with hot soup and sandwiches their wives had prepared for me. And the nicest touch: On the second night, the first policeman gave me a hot water bottle, courtesy of his wife.

What was all this leading up to? What did the French do with teens like me who were under eighteen? I couldn't imagine they just let us free to wander about. And they couldn't send us to Switzerland.

I was sure this path led eventually to a German concentration camp. Perhaps this particular path had a few flowers along the side, but the end result had to be the same. So I enjoyed the cheese sandwiches and vegetable soup the policemen's wives sent along.

Reunion

A T 9 A.M. on the third day, one of the policemen took me to a courthouse, a small but distinguished building with two decorative columns in front in another small town near Annemasse. About a hundred people crowded inside the overheated courtroom.

This was a huge crowd of defendants for such a small town. But these weren't ordinary criminals — rather the spillover from a war. The charges against the defendants fell into two categories: illegally passing the French frontier and trading in the black market. The sentences meted out for both types of offense were insignificant — a small fine or a brief prison term of a few days or weeks.

After about an hour, as the crowd began to thin out, I spotted Walter, six rows in front of me, with a policeman at his side. He did not see me and, as might be expected, was not looking around in anticipation of meeting someone he knew. I immediately decided to stare so hard at Walter that he would feel my look and turn around. But my efforts were interrupted when I caught sight of Madame Barrow of the Swiss Red Cross home near Annemasse, from where we had begun our journey. She seemed as upbeat as ever and smiled encouragingly as I caught her eye. She sat within a few feet of Walter but didn't alert him to my presence, so I dropped my plan to stare Walter into noticing me; possibly she feared it would inadvertently disrupt the court proceedings when Walter noticed me.

I wondered who else I knew might stumble in on this improbable scene in the rural French courtroom. Seeing Walter was a wonderful, chance occurrence, but it was truly noteworthy that Madame Barrow was obviously following our travails and still trying to help. Perhaps my encounter with Walter was not entirely serendipitous.

Why would she still care about what happened to us, after all the trouble we had caused? Surely she must have had more important things to tend to with the flood of refugees taxing Swiss Red Cross resources.

I focused on the main event — the ongoing court proceedings. My primary concern was to be sure I heard our names as the cases were called. I worried because Walter and I both had very un-French names, and the French pronunciation might make them unrecognizable. At noon, a court assistant announced a two-hour recess, but surprisingly, he concluded by calling out Walter's and my names, very recognizably. We were told to present ourselves immediately in the judge's chamber.

The moment Walter realized I was also in the courtroom, his face broke into a broad grin and tears filled his eyes. He brushed hair away from his forehead — he badly needed a haircut. Madame ambled over to Walter and began discussing matters with him while the policeman who had brought me to the courthouse and had remained with me escorted me outside the courtroom to wait for them. We then walked up the narrow village street a short way — Madame, Walter, me, and our two police escorts. Walter quickly whispered, "Just agree with everything that is going to be said, regardless of whether or not you understand it."

The judge was a small, wiry old man, probably sixty-five or so, with a strong voice that resonated in his tiny, personal office. He looked very serious in his black robe and spoke to us sternly for five minutes about how important it was for foreigners to obey all the laws of France, particularly in this dangerous climate. "We must have order," he admonished us at one point.

After his speech we were asked to swear to something very official sounding I could not understand. Then the judge turned to Madame and told her he was going to show leniency and free us — provided a member of the Swiss Red Cross personally escorted us back to Château la Hille.

Walter and I stared at each other, mouths agape. Return to Château la Hille? And someone would have to come and get us? It was far-fetched. Why would the Swiss Red Cross want us back at Château la Hille after all the danger we had created? And even if they were willing to take us back, why would they send someone on a grueling eighteen-hour, one-way trip to get us? And then take the same trip back?

But Madame was all smiles. She thanked the judge profusely, explaining how she was going to take care of us and make all the necessary arrangements. She then chatted with him about his work and his family. She inquired about the health of one of his daughters, whom Madame knew indirectly.

Once outside, Madame asked the two policemen still with us whether she could speak privately with us. She then told us that early the next morning we would be returning to the château. We would take a train to Toulouse, accompanied by Anne Marie, and she would escort us to Château la Hille.

"Do the people at Château la Hille know about this?" I asked. "Are you sure this meets with their approval?"

She laughed. "It was their idea. They offered this solution to the French court and will be pleased it has been accepted without difficulties."

Since we were discussing official matters, I seized the opportunity. "I have one more question. . . . Is there any word about our three friends who were arrested by the Germans?"

The smile faded from Madame's face, replaced by a puzzled expression. She was probably surprised I had brought up such unpleasantness. "The Toulouse office inquired, and the Germans are refusing to release them. In fact, the Germans say the three are no longer even in Annemasse."

As she bid us good-bye, she explained we would stay overnight in Annecy because it was not wise for us to be seen near the Annemasse Red Cross home.

Should I have been more insistent in my inquiry about Dela, Inge H., and Manfred? I sensed the Swiss Red Cross was already going far beyond the call of duty. But still. Maybe they could push a little bit harder, as Maurice had done for us at le Vernet.

Walter and I were taken back to the police station so familiar to me by now, and the afternoon passed quickly as we updated each other about our experiences during the past week. Walter recalled, with amazement, how considerate the French border guards who arrested him had been. When they discovered he had some money, he told them he had stolen it, so as to avoid mentioning Rösli and Château la Hille. Walter was quite clever that way.

He had a one-word reaction to my story: "Unbelievable," he remarked. "Unbelievable." He repeated it three or four times as I told my story.

What was it that astonished Walter? That I escaped? That I left Dela, Inge H., and Manfred? That they were deported by the Germans? Walter never said, and I never probed him.

I sensed he was trying to sort it out, to ask himself what he would have done under the same circumstances. Little did I know I would receive a most emphatic answer a few months later.

Being reunited with Walter made me feel better that afternoon than I had felt for the past week. I could see the strain on his face was slowly diminishing.

Toward evening, a policeman informed us he had to take us to our respective quarters for the night — Walter to a YMCA and me to a local convent. I slept in a small, simply furnished room; above all, it was warm and dry.

The next morning, we met Anne Marie at the train station. When I apologized to her for having to make this trip with us, she said that, quite the contrary, this trip was an unexpected vacation for her. After taking us to Château la Hille, she was going to spend some time with her sister, who worked at the Swiss Red Cross office.

The journey was as long and tedious as I expected. The train was so crowded with soldiers on furlough we had to stand during the first hours. Afterwards, we sat and dozed. Then, we had to wait in the Toulouse station for much of the night and catch a very early morning train that would drop us at a small town near the château.

As we started our one-and-a-half-hour walk from the station toward Château la Hille, I had mixed feelings. It was nice to be able to return to this familiar and welcoming place. But at the same time, a sense of failure weighed me down.

I dreaded facing Rösli. I had made her life so difficult. And the other children? They must hate me. I had screwed up their chances for escape. And then there was the matter of notifying the families of Dela, Inge H., and Manfred. I didn't even know these families. How would I inform them their children had been captured by the Nazis?

Rösli and the other administrators anticipated our state of mind and warmly welcomed us back to la Hille. How did they really feel? I'll never know, but I imagine Rösli was quite angry. The children who preceded us had successfully escaped to Switzerland. When Rösli entrusted the same responsibility to Walter and me, we failed in disastrous fashion. And, as I was to discover, Rösli took the heat.

Two days later, Walter and I accompanied Anne Marie back to the station; our farewell wishes couldn't fully express our gratitude to her.

Reflection

L IFE AT la Hille continued as usual in the winter of 1943. No one else had left the château since our ill-fated venture. I kept trying to find out about Dela, Inge H., and Manfred. Rösli was good about following up, pushing the Swiss Red Cross office in Toulouse to check with its French and German contacts. At one point, I learned they had been taken to Gurs, a camp in southern France. "Our people who visit Gurs will see what they can do to obtain their release," Rösli told me.

But either the Swiss Red Cross representatives couldn't find my friends or they were no longer there. A few weeks later, Rösli took me aside after I brought wood in for our stove and said, "I have done some more checking. The news about the three isn't good. They have been taken from Gurs and sent east."

No one ever heard from them again.

I FOUND MYSELF mentally playing and re-playing the events around our capture. Would everything have turned out the same had I not resisted the commander and then escaped? Might the Germans then have been more receptive to Swiss Red Cross requests for our release? The French border authorities had certainly been cooperative in their handling of Walter, and later of me.

Or suppose I had been executed as planned the morning after our capture. Might that have satisfied the commander so that he might have released Dela, Inge H., and Manfred?

And then I thought about the three of them. Dela especially. I remembered her last words to me, "You don't just abandon your closest friend." Her empty place next to mine in the onion cellar where the older children still slept was a regular reminder of her departure. I thought about little things — how she still took her small, wooden doll, Gretchen, to sleep with her. I couldn't find Gretchen and assumed Dela had taken the doll along on our attempted border crossing. At meal times, I contemplated her empty chair next to mine and remembered how she gave me her portion of the carrots she so despised.

I thought about our common attraction to Walter. And the fact that when Walter showed a preference for me, she refused to let it affect our friendship. She didn't act mature overall, and she was self-centered in many ways, especially when it came to her creature comforts. But on this central, and sensitive, issue, she was more mature than I'm sure I would have been had Walter chosen her.

I began to weep as I ran through this train of thought, waiting for sleep to overtake me. Even now, I think about Dela enduring the cold and starvation of whatever concentration camps she was sent to. I think about how life would have been had she become an adult, how we would have laughed and joked about our fun together in Brussels and at la Hille. I wonder what career she would have chosen. Whether she would have married Manfred Kamlet. If she would have had children.

As for Inge H. and Manfred Vos, I couldn't forget them even if I wanted to. Shortly after our return, Walter Kamlet, our intellectual pianist, actually sought me out — the first time that ever happened — inquiring about our misadventure. I told him the story of our capture, my escape, and how the Swiss Red Cross tried to obtain the release of Inge H. and the others. He listened, asked no questions, and offered no commentary. I was slightly relieved, since it spared me having to tell him about Inge H.'s tearfulness under pressure and her poor efforts to make believe she was a French Swiss girl after our capture. After that, he avoided me even more scrupulously than he had before.

I thought about the fun Inge H. and I had had together in Brussels. About her bed-wetting experience in Seyre. Even though we had grown apart since then, we had maintained a decent relationship and done nice things for each other. I had tried to help her with her French. She would loan me clothes from the remains of her elegant collection, and I believe it is her dress I am wearing in the photo I have of Walter and me. I thought about the terrible irony of that precious, but useless, American visa that awaited her when we returned from le Vernet. One day we might have met up in the United States and become good friends again.

The worst daily reminder of the three was Manfred Vos. He had an eight-year-old brother, Henri. Probably because they were ten years apart in age, they weren't close, and I had taken even less notice of Henri than of Manfred. But when I returned, I was struck by how much Henri looked like his older brother. It was like seeing a miniature Manfred, every single day.

Shortly after our return, I asked Rösli how much she had told Henri about his older brother. Rösli said Henri knew his brother was trying to escape and had been captured and that Rösli and others were attempting to get him released. Rösli said they had painted a hopeful picture of the possible outcome. I tried to do that as well when I approached Henri later the same day.

"I was captured with your brother," I said. "Manfred was very brave. I know the Swiss Red Cross is trying hard to get him released. Rösli thinks there is a good chance of helping him." I avoided telling him how Manfred endured a brutal beating.

"Why didn't he escape with you?" Henri asked.

"We were separated," I said. "The guards kept me apart from Manfred and the others. So I couldn't tell him I was going to try."

Henri didn't ask any more questions or comment any further.

Dela's boyfriend, Manfred Kamlet, the nice brother of Walter Kamlet, was still at la Hille. I don't remember much about his reaction to Dela's deportation, except that he was quite upset yet also seemed reasonably friendly toward me. He accepted the knowledge that a risky situation didn't quite work out.

There remained the question of how to inform the relatives of Dela, Inge H., and Manfred (in addition to his brother). I knew Dela had lost contact with her parents in Siberia. But I did have an address for her older sister in Palestine.

As for Inge H., she was an only child, and her mother was in England. When I asked Walter K. for the address, he looked it up, wrote it down, and handed it to me, entirely in silence. I couldn't find any information about Manfred's parents; they had been deported, and no one knew whether they were alive or dead.

None of it mattered, though, because in the end, I didn't contact either Dela's sister or Inge H.'s mother. I couldn't come up with something to write that made sense. To someone who hadn't been there, wouldn't it raise unanswerable questions? The Swiss Red Cross communicated the barebones facts to the families: The children were missing.

When, a few years after the war, I saw Hanni Schlimmer, my Brussels confidant, in New York City, she told me she had attempted to visit and console Inge H.'s mother in England, but the older woman wanted nothing to do with her. "Why did you and the others survive but not my Inge?" she asked Hanni. "I can't understand it."

Jewchildren

ABOUT TEN boys and girls near or past the age of eighteen remained at la Hille. Many of the others who didn't escape, like Ruth and Lixie, used the time while Walter and I were being held near Annemasse to scatter deep into the countryside and try to find shelter with farmers or nuns. We who remained were at a loss as to what to do next. The only choice seemed to be to stay where we were and wait for further developments.

I tried not to dwell on our bungled escape attempt, but its true impact became painfully evident to me one day in early February, when I was doing some filing in Rösli's office. Away in Switzerland for extended periods after we returned, she was always vague about the purpose of her trips. She usually said something about having to go to Bern "to take care of some personal things."

I didn't think much about her trips until I picked up a particular package of documents from the Swiss Red Cross. I don't know why these documents were sitting on her desk amid a pile of routine records. Given their explosive content, I'm sure she intended to keep them confidential. Or did she? The papers were an official report about our escape effort.

The papers went on and on about various officials referring things to one another, names I didn't recognize, very bureaucratic. The documents were in draft form with lines crossed out or edited. But one paragraph seared itself in my memory:

"Jewchildren from Château la Hille of the Swiss Red Cross Children's Aid were sent away by the director, Miss Näf, to illegally cross the border. . . . On the night of January 6-7 four of the children were taken into custody by the German border patrol. They notified German customs officials in Lyon. This behavior by the home's director was viewed as politically foolish and humanly inconceivable, given the wintry conditions. Unanimously agreed the Swiss Red Cross needs to totally distance itself from the director. Suspicions about whether Mr. Dubois was involved in these happenings. . . ."

When I finished reading, my legs were wobbly, my stomach queasy. The use of the term "Jewchildren": Was the report meant for German consumption? So many ordinary people had risked their lives for Walter and me, yet their superiors viewed us as troublesome Jews.

Then there was the matter of Rösli. Now I understood why she was away so much. Obviously she was in big trouble. She had been turned into a scapegoat. Her career with the Swiss Red Cross was likely over.

From the larger perspective of our situation in early 1943, the report strongly suggested the Swiss Red Cross was under the microscope and all its actions and decisions were closely monitored from headquarters in Bern. This also implied the Swiss Red Cross was probably impotent to help us any further. Once again, I had underestimated the ability of brave individuals to make a difference.

The information I gleaned confronted me with two immediate decisions. Should I let Rösli know what I had learned? But because of her natural protectiveness, she would probably minimize the whole thing, at least to me. What would be gained from going through the exercise of revealing my knowledge and having her regret that I had seen such an awful report? Nothing, I decided, so I simply filed the papers away and did not mention them.

My second decision was whether to tell Walter. Here I felt more conflicted. We followed an unwritten rule to share with each other all information relating to our situation — news about the war, about relatives, about what other children were planning, about our Swiss Red Cross supervisors. Since our return, however, our relationship had changed subtly. We were as close as, perhaps closer than, we had been before. The earlier awkwardness of our relationship had given way to a natural togetherness — an intimacy stemming not only from our shared experiences, but also from each of us expecting to be first and foremost with the other.

At the same time, I sensed a void — an unspoken bundle of feelings about some topics pushed off to the side. One was the escape attempt. Walter never brought it up; in fact, he avoided speaking about it, and I took my cue and never brought it up either.

So for several days, I instinctively hesitated to give him the news about Rösli. I know why now: I was afraid if Walter learned how much trouble our fiasco had caused, he would avoid any and all future risks associated with escape for fear of creating more problems.

TIME ACTUALLY passed quickly. The winter was unusually cold for southern France, and we kept quite busy with the usual chores of cleaning and chopping wood, divided now among only a handful of us. One milestone during this period was Walter's eighteenth birthday on February 5. I presented him with a small bar of Swiss chocolate Herr Lyrer was able to bring back for me on one of his trips. This was the only celebration we enjoyed. It was a bittersweet event we didn't want to discuss very much or publicize, since turning eighteen made Walter even more vulnerable to arrest.

I hoped the French and German authorities, once they had completed their internal investigations and communications, would forget about Walter and me. But I learned differently one day in mid-February.

Late in the afternoon, I was returning from Palmiers, a town about five or six kilometers away, with a small French boy whom I had accompanied for treatment of a badly infected eye. As I approached within about three kilometers of the château, I saw Eugene Lyrer, the Swiss instructor, standing in his overcoat, flapping his arms to keep warm in the brisk winter wind, waiting for us.

He looked directly at me. "I have bad news for you, Inge," he said.

My first thought was of Mutti, whom I had not heard from for weeks. "Is it my mother?" I asked. He shook his head. "A problem with my father?" Another shake of the head. Tears formed in Herr Lyrer's eyes.

"It is Walter. He was arrested, together with Ernste, Manfred Kamlet, Bertrand Elkan, and Henri Brunell. It happened about three hours ago. French gendarmes appeared just before all of them were to return from gathering wood. I wanted to warn them. . . ." Herr Lyrer's voice broke and he stopped to compose himself. "But they held me back, threatening to kill me."

"Where have they been taken?" I asked.

Herr Lyrer looked down at his shoes and shook his head.

Returning to the château, I understood why Herr Lyrer had met me on the road. The situation was chaotic, and he had wanted to be able to tell me the awful news privately. Many of the younger children were crying, but the worst was Frau Schlesinger. She was inconsolable. Her husband, Ernste, had been taken, which was upsetting in and of itself, but once I learned the exact circumstances of how he was taken, I understood her extreme distress.

Walter and the three other boys had been out in the woods doing their daily wood-gathering chore. But Ernste Schlesinger had been inside the château. When the gendarmes approached, someone had rung the warning bell, as planned, and he had done exactly what he should have done — hidden in the onion cellar.

As the gendarmes waited for the four boys to appear, they quizzed Frau Schlesinger about the whereabouts of her husband. She, of course, said she didn't know where he was. "We need him to examine some tobacco for us," one of the gendarmes said. "He has helped us before. We need his expert advice as to whether or not the shipment we have is diseased. It is routine. We will have him back in no time."

Unbelievably, Frau Schlesinger fell for the trick, probably because she wanted to curry favor with the local officials and forestall real trouble for her husband. So she went back into the château and signaled to Ernste to come out. When the other boys appeared and it became clear this was a straightforward arrest and likely deportation, Frau Schlesinger realized she had been duped and she fell apart.

I tried to console her, and in doing so, I temporarily reduced my own sense of panic and upset. "We all make mistakes," I told her. "Look how Walter and I made such a mess of our escape."

"But you didn't do something as utterly stupid as me," she wept. I kept my arm wrapped around her shoulder.

Where was Ilse Brunell, our spy, who was supposed to warn us of possible arrests and deportations? For some reason, she wasn't working during these particular days. Perhaps the French officials knew enough to keep such information away from her.

All that was silly speculation. If there were a way for things to go wrong, they would. All that was necessary was some association with me. My mere presence cast some spell that made plans and hopes fall apart.

I was glad of only one thing — I hadn't told Walter about the horrible Swiss report on our escape fiasco. Maybe he would find a way out of his new predicament.

Peace

S EVEN DAYS after Walter was taken, I received the following postcard from him, written in French:

Dear Inge,

I hope you received my letter from Gurs camp. In the meanwhile, many things have happened. Since this morning at seven o'clock, Ernste and I are on a train and we will probably arrive tomorrow noon at Droncey.

I am in no way fatalistic, despite the fact that before two o'clock I was still firmly committed to following your example, even though it would have been almost impossible. But I changed my mind. Some people not without importance and with more experience than me, managed to persuade me that it is better for me to follow Dela. Those who are capable of working will have their work and I am happy that I am among the first of these.

If I had written to Leo, I do not think he would have been able to help a lot, because his position today is not any more sure than that of our sisters. As for the FF, I have nothing more to ask of them. They have already done too much for me.

The girls have nothing to fear for the moment. Don't worry about me.

For a long time, I have not been as much at peace as I am at present, now that I managed to decide to stay.

Best regards to everyone. You must excuse my handwriting, for this is written in the middle of a train. The shaking of the train makes it impossible for me to write any better.

Best wishes to you and Mme. Schl.,
From Walter and Ernste

Frau Schlesinger, Rösli, and I took turns trying to make out the shaky, cramped handwriting, and we theorized Walter threw it out of the train at a station and that someone had mailed it for him. I never received the earlier letter he referred to.

In his convoluted style, no doubt deliberate to prevent the authorities from making much sense of his meaning, we agreed Walter's statement that he "was still firmly committed to following your example" was a reference to my escape from the Germans two months earlier. But beyond that, we were confused about a number of his other allusions and concluded he felt he could survive as part of some kind of work group.

I wasn't willing to drop the matter so easily. When I was alone, I spent countless hours, in the days after receiving the postcard, interpreting it and re-interpreting it. Periodically over the years, I have returned to it, nearly as often as to the photograph of Walter and me. I believe I now understand nearly everything he is saying. I was able to make sense of most of it.

As for Walter's decision not to try to escape, I imagine some of the camp veterans in his barracks or on his train convinced him that survival was possible if he was strong and willing to work hard. Walter was both. Thus his reference "that it is better for me to follow Dela. Those who are capable of working will have their work and I am happy that I am among the first of these." Possibly someone even convinced Walter that a labor role could be arranged in advance. Was this Walter's naivete, or was he just trying to reassure me?

His reference to "Leo," I concluded, was really a reference to Maurice Dubois and his success in gaining our release from le Vernet. And his reference to "our sisters" was a reference to Rösli and other Swiss Red Cross nurses. In saying that Leo's "position today is not any more sure than that of our sisters," Walter was suggesting the fallout from our escape attempt had significantly weakened their authority within the organization to the point he didn't want to even ask them to try to help.

His statement, "As for the FF, I have nothing more to ask of them. They have already done too much for me," must refer either to the Swiss Red Cross or the French Underground. This was typical Walter — fretting he had taken so much from others that it would be unseemly for him to take more. His suggestion that "the girls have nothing to fear" must have been based on some information he obtained from the arresting police or other authorities that they likely wouldn't arrest the older girls remaining at Château la Hille.

Most puzzling to me, though, was his statement, "For a long time, I have not been as much at peace as I am at present, now that I managed to decide to stay." How could his decision not to escape have left him with such a wonderful feeling?

There was no doubt in my mind he should have at least tried, for he was undoubtedly on his way to a German concentration camp. Deportation meant certain death. Attempted escape could make all the difference — and if he was caught, the only consequence would be an even earlier end to his existence.

I communicated with Walter at this point by sending him twenty-five-word messages through the International Red Cross. However, there was no way to know if he was actually receiving them.

Some time in early April, we received another surprise: Two of those arrested with Walter — Henri Brunell and Manfred Kamlet — returned from Gurs to Château la Hille. Because each of them was seventeen, the Swiss Red Cross was able to arrange their release. Henri, a small but handsome teenager (and brother of Ilse Brunell) I didn't know well because he tended to stay to himself, told a tale of near-calamity similar to what we had experienced at le Vernet. He was separated from his four la Hille comrades and was in a barracks with other prisoners. One morning the prisoners were ordered to pack their things and line up outside the barracks. Names were called and people were loaded onto boxcars, but when the dust had cleared, Henri was all alone in his barracks, in tears, wondering what special fate was in store for him. At that point, Maurice Dubois appeared to tell him everything would be all right — the Swiss Red Cross had managed to keep him off the train.

I REMEMBER LITTLE ELSE about the time following Walter's arrest, not even the emergence of spring and the wonderful fragrances of the wild flowers that grew in such abundance around the château. Because my closest friends were all gone, I spent much of my time alone. I was casual friends with a few girls at la Hille, like Edith Goldapper ("Omi") and Inge Schragenheim. I didn't feel much like talking or otherwise interacting. I oversaw the planting of a vegetable garden, but I lacked the enthusiasm Rösli used to bring to the effort. She was rarely around.

Much of the supervision responsibilities of the château had been assumed by Rösli's second-in-command, Margrit Tännler, who had arrived with little fanfare the previous September, shortly after our return from le Vernet. She was a much more modest and low-key person than Rösli and very kind. She was a small woman with a round, almost cherubic face, probably in her mid or late twenties. She had been a teacher before joining up with the Swiss Red Cross, but I sensed from her selfless demeanor that if she hadn't been teaching or supervising us, she might have been a nun.

In late May I received a second card from Walter, this one written in German:

I am glad that I can write this brief note. I am in the best of health. I hope that you all don't worry about me. Please answer if possible and write to my relatives not to worry. Greetings to Fräulein Näf and Herr Lyrer if they are not there anymore.

Yours,
Walter

Walter's return address written on the front of the card, "Lublin, Maidenka," turned out to be in Poland, close to the Russian border. While the card's content was noncommittal, almost certainly because of censorship concerns, I inferred a disturbing reference. For Walter to say he was "in the best of health" had to be a lie, an effort to reassure. My unhappy guess was that the exact opposite was true.

Judgment

I RECEIVED NO FURTHER written communication from Walter, and no one heard from Ernste or Betrand Elkan. Shortly after I received the terse postcard about Walter's health, we had a visit at Château la Hille from a Swiss Red Cross nurse who stopped by occasionally. Her name was Elzbeth Kesler, and she spent much of her time trying to help inmates in the huge Gurs camp. That particular camp was probably the largest French concentration camp, and while its living conditions may have been slightly better than le Vernet's, food there was in short supply and disease was rampant.

Elzbeth spent much of her time trying to arrange for additional food and emergency medical supplies to be brought in. I knew she had achieved some surprising successes — in particular, obtaining powdered milk for pregnant women and organizing classes for young children led by Jewish teachers in the camp. For individuals, she had been extremely helpful as well. She had helped get Walter Kamlet released in 1940 to Alex Frank. Later, she had helped ensure delivery of our food packages to Walter S.'s brother, Siegfried. All these and other heroic efforts she performed had earned her the nickname, "The Angel of Gurs."

I hadn't had much to do with Elzbeth on her previous visits to la Hille, since she usually spent most of her time with Rösli and Herr Lyrer. But on this visit, Rösli ushered me into the dining room to introduce me to her, explaining that Elzbeth had seen Walter in Gurs shortly after his arrest.

"Elzbeth wants to tell you about her time with Walter and about his heroism," Rösli said.

Coincidentally, Elzbeth was sitting in Walter's customary seat, near the dining room door. As I shook Elzbeth's hand, I was struck by both her physical beauty and spiritual presence. She was a diminutive, dark-haired woman with soft features, high cheekbones, and full lips. Most striking, though, were her sparkling, brown eyes. They gave her a unique aura, a sense of tranquility difficult to describe. Though she looked directly into my eyes, she radiated a presence that indicated her mind was fully present in a thousand other places at the same time.

"Rösli minimizes the entire episode," Elzbeth said in a full, deep-toned voice. "When I learned Walter and the others had been arrested, I visited him. I knew how special he was to so many people, and I also knew he had just turned eighteen and was beyond any legal remedies the Swiss Red Cross might propose. I had arranged what I thought was a possible way for him to escape from Gurs. I possessed an extra set of Swiss Red Cross identification documents, including the white overalls our trainees wear to identify themselves. I proposed to Walter that he take the identification, put on the overalls, and leave with me. It would be very simple and he had a good probability of success."

I was afraid to ask what happened next, but I did. "What was Walter's reaction?"

Elzbeth's eyes brightened. "He said nothing for several minutes. Then he asked me, 'What if I get caught?'

"I told him that likely wouldn't happen. But if it did, I would tell the guards he was assisting me on some special projects and would be returning after we were done. I didn't think it would be a serious matter. Walter thought some more, and then said, and I remember his exact words, 'Fräulein Kesler, I appreciate your interest in my situation and your generous offer. I would love to accept it. But I cannot. I cannot take the risk of another debacle like the one I had at the Swiss border. I don't worry about myself. I worry about the others. It would place too many children in danger. I can't have it on my conscience.' I pleaded with him to consider it further, but he told me that his mind was made up, his decision was final. He said he was fully at peace with himself."

Elzbeth continued smiling softly at me, as if also at peace. I think she expected some affirmation from me of Walter's selflessness and heroism. Yet as I stared at her sitting in Walter's place, all I wanted to do was to spit, to tell her what a stupid fool Walter was. I wanted to scream at her for even telling me this pitiful story. But of course I didn't. I didn't say or do anything.

Walter's message couldn't have been clearer if he had stood in front of me telling me himself. Walter had rendered his verdict about my behavior at the Swiss border. He had said: "Unbelievable." When a door opened slightly for me, I had jumped through, without thought for anyone else. When another door opened slightly for him, he had closed it and walked away.

THERE COMES A TIME in one's life when the imminent future seems impenetrable — impossible to conjecture. During the following days, weeks, and months, I simply existed.

How could I not be depressed? Walter had accepted his death sentence.

Despite all this, I was stubborn. I would try to fight the feelings and the situation, just as I had fought the German commander. I would make the Germans work harder to get me than Walter had made them work to get him. What other choice did I have?

Bicycling

Rösli DEPARTED Château la Hille in late May of 1943 to return to Switzerland. It was a sad farewell, as she bid me a private good-bye to avoid any formal, group leave-taking. She explained she had a new assignment. She didn't say anything about the real reason for her departure, and I didn't try to get her to confirm what I already knew.

As we stood in her small, high-ceilinged office, she said: "I know you have been through a lot, Inge. But you are very strong, and because of that, I believe you will survive. Be brave."

Most of the other children didn't know she was gone until well after she had departed. Margrit Tännler, her assistant, took over as director. She had arrived the previous September, toting a spinning wheel that she set up, and in old-world fashion, she had begun spinning yarn. She was also an expert cook and often helped Frau Schlesinger. Perhaps because she was so low-key compared to Rösli, I hadn't had much to do with her. I did observe, though, she was the most devoted church-goer of all the Swiss Red Cross representatives, dressing up each Sunday and walking several kilometers to the nearest church.

Margrit took notice of me and, for some reason, liked me quite well. She went out of her way to inquire about my well-being and the state of the garden. Perhaps Rösli had informed her of my misadventures and she pitied me.

Only a few of the seventeen-year-old girls remained, and we had assumed more responsibility for the smaller children. I continued to spend many hours in the garden, for we depended more than ever on our own vegetables. The French farmers felt the German occupation more directly than before because they were required to give up a high percentage of their produce to the German forces. It left them with little to sell. The garden also gave me some measure of solace — a place of peace in a tumultuous and threatening world.

Much as I tried to avoid thinking more about escape, the subject continued to rear its ugly head. In June, a particularly unfortunate incident took place. Five la Hille boys, who had gone off to live with area farmers in April, got together to attempt an escape over the nearby Pyrenean Mountains into Spain. The Pyrenees were, of course, much closer to us than Switzerland. And Spain appeared more welcoming of Jewish refugees than Switzerland. The previous winter, Alex and Elka Frank had made it to Spain along with three la Hille teens. But the trek through the mountains was physically grueling. It was important to have a guide to avoid getting lost in the barren mountains.

The five boys pooled their meager savings and arranged for a Spaniard to lead them through the rough terrain. The main problem with such arrangements was that you couldn't be sure the person you were dealing with was honest. If he wasn't, he might take your money and then earn additional bounty by turning you over to the Germans.

In this particular situation, one of the boys became suspicious of the guide and turned back. The other four continued on and were betrayed. They ended up in Auschwitz.

ONE MORNING early in August, Margrit took me aside in the garden and explained there was an opportunity for me to leave Château la Hille, if I chose. A French official of a small community about twenty-four kilometers away from la Hille, who was trusted by the Swiss Red Cross, had offered to provide temporary housing to one of us. I was impressed that Margrit selected me.

Even with the Nazis obviously closing in on the older children, I was undecided. When she posed the possibility, I realized I was still shaken from my own and others' experiences — and I told Margrit so. She encouraged me. "Your eighteenth birthday is next month," she said, urgency in her voice. "This effort is not without risk, but I feel it is the wise thing to do under the circumstances."

I thought about it for a few moments and concluded that Margrit was thinking more logically than I was. Much as I would have preferred to avoid escape, I knew remaining at Château la Hille as an eighteen-year-old was not the answer. And beyond that, I sensed this serious, church-going woman wouldn't commit to any such venture without feeling very confident about the people involved.

"All right," I said. "I'll do it, but with one condition. I want to go alone. No groups. I don't want responsibility for others." I was surprised at my own boldness in setting conditions and worried I had angered her.

Margrit looked at me blankly for a few moments. Then, in a soft voice, she replied. "No groups. Just you."

"When do I leave?"

"Tomorrow morning."

That night, I packed my few personal belongings into a rucksack. I assumed my departure, like those of others who had departed suddenly, was a confidential matter, and I didn't discuss it with any of the other girls. As I climbed into the onion cellar, I knew this was my last night at Château la Hille. I felt little nostalgia or sadness. I had already detached myself.

The next day was already blazing hot by early morning as I rode off on a bicycle, which was to be returned to the château at a later date. Much more than in January, I felt as if I were heading off into the great unknown. Then, I had known the schedule and itinerary. I had been brimming with confidence about our expected success. Now, everything was uncertain and meandering.

I had never heard of the town to which I was going, let alone been there, but I had no difficulty locating the right address when I arrived. The family I stayed with was quite ordinary — a squat, balding, middle-aged father, Edgar; a thin, energetic wife, Bettina; and their son and daughter, the son about ten and the daughter about seven. They immediately welcomed me as one of them. Probably because Edgar was a local official, he had access to enough food and I enjoyed the ample helpings of potatoes and vegetables. I helped in the garden and household.

Any doubts I might have had about the allegiances of my hosts were eased the day after my arrival. At about 3 P.M., three or four men of varying ages stopped in at the house to see Edgar. They gathered in the parlor, closed the windows, and tuned in to the BBC, transmitting uncensored news. This was, of course, strictly *verboten* in occupied France. I was not invited into the parlor, but the fact they let me witness their gathering told me I was fully trusted.

Even more heartwarming, I realized after a few days, was that this ritual was a daily event. After one of these broadcasts, Edgar informed me he understood Italy's Il Duce had surrendered to the Allied forces.

The local newspapers that evening said nothing about this; days later, one paper reported Italian troops had retreated.

One afternoon, after the daily radio listening group broke up, Edgar directed me to accompany one of the participants. He took me to a photography studio located over a bakery, where a photographer snapped several photos of me and congratulated me on my upcoming "graduation." I thanked him. Edgar said nothing about the event, and I decided not to inquire further.

I was quite certain I was living in a community made up primarily of members of the French underground. But after about ten days, before I could become too comfortable, Edgar informed me I was to meet that afternoon with Margrit. She was passing through the town on her way back to la Hille.

Edgar gave me detailed instructions on where and when I was to meet Margrit. He didn't say so, but I inferred from his serious demeanor this was risky business — Margrit didn't know if she was being observed, and the last thing she wanted was to be seen helping one of the la Hille children escape France.

The place we were to meet was a few kilometers away, far enough away that I needed a bicycle to reach it. As I departed, Madame handed me a box. It contained several dozen eggs to be given to Margrit for the children at the château. In the food shortage faced by la Hille, this box was the equivalent of gold. So what happened on my way out of town? I slipped in the road and only by sheer luck had the sense to lift the box of eggs before the bike hit the ground. I chuckled at my clumsiness. Margrit wanted eggs, not omelets!

I spotted Margrit at the appointed place on a lonely road, and we pushed our bikes through some bushes so we would not be seen by anyone passing by. She was obviously nervous. We exchanged no pleasantries, and in a hurried whisper she told me Edgar would be taking me to Toulouse the next morning, and from there I would be going someplace alone and under an assumed name.

"I know nothing about where you will be going, but I will find out through Edgar. In any event, do not write or otherwise try to contact me at la Hille." Then, for the first time, she smiled and took one of my hands in both of hers. "Good luck, Inge. You will be fine."

I was so choked with emotion at her genuine concern for me all I could do was nod my head.

When I returned to my temporary home, Edgar informed me we were leaving early the next morning and told me to be ready by 6:30 A.M.

Irene

OUR TRAIN to Toulouse was slow and crowded with German soldiers. It stopped at the tiniest of stations. By 9 A.M., we arrived in Toulouse, the all-too-familiar site of my longest day the previous January. Edgar got off the train with me, and as we walked with the crowd of soldiers and civilians alongside the train toward the main station, he nudged my arm and motioned toward a slender, young man wearing a black beret. Edgar bid me a hasty good-bye by shaking my hand and saying, in an even tone of voice, "Give my regards to everyone."

I followed the man with the beret, but he walked so fast I had difficulty keeping up. About five blocks from the train station, we entered an apartment building and climbed up three flights of stairs. There, the man, whose name I never learned, asked me to enter a small back room in a lengthy, run-down apartment.

He appeared to be in his late twenties, with disheveled, brown hair and a week's growth of beard. He closed the door and, in a matter-of-fact way, explained the French underground had ways to provide false papers for individuals who were in need of them. These papers consisted of a "carte d'identité" and "carte d'alimentation" — identification and food cards, both vital for life in France during the war. Knowing how desperate the food situation was in France, I sensed that having an extra food card would be incentive for someone to take me in, since I would give them access to more groceries.

The young man told me he was about to obtain both cards for me, stamped by an Alsace-Lorraine "préfecture," but that first we must agree on a name. "It is wisest to keep your same initials, I. J.," he said. He was at once distant yet intensely serious.

After a few minutes we decided to call me Irene Jerome. My date of birth would be changed to September 19, 1926, to make me seventeen rather than eighteen to possibly gain me some leniency should I be arrested.

"If questions should ever be raised about your papers, you must not under any circumstances reveal their source. Many people could be hurt. Now, I must leave. Do not answer the doorbell if it rings. And do not worry if a young woman appears in the apartment. I will be back by eleven o'clock, since your train will be leaving before noon." With that, he was out the door, leaving me to wait alone.

I sat on the edge of a worn couch and waited, not quite knowing whether this provided me with my best chance for survival or whether it spelled yet another disaster. What weighed on my mind was the young man's warning about the possibility my false papers could be questioned.

I knew that I could rely on myself in this respect. I had proven that in my encounter with the German border commander. But what if the authorities questioned my documents and discovered their source independently of me? The possibilities and variations raced through my mind. I lacked both the enthusiasm and sense of adventure I should have felt at this point. I was not exactly afraid for myself, but rather for the possibility that my actions could somehow injure others. I recalled my optimism at the time of our first attempt to enter Switzerland. Now I could only shudder and try to pull myself together as I wept a little, dabbing my face with an embroidered handkerchief Mutti had given me. How could I manage in this situation? There was so much to remember. My new name. My new address. My background, whatever it was.

And there was so much to try to forget. The town where I had spent the last ten days. The family that sheltered me. The location of this safe house. What would happen if I was captured and the Germans decided to do what they had done to Manfred, to beat the information out of me?

SHORTLY AFTER 11 A.M., the young man reappeared. He handed me both sets of identification. On the carte d'identité appeared one of the "graduation" photos taken of me in the studio the previous week.

But I was shocked to see the documents did not appear to be new. "What is wrong with these? They look as if they have been discarded. Why don't I get new documents?" I asked gruffly. I must have been very gruff, because for the first time the man appeared startled.

"You must understand these official stamps are authentic but that the people who prepare the cards try to make them look as if they had been used for years. That way they are less likely to be questioned. The preparers are experts; they have much experience."

I must have continued to look dubious because he smiled slightly, a warm look on his face.

"You need not worry. We selected you now for a reason, because we know you are up to handling difficult situations."

I wondered how much he knew.

He handed me an envelope. The envelope was very important. It was to be given to Anna, the oldest daughter of my new family and first employer.

"You will get off the train at Jarnac, a village north of Bordeaux. Anna will meet you. She is about your height, with long brown hair pulled up in a bun. She will be wearing a black skirt and white blouse with a yellow, silk scarf. From this point on, you are not to discuss anything about your previous life with anyone. If questions should come up, you can say that you had been living with friends of your family near Toulouse. Only Anna will know that you are there under a false name and papers, but the rest of the family will think that you are the family's new housekeeper. If any unforeseen trouble should arise on the train, first try to get rid of the envelope, because it contains information we cannot send by mail."

He then handed me a train ticket, and we hurried to the Toulouse station. A few minutes after I got onto the train, it pulled out. The ride was going to take about six hours. As I settled into my seat next to an elderly woman, I no longer worried. Somehow, a feeling of *que sera, sera* had come over me.

THE TRAIN ROLLED through beautiful countryside. It was harvest time and the many vineyards were dotted with workers picking grapes. Southern France offered beautiful scenes during the late summer. We passed rows and rows of olive groves interrupted by vast cornfields and patches of trees laden with chestnuts. The hours passed peacefully and I dozed a bit. There were no identity checks and few German soldiers.

Eventually, I needed to pay full attention to the train stops in order not to miss my destination. When I descended from the train, a young woman in her early twenties, dressed as expected, approached me.

"Hello, I am Anna. You must be Irene."

I was about to correct her when I caught myself and nodded.

"Welcome to Jarnac. I hope you will like it here."

It took us about fifteen minutes to walk through the town to her house, but I barely noticed the town since I was trying to concentrate on what Anna was telling me. I was to help her mother with the housework and garden. Anna herself was a social worker. She had three other sisters who were away at boarding school. A fifteen-year-old sister lived at home and was finishing her school vacation, and another twenty-one-year-old sister held a job in town and lived at home. I counted six sisters.

She explained her father was away most of the time and returned only two or three times a month over weekends, but she said nothing about what work he did. She also said nothing to acknowledge the special circumstances of my visit.

The residence was a roomy, French country-style house, very comfortably furnished, with about eight rooms. It was dinnertime and after brief introductions, we sat down to eat a very satisfying meal of an omelet and fresh green beans, tomatoes, and cucumbers. For dessert there were fresh, ripe peaches. This was obviously a special meal on my behalf.

After dinner, I approached Anna privately in the living room and handed her the envelope. She took it without a word, and I felt much relieved. Finally, I had achieved a success. Was I going to be asked to carry out other such missions? Or was I given this mission as a matter of convenience on my way to escape? There was no one to ask.

MADAME SHOWED ME where to do the dishes, and from there on I was pretty much on my own. The hardest part of my assignment, I think, was getting used to being called Irene. More often than not in those first few days, I failed to answer immediately when Madame or one of the other sisters called for Irene. Once, Madame said, "What is the matter, Irene, are you hard of hearing?"

Madame was a plump woman in her fifties who had been quite wealthy before the war. She told me on my first full day, with an air almost of apology and resignation, this residence was one of the family's summer homes; it had become the family's permanent home because living conditions at the present time were preferable in this town. She resented the old house, although it was quite roomy and luxuriously furnished with dark-wood antiques and oriental rugs. Surrounding it was a large garden where

I spent three hours a day harvesting vegetables, pulling weeds, turning the earth, and watering. The rest of the time I helped with the cleaning, washing, and cooking.

Aside from the confusion about my name, I worried during these first days about official acceptance of my identity — especially after Anna took my carte d'alimentation to the "préfecture," where it had to be registered in order for the family to obtain food rations issued to me. Fortunately, no questions were raised, and my life as Irene Jerome developed into a quiet, but also very lonesome, existence. Some evenings, the family took me along to visit friends or to shop for food in the country. During the day, Madame sent me on errands to the post office, dry goods store, and assorted other places. I was never quite at ease during these excursions and tried to speak as little as possible. The last thing I wanted was extended conversations and questions about my background.

It was difficult enough when Anna's fifteen-year-old sister, Véronique, a mischievous adolescent, tried to question me about my past. "Do you have brothers and sisters?" "How old are they?" "Where did you go to school in Toulouse?" "Is your father in the army?" I told her the truth — I had one older sister, I went to a small private school outside Toulouse, and my father was like her father, away much of the time. But each time she questioned me, I sought to quickly excuse myself to complete various household tasks.

The town of Jarnac had a few thousand people. The month of September was especially hot, and walking at mid-day or early afternoon through the sleepy streets, lined by gray and white stucco houses, I felt as if I were in an abandoned town. It was almost eerily quiet, and rarely did I see small children.

The days turned into weeks. My eighteenth birthday, on September 19, was just another day, since no one knew, and I wasn't going to bring it up and encourage questions about my family and past.

I was completely out of contact with la Hille. I did not write to Papa or Lilo in the United States because of potential problems in both sending and receiving mail. For one thing, I wouldn't be able to explain my new name to my real family, since all mail was censored. What if they didn't notice my new name in the return address, and sent a letter to Inge Joseph at my new address? And even if they did get my name right, how would I explain my American connection to my new family? It was all too complicated, so I followed my instincts.

As time went on, I wondered: Could I actually last out the war here in Jarnac? Much here appealed to me, even if I couldn't be in contact with people I knew. I was relieved not to have to deal with the social pressures of la Hille. I liked not having to worry about the police possibly surprising us with a special visit and arrests. In Jarnac I could be the ultimate loner. I could go about my business and not seriously interact with people. Here was a place where I could simply enjoy the present.

Lamb

ONE DAY in October, I received a short letter from Margrit, the first and only letter addressed to Irene Jerome. She was returning to Switzerland and would stop by to see me. Coming to see me meant many hours of detours for her. While I truly appreciated her thoughtfulness — it had been nearly two months since I had spoken with anyone from my "real" life — I knew there was more to this visit than simply a social call. She had news of some sort that would likely disrupt my quiet, comfortable life.

She arrived in the early afternoon and checked into a small hotel. We met there and took a walk to an area of fields and woods on the outskirts of town, where we could talk without fear of being overheard. She explained to me she would be there only overnight. In fact, she was returning to Switzerland for good, having left her post at Château la Hille.

Then she revealed her plan: The mother of a French girl working at a Swiss Red Cross office near Lyon lived in a house right next to the Swiss-French border. I was to travel there and use the house as a launching point to cross into Switzerland. There I would be met by the father of Anne Marie Piguet, a roving instructor at a number of Swiss Red Cross refugee homes as well as an aid in French concentration camps. Her father was a Swiss forester in the area where I was to cross the border, not far from Lausanne, in French-speaking Switzerland. He would make sure I made it far enough into Switzerland without encountering soldiers or police.

What was left unstated was this would likely be Margrit's last chance to help me. Yet as she sketched out her plan, my heart sank. Switzerland seemed unattainable. I was convinced I was destined not to make it. I didn't want to tell her this, though, so I went in another direction:

"Don't you think the Rousseau family might object to me giving such short notice?" But even as I said it, I knew too well this was not a valid argument, and Margrit said so.

"Anna was informed before you arrived you might be here only six to eight weeks. We are right on schedule."

"The other thing that concerns me is possibly creating problems for you and the Swiss Red Cross. I don't want the same thing that happened to Rösli to happen to you."

Margrit was clearly perplexed by my hesitancy. I was sounding like Walter. We walked in silence for some moments.

"If you are afraid, Inge, it is understandable. You should know, however, that you will not be the first la Hille person to take this route. Several of your friends have already taken it and no one has had any trouble. Last month, Addi Nussbaum made the same trip so he could be reunited with his sister Lotte. He made it fine, and now they are together in Switzerland."

"Yes, and that was what they told us when Walter and I and the others tried to cross in January. And even when I made it into Switzerland, the police sent me back."

I sensed Margrit was beginning to think I did not appreciate her substantial efforts. I knew I was not being rational. I was well aware that in all of Europe, Switzerland was the only country where one could safely hope to see the end of World War II, regardless of its outcome. As I walked in a small town in occupied France in 1943, that outcome did not look as hopeful as it may have from the American continent.

I also sensed I may have insulted Margrit. To her, Switzerland was not only home but a country proud of having accepted refugees for centuries.

"Let me think about it some more," I told her. But we both knew what my decision would be.

LATER THAT EVENING, I approached Anna about leaving the next day. Not surprisingly, she encouraged me to do so. She even offered to tell her mother, so all that was left for me was to pack my few belongings into my rucksack and get ready to move on once again.

It was with an odd sense of regret I left Jarnac. It had been an anxious holding pattern but a strangely satisfying one. It's not often you can escape your life so fully you actually become another person. Now, even though I was carrying my Irene Jerome *carte d'identité*, I was leaving Irene Jerome behind. When I was with Margrit, I was once again Inge Joseph.

THE NEXT MORNING, I boarded the same train as Margrit, but we sat in separate cars. In Lyon, I was to transfer to another train while Margrit continued directly toward Switzerland. While waiting for my train to leave, I wandered the streets of Lyon surrounding the railway station. That area of the city was very sinister — crowded and dilapidated, populated with many refugees and Gypsies, and probably undercover police.

A nearby bookstore beckoned. It had been so long since I had been able to browse through one, I couldn't resist. I used some of my meager housekeeper earnings to purchase a paperbound edition of an introduction to psychology. It was written in an easy-to-understand style, and the subject had begun to interest me. I considered it a safe object to bring along with me on my upcoming Swiss adventure.

My next train ride, from Lyon to St. Claude, was only about two hours but noteworthy because of an identity check. It came without warning as officers boarded the train in a small town and snaked through each car, demanding everyone produce a *carte d'identité*. My "Irene Jerome" card was to get its first real test.

A middle-aged policeman quickly scanned my card, glanced over his reading glasses at me, and then back at the photo. He hesitated a moment. It felt like forever, though it was only a few seconds. He silently handed the card back to me and moved on to the next person. I breathed a sigh of relief and leaned back in my seat.

It was evening when I arrived in St. Claude, just thirty or forty kilometers from the Swiss border, where Madeleine Cordier, a sister of the Swiss Red Cross employee in Lyon, Victoria Cordier, was meeting me at the station. She was a very cheerful individual, slender, with brown hair past her shoulders that she wore loose. We spent a pleasant evening in the small apartment she shared with her girlfriend. We made no conversation about my real purpose here, presumably because of the roommate. Madeleine had to work until noon the next day, Saturday, at her job as a cook, so I spent that morning ironing her laundry. She didn't ask me to do it, but I was anxious to stay busy.

By 1 P.M. we were ready. "I think it is time to visit my mother's house," Madeleine said in the first allusion to the business at hand. "Be sure you have your identification. The Germans are everywhere in this three-kilometer zone, trying to prevent unauthorized border crossings. Remember, we are just visiting my mother and bringing her some groceries.

"There is one other thing. Everyone who enters the zone must have a special permit. We don't want to take a chance using your identification to obtain a permit because they will check everything very closely. So you will have to avoid the roads, which are patrolled by German soldiers, and approach the house indirectly."

This entire scheme was beginning to sound ever less safe. But it was too late to turn back.

First we took a streetcar to the outskirts of St. Claude. Then we embarked on a four-hour walk through the forest. Madeleine carried a rucksack with groceries. She gave me some groceries to carry in my rucksack as well.

Walking through the forest, we chatted and pointed at trees and birds, and the few people we encountered probably took us for excursionists. Madeleine was very proud of a certain type of pine she pointed out. It grew only in a certain type of soil and was rarely found. I had difficulty concentrating on anything she was saying. This forest was too much like the one where I had been caught last January, even though it was far away and there was no snow.

At about 5 P.M. we came to a clearing and Madeleine pointed out her mother's house to me — a fairly ordinary, two-story farm house — about a kilometer away in a field with a hill in back. Madeleine would continue along a dirt road toward it, but I was to approach via some fields during the next hour when dusk turned to darkness.

From behind the large fir tree where I was hiding, I had a good view over and down the road. If someone approached, I would have to retreat deeper into the forest.

After about twenty minutes, I saw a herd of cows guided by a boy of perhaps eleven or twelve coming toward me and heading in the direction of the house. The boy was singing. I made an instant decision to help the boy bring the cows in from the fields. Neither the boy nor the cows seemed to mind. I dropped out from this little party as we moved past the house.

I was greeted by Madeleine's mother and, as she opened the door, by a pungent sweet smell — a smell that took me back to Papa's rendering plant in Darmstadt. Madeleine's mother had killed a lamb during the afternoon — which was strictly illegal without a permit. After slaughtering the animal, she dragged it from the kitchen into the living room and covered it with an old rug. Still breathless, the petite, dark-haired woman animatedly recounted how either the sound of the animal being slaughtered, or the smell, had attracted the attention of a passing German soldier who had stopped by twice and peered through her kitchen window.

Madeleine did not want to take any chances with soldiers and directed me upstairs to the attic. She helped her mother cook the lamb and, by the time we ate, everything had been cleaned up, including the smell.

It was a bittersweet meal. The lamb was delicious and should have been a very special treat, coming as it was more than two years since my last meat-based meal during those French farm dinners after stomping grapes. But I could only pick at the food because my stomach was in shambles. Madeleine's mother was obviously disappointed in my poor appetite.

As I sat there, I had the feeling a condemned prisoner might have eating her last meal. I should have enjoyed it, but my mind was on the upcoming execution.

Leaves

AFTER DINNER, Madeleine asked me to follow her up to the cramped attic. She said little as we sat there for several hours in the dark. The activities around the house spoke louder than any words. At approximately one-hour intervals, details of soldiers passed the house. Unlike ten months earlier, near Annemasse where the border was patrolled by both French and German soldiers, the soldiers here were all German. They toured the road with three or four soldiers in one or two Jeeps. Sometimes they stopped and randomly poked around in the woods. A revolving spotlight from a nearby tower or hill illuminated the area around us in white light about every five minutes.

Madeleine pointed toward the border separating France and Switzerland, a scant two hundred meters behind her mother's house, up a steep hill. So near, yet so far.

At about 11 P.M., Madeleine took her leave of me. I was to remain in the attic and sleep on an old bed with a fluffy down comforter. I was too rattled to sleep. I kept thinking about the Jeeps and soldiers and spotlights, and I wondered whether I could go on.

As the minutes ticked by in the silence of the night, I wished more than anything I had refused Margrit's offer. I wished I had insisted on staying in Jurac and trying to last out the war as Irene Jerome, the maid.

THE NEXT DAY, Sunday, was a beautiful, clear October day. How I wished I could have immersed myself in it by walking freely in the woods, breathing in the crisp, pine-scented air. However, I was to meet the forester across the border behind the house, in Switzerland, at noon. That meant I should leave the house at 11:30 A.M., Madeleine and her mother agreed. Yes, I had an appointment in Switzerland, and I didn't want to be late.

The growing terror I was feeling must have shown on my face, for after breakfast Madeleine's mother insisted I take a drink. Homemade whiskey from her small flask would give me the little push I needed. But I didn't dare to complicate matters any more than they already were by drinking whiskey. I settled for a cup of strong coffee, which tasted suspiciously fortified!

And then it was time to part. I asked Madeleine to give me back my *carte d'identité*, which she had taken the previous day before our walk to her mother's house. She shook her head. "It will do you no good."

"Why not?" I asked. "If I am caught, at least I can pass for being a French girl who lost her way."

"If you are caught, the card will be useless since you have no permit to be here or to cross the border. It would only make things worse, because the Germans might examine it closely and realize it is a fake. Then they might try to get the information about the card out of you. No, you are best off being a poor refugee. They might just bring you back into France and let you go. Besides, someone else can use your identity card now."

The way was simple. I was to walk about seventy-five meters straight across a meadow behind the house and then up a steep hill, about one hundred meters high. Madeleine had warned me about the hill — I was to take it easy on the climb up because it was covered with fall leaves, which could make noise. On top of the hill was a road. It belonged to France. The forest on the other side of the road was Switzerland. There was no barbed wire on either side of the border. But the border road was well patrolled by the Germans. Once in the Swiss forest, I should look for a dilapidated, wooden structure, an abandoned barn, with the unlikely name, "Hotel Italy." There I was to meet the forester.

I strolled through the meadow and reached the bottom of the tree-covered hill. It was peacefully quiet — too quiet. I took a few steps up the hill and stopped, horrified. Each time I stepped, the autumn leaves crunched and rustled — in my anxious state the sound seemed as if it were being broadcast far and wide. I darted from tree to tree to stay hidden. Half way up the hill, I was relieved to find the trees and leaves gave way to rocky terrain. My relief was short-lived. Each step now sent stones rolling down the incline. I had no choice but to wait until they reached the meadow below me and the noise died down. Though it was cool, I was sweating and out of breath.

I carefully scanned above and below me to make sure I was not being observed. My heart was pounding in my throat. Never before had I been so terrified, not even after jumping out the bathroom window. What if a soldier on the road above me had heard the noise and was waiting in hiding for me to reach the top? I had no way to know what was happening on that road above — the hill was too steep for me to see anything.

I was just a few meters from the road. This was the point of no return. Either I made it this time, or I fell into the hands of the Germans and was taken away. It was as if I had spent hours on the hill. I glanced at my watch — ten minutes past noon. I was already ten minutes late for my meeting with the forester. How long would he wait?

I needed to do it and do it quickly. I was only a few steps from the top. I made up my mind. No matter what awaited me on the road, I was going to dart across it into the Swiss forest. If I ran fast enough and hid behind a tree, perhaps not even a German's gun could reach me.

Taking one deep breath, I dashed — GO! — across the two-lane paved road and about fifty feet into the adjoining Swiss forest. It was very quiet for a moment. Then I heard a deep man's voice: "Inge? Inge Joseph?"

Within a few seconds, a tall man in a green uniform approached me. "Welcome to Switzerland."

He laughed. "I watched you run up the hillside and cross the road. Never have I seen someone run so fast."

I laughed, too, for otherwise I might have cried.

I should have been ecstatic but I was numb. Besides, Walter should have been with me. We should have been celebrating together, looking forward, at long last, toward our future, toward washing machines.

Regulations

I HAD COMPLETED the most difficult part of my journey, but it wasn't over. The forester, a sturdy, well-sculpted man in his fifties, explained that while I was safer on the Swiss side of the border, I still faced possible danger. Unless I made it twenty kilometers into Switzerland, I could be arrested and returned to France.

"The roads are well-guarded by Swiss soldiers," he explained. "I know many of the men, but not all will necessarily cooperate with me. So we will walk directly through the forest, bypassing the roads. It will take about three hours. If by chance we should meet any official during our walk, I will introduce you as my niece."

At one point, we heard some men's voices coming toward us, and we silently moved off our path, deeper into the woods. It turned out to be only a group of hikers.

It was about 5 P.M. when we reached the forester's house. Waiting there with his wife was Margrit. We hugged and she was crying. I could not thank her enough.

Much as the three of them encouraged me with a wonderful meal and wine to celebrate, I had little such inclination. I was so exhausted that I was poor company. It was a relief to lie down to sleep.

The next day, I inquired about contacting Papa and Lilo. Not so fast, I was advised. I was not entirely out of danger. As they explained it, an unwritten Swiss law required six weeks of residence in Switzerland, after which one was automatically granted permission to stay. If a refugee was discovered more than twenty kilometers within Switzerland and had been in the country for less than six weeks, he or she could, theoretically, be expelled. In practice, such refugees were often allowed to remain. But I needed to continue lying low.

The next day, I was on the move again, traveling with my hosts to the village of Hohflu in the Berner Oberland. I got my first glimpse of the Switzerland of picture postcards. What a compact, picturesque country! Hohflu was a village near Interlaken in the midst of the Alps, where most of Margrit's relatives lived. Two of her older aunts owned a hotel there, which they were about to close for the season when we arrived. During my stay there, I helped with the housework and the many details of life in a well-ordered Swiss household.

My most wonderful times were up in the mountains. In the company of an aunt and uncle of Margrit, I journeyed up, by way of a small cog rail, almost daily for two weeks. There, we raked fall leaves and stored them in the cow barns for the next spring. The leaves were spread under the cows instead of straw. While we were up there, the aunt and uncle also boiled cheese in a kettle hanging over an open fire. On the day of our final visit, when winter snows became a threat, we brought the cattle down with us to spend the winter in the valley.

I spent six glorious weeks in Hohflu, after which Margrit registered me in Bern with the proper authorities. I was to apply for a job on a farm because, during the war, the only work permits Switzerland granted to refugees were for farm work and household help. My application to a farm was promptly approved. I was now "official" in Switzerland.

Thus, I departed Hohflu during the first weeks of December 1943. By that time, snow fell every day. I will never forget the fiery-red sunsets that made the white mountain tops glow.

LIFE ON THE FARM began for me in Gampelen, a village about an hour's train ride from Bern, toward France. The family I stayed with was very nice. Grandpa Kaegen, along with his son, Wilhelm, and wife, Giselle, ran the farm. They had two small children, Gerhard, five, and Susie, two. Gerhard died not long after I arrived, shortly after Christmas, of congenital heart disease. This was a terribly sad event, though not quite as sad as I might have expected, perhaps because it was long anticipated. I also sensed farmers had a keen understanding of the ebb and flow of life. Or perhaps I had just become more hardened to death in the last few years. This left the family with Susie, who was a robust, red-cheeked little girl.

Wilhelm ran the place with the help of Swiss and Italian farm hands. My duties were to look after Susie, wash, clean the house, cook, and care for the pigs, rabbits, and chickens. I loved this life on the farm. The Kaegens carted their produce, mainly vegetables, to the market at Neuchâtel twice a week. I helped prepare baskets and baskets of spinach, beans, carrots, and beets.

While doing such peaceful work, I slowly accepted the fact that I really was living in a country not at war. No more sleeping in an onion cellar. No more worries about using a forged identity card, of answering to someone else's name. No more watching out for soldiers on guard duty. Five years of flight from the Nazis had finally ended for me. It had meant separation from my family and the loss of my friends. At the age of eighteen, I was by myself in a safe country.

Yet as I marveled at my freedom, it also felt peculiar to be by myself without my family in a tiny country, surrounded by other nations fiercely at war. Especially such nations as Germany and Russia. Although Switzerland had declared neutrality, the population eagerly anticipated any Allied advances. How was this all going to end?

Geopolitics aside, I naturally expected to feel profound relief over having escaped France with my life. But weeks into my new life, I wasn't feeling anything like that.

Debt

I N EARLY 1944, Margrit approached me with an unusual request — one I
understood to mean very much to her personally. She was a deeply religious person with an unquestioning faith in God and the writings of the
Bible. She valued this fundamental component of her existence as highly
as her proud Swiss citizenship, probably more.

I was deeply indebted to Margrit. Not only had she risked her own life
to help me, but she had made it possible for me to settle into a new, peaceful country. That is why I agreed to join the Lutheran Church.

Once I made my decision, I found myself thinking much about what
religion meant in my life. I thought back to Brussels, when I lived with
cousin Gustav, and about how adamant he had been about the Jewish law
being obeyed exactly as it had been written. But as time went on, I observed that people who adhered closely to religion did not differ from
those who took a more independent stand. My conclusion: Religion did
not necessarily make people better.

During the years in France I didn't adhere to any type of religious life,
aside from the Christmas celebrations and Ruth's Friday evening services
in Seyre. I occasionally discussed the subject with Walter and Ruth, and
we all reached the same conclusion: If religion was a universal basis for
human life, it was extraordinary to see how many versions and interpreta-
tions of it had appeared over the centuries. Mainly, it seemed important
for people to have some sort of ethical code to live by.

My decision was almost casual, and maybe changing religions is a
strange "request" to make of someone in your debt. In the context of all

that had happened, though, it wasn't so unbelievable. Her request had the flavor of that first Christmas in Seyre when Maurice Dubois and others in the Swiss Red Cross communicated a missionary zeal. They had risked their lives for me. If a change in my religious affiliation was what they wanted so badly, and it wasn't difficult for me to give, then why not?

So when Margrit proposed I adopt the Protestant religion, I felt it was the decent thing for me to do. The pastor of the village of Gampelen instructed me twice a week in the teachings of the New Testament. It held little real spiritual impact for me. After about three months, I was baptized and during the Easter season of 1944 I took part in the colorful confirmation exercises. I became a member of the Swiss Lutheran Church. Whenever the question arose on application forms and questionnaires about my religion, however, I always indicated I was Jewish. Since then, my main gesture toward Margrit and my new religion has been to decorate a small Christmas tree each year. Though the tree annoys my sister Lilo no end, I haven't tried to explain it to her because I don't think she would understand. I have never taken steps toward any other kind of religious affiliation, even though I married a Jew.

And now, as I waste away, religion continues to offer nothing. No kind of logical explanation for all the terrible things I experienced. No solace. No view of the world to guide me out of the darkness which engulfs me.

I had re-established contact by mail with Papa and Lilo in the United States a few months after arriving in Switzerland. During the spring of 1944, I made the mistake of writing Papa that I was about to be baptized. Not surprisingly, he became terribly angry. He wrote back, demanding I reverse my decision and threatened to contact the head of the Swiss Lutheran Church to object. I wrote him that it was my decision and he should not get involved; he eventually backed off.

Mutti?

L IFE CONTINUED for me in Switzerland. I enjoyed working on the farm.
I liked being alone and on my own. I didn't necessarily want to spend
the rest of my life doing manual labor — I still had it in mind to be a nurse
or a psychologist.

Papa and Lilo tugged at me. I corresponded regularly with them, and
they were anxious for me to come to the United States. They even traveled
to Washington to launch the process for my American visa.

I wasn't anxious to pick up and leave Switzerland and go to the United
States. I had done enough picking up and leaving to last a lifetime. I just
wanted stability. I wanted to remain with the people who had risked their
lives for me and valued my presence.

And why should I want to be with my own family? When Papa had
come through Brussels on his way to England, I was far down on his prior-
ity list. And I stayed that way, for him and for Lilo, throughout the war.
They hadn't pulled strings to get me out of France as other children's relatives had. They didn't always answer my letters.

And then there was the awful unspoken question: What had finally
become of Mutti and Walter, as well as Dela, Inge H., and Manfred? I assumed they had died, but after the war I began hearing news about displaced persons' camps and incredible stories of relatives and friends who,
presuming each other dead, miraculously found each other. Could something like that happen to me?

IN JULY 1945, following the Armistice, I left the Kaegen family to take a new direction. I decided I wanted to be a nurse. That desire stemmed from my admiration of Rösli. More specifically, I wanted to be an obstetrical nurse, because I wanted to help start lives instead of ending them. Margrit and the Kaegen family were very supportive of my decision.

I enrolled in a nurse training program at Zollikerberg Hospital in Zurich. It was a very large hospital. My "training" consisted mostly of doing menial work like cleaning rooms, sorting laundry, and emptying bedpans. I lived in a dormitory with other young women. I liked living with other women who had the same aspirations and enjoyed being around expectant mothers and newborn babies. I received my room-and-board in exchange for work.

I was settling into my new life when I received a huge surprise. The International Red Cross in Geneva alerted me that my maternal grandmother, Oma Josephine, was looking for me. According to the message, she had recently arrived in Switzerland.

It was as if a ghost had suddenly appeared. I had assumed that Oma Josephine had perished, along with Mutti and my Aunt Martha and Uncle Hermann. My last memories of her were of a spry, diminutive, seventy-five-year-old who retained her positive outlook on life even as the Holocaust closed in on us in Darmstadt. If Oma had survived, was it possible that somehow, some way, Mutti had also survived? I dared not think the question, let alone ask it.

I visited Oma at an old-age home in Geneva. She was now eighty-two years old. What a reunion! Other than looking thin, and having lost much of her hearing, she was remarkably cogent. She was most curious about me — about my health and life in Switzerland. She asked me little about my life on the run and I took my cue, partly because she had lost much of her hearing and had difficulty understanding what I was saying, and partly because I didn't feel like reconstructing the story.

What I gathered from her was she was deported to Theresienstadt, the Nazi "show camp," in early 1944. The Nazis had used Theresienstadt, in Czechoslovakia, as a propaganda tool, periodically improving conditions there and allowing international observers in to suggest the Nazis really weren't mistreating the Jews.

For the most part, conditions there were nearly as deplorable as at other camps with disease and starvation. Oma Josephine recounted how her sister, Emilie, died of typhus while lying next to her.

Somehow, and she never fully explained how, Oma Josephine and about a hundred other elderly individuals survived, and at the end of the war they found themselves in a displaced persons' camp. The English or American occupation forces must have arranged for their transport to Switzerland.

I visited her several times in the month or two that followed, and on my second or third visit, I began to inquire about what happened in Darmstadt after I departed. She told me she saw my mother and Aunt Martha deported together to Piaski, not Mutti alone, as I understood, in late 1942. She said she didn't receive any communication from them; the one message I received was the only one that got through. My Uncle Hermann was deported later, in early 1944, because he was married to a non-Jewish woman. Perhaps because of her age, Oma Josephine was deported last, and that may explain why she was able to survive. She told me that from Theresienstadt she was able to correspond with my Uncle Hermann's wife in Darmstadt and from her she learned, late in 1944, that he had died in Auschwitz.

At the end of that discussion, I gathered the courage to ask Oma Josephine the question weighing on me. "Is there any chance, any possibility, Mutti might have survived? Could she be in a displaced persons' camp somewhere?"

Oma said nothing. Tears welled up in her eyes. She stared at me with a look of pain such as I'd never seen before. I never again dared to speak to her about Mutti.

Oma, an eighty-two-year-old woman, a mother, lost not only her home and material possessions, but also all three of her children. If she could have traded her life for one of her children's, she would have done it. But she didn't have the choice. It gave her much satisfaction to see I had survived, to know that the family would carry on despite the loss of one generation.

I finally dispensed with any illusions I might have held that Mutti, Walter, or any others had survived. I knew for certain how this part of my journey had ended, who had lived and who had died. But how was I to carry on?

Advancement

M Y MOST SATISFYING experience in Switzerland came from helping Oma Josephine enjoy her last years of life. Sometime in late 1945, she wrote me she was about to be sent to Italy. Switzerland wanted to be rid of her. The administrator of the old-age home where she was staying confirmed the news.

I decided to take matters into my own hands, à la Rösli. I traveled to Bern and sought appointments with the officials in charge of immigration. A low-level bureaucrat tried to derail me, telling me that Oma Josephine's imminent departure was "in line with regulations." But I had learned not to take "no" for an answer and insisted on seeing the official in charge of immigration. To my surprise, he was extremely friendly. When I told him about Oma Josephine and how she came to end up in Switzerland, he asked me some questions about her and me — about whether we had family in Switzerland, about her health, and so forth. Once he had heard the details about our family, he silently pulled out a list of names from a file of individuals destined for deportation and crossed out my grandmother's name.

As a result, she was able to spend the last ten years of her life in a beautiful old-age home in Vevey, Switzerland, on Lake Geneva. In achieving this small victory, I had acted as I wished my relatives had acted on my behalf years earlier. I had challenged the system, and with enough determination, I was victorious. No one had ever done that for me until Rösli walked into le Vernet.

ONE OF Oma Josephine's most fervent wishes, aside from wanting to remain in Switzerland, was to see me go off to the United States. "This is no life for you, alone in a strange country," she said more than once. "You should be together with your father and sister. And besides, there is much more opportunity in the U.S. for a young person like you."

I resisted her entreaties through the rest of 1945 and into 1946. But later in 1946, months after Lilo and Papa finally obtained a visa for me, I found it increasingly difficult to say no to all three of them. I asked Lilo and Papa to secure a visa for Oma Josephine, too, but it was impossible, apparently because of her age and serious hearing loss.

So in May 1946, as I was nearing completion of my first year at Zollikerberg Hospital, I departed Switzerland for the United States. Everyone I knew in Switzerland, including Oma Josephine and Margrit, encouraged me to leave, but I was sad about leaving familiar and welcoming Switzerland.

I settled initially in New York City, renting a room in an old Upper West Side apartment building, not far from Papa's small apartment. I quickly took advantage of the educational and professional opportunities possible only in the United States. At age twenty-one, I began special extension high school classes and completed the entire curriculum in one year, passing Regents exams in all subjects so I could meet the requirements to go on to college and professional training. I had some strengths in areas like foreign languages and literature, but also I had some weaknesses, not the least of which was my limited knowledge of English.

I didn't care for New York. Aside from being crowded and dirty, the city held too many reminders of my days on the run. Seeing Papa once again, alone and destitute, as he had been in Brussels eight years before, only reinforced Mutti's absence. He was working at a menial clerical job one of his relatives had helped him obtain. And he was living with a woman about his age whom he wasn't inclined to marry.

And then there was Gustav Wurzweiler, who, as I had expected, was living in a fancy building on the East Side. I saw him and Loulou only once, at a dinner at their apartment with Papa and some other relatives. They didn't want to know about my experiences following their departure from Brussels, and I didn't have the energy, or inclination, to challenge them about their wartime behavior.

On occasion, one or another of the la Hille children would pass through New York and contact me. Once I was visited by Frieda Steinberg, my friend from Brussels and la Hille.

"You're lucky," she told me as she described how nearly all our friends had lost their entire families. "At least one of your parents survived."

"I'm not so lucky," I replied.

One other piece of news emerged from one of these visits, although I don't remember who told me: Werner Epstein, one of the boys who had been deported after a failed escape attempt to Spain, survived Auschwitz! Moreover, he had met Walter there. The story had it that he had offered Walter some extra food Werner had hoarded, and Walter refused it, encouraging Werner to give it to someone else. Werner knew for certain that Walter had perished at Auschwitz.

After obtaining my high school diploma, I moved to Chicago, where Lilo had settled. There, I completed three years of nurse's training at Michael Reese Hospital on the city's South Side, followed by two years of studies leading to a Bachelor of Science degree from the University of Illinois.

By the early 1950s, I acquired nursing positions and, eventually, the job of maternity supervisor at Chicago's Weiss Memorial Hospital on the North Side. All this was available, not because there was money at my disposal — on the contrary, I worked my way through school — but because in America, anyone who is willing to work can climb up the ladder.

Living in Chicago was much more comfortable for me than living in New York. When I arrived in late spring of 1947, there was much family joy because Lilo had given birth only five months earlier to her first child, David. I very much enjoyed babysitting him and watching him grow.

But even in Chicago, I couldn't fully escape my past. Sometime in 1953 or so, when I was working as a nurse, I received a call from, of all people, Gustav. He spoke as if we were lifelong friends and said he was calling me because I had always impressed him as extremely competent and smart. He knew I had become a nurse, and he hoped I would now be able to help him. He was seriously ill with cancer, he explained, and wanted me to come to New York to care for him. He would pay all my expenses and compensate me much more generously than any hospital.

I didn't even hesitate or inquire about the compensation details. I was too busy, I told him, which was true. But I knew in my heart there was no way I was going to care for him, for all the money in the world. He died a year later and left a huge amount of money to Yeshiva University, in New York, which established the Wurzweiler School of Social

Work, and to Bar-Ilan University in Israel, which built the Wurzweiler Central Library.

On December 1, 1959, Papa died suddenly of a heart attack. I went with Lilo to his funeral in New York, and she talked about postponing David's bar mitzvah, scheduled to take place a little over three weeks later. I argued against it. We should try to celebrate happy occasions, I argued, no matter what the timing. She went along with my reasoning.

My relationship with Lilo was better than it had been with Papa. Even with her, though, there was a heaviness, a tension, probably a result of my resentment about our wartime separation and the long silences marking that period. I told her little about my experiences. If she wasn't interested when they were happening, why would she be interested later?

My most satisfying family relationship was with David, as he grew into a teenager and a young professional. He was warm, sensitive, and very bright — in certain respects like Walter. He liked to write and sometimes flattered me by asking for my opinion on one or another of the essays he had written for school. He could be anxious, as well, and preferred confiding in me, rather than Lilo or Lutz (his father), about grades, or painful social situations, or applying to college. What drew us together, more than anything, was that he had the same disdain I did for groups and conformity. He was a loner.

Optimism

A FTER I SETTLED in Chicago, my life went very well. I was inspired by my professional success. Then came some measure of family happiness. I married Frank Bleier in the late 1950s. He was a pleasant Austrian, not nearly as arrogant as many Austrians I have known. He was like Walter in a few ways — he had a good sense of humor, with a wonderful deep laugh, and he loved sports like tennis and Ping Pong. As an engineer, he was mathematically and scientifically oriented. However, he wasn't as interesting or generous or charming or thoughtful as Walter. By then, I had forgiven Walter.

After we were married a few years, Frank and I decided we wanted to begin having children. I became pregnant and, three months later, had a miscarriage. A year later, I became pregnant again and, four months into the pregnancy, had another miscarriage. Because I worked in a place where women were giving birth every day, I tried to convince myself I could do the same. But deep inside, I sensed it wasn't going to happen. The poor diet and other deprivations of my adolescence had wrecked my insides. There was no way I could bring a child to full term.

Frank was supportive, and after the third miscarriage, he began pushing for adoption. I agreed, and in 1963 we adopted a beautiful infant girl, Julie. For a while, I liked having my own family. Occasionally, I was able to pull myself together for family gatherings and took much pleasure in buying fancy meats and salads and breads and pastries for them (more than Lilo and her family — and several other families — could possibly eat). I loved to watch them "ooh" and "aah" about the treats, as we did in France at Christmas when the Swiss Red Cross re-galed us.

As time went on, Frank began to grate on me, perhaps for who he was, and wasn't, and for who I was. He never understood why I became so moody — why I'd be lovely and engaging one moment and have temper tantrums the next moment. Nor could I understand it. When the adoption agency contacted us in the early 1970s saying another infant needing parents had just been born, I turned down the offer, even though Frank was favorably inclined. I couldn't be further burdened.

No matter what I accomplished professionally, and it was a fair amount, I felt worse and worse as the years went on. After receiving a full scholarship, I earned a master's degree in journalism from Northwestern University in the late 1960s. During the 1970s, I applied my journalistic skills to writing two textbooks on nursing that were widely adopted in nursing schools. I advanced further at Weiss Memorial Hospital and headed the obstetrical nursing area.

As my wartime experiences became more and more a part of my distant past, I lost contact with Margrit. Still, she epitomized my conviction that in a world of tyranny a sufficient number of decent people existed and cared. My only connection to la Hille over those years of the 1960s and 1970s was Alix "Lixie" Grabkowicz, one of my roommates, who had married and become Lixie Kowler. I don't know why I stayed in touch with her, since she wasn't my closest friend at la Hille. She was diligent about staying in contact with me and lived in Western Massachusetts, a couple of hours from Hilde Loeb Lieberg, my dear cousin (daughter of my Aunt Martha), who lived in Newton, outside Boston. So when I visited Hilde, I would see Lixie, and when she came to Chicago, she would look me up. When Hilde died in 1975, I stopped going to Massachusetts, but Lixie stayed in contact and stopped in during her occasional Chicago visits. We went out to local restaurants and talked about our current family lives. But I didn't confide how much my personal life was deteriorating. She was so well adjusted to living in America, raising her children, and building a guesthouse business in the Berkshires, that I felt like a failure.

Even more odd about those meetings was we didn't discuss the past. In fact, I spoke little about it with anyone. After I completed my journal in 1959, I submitted it to a few publishers. Most returned it in the self-addressed envelope I included, together with a form letter of rejection. But one editor, I don't remember who, actually wrote me a personal letter of rejection, explaining the publication of *The Diary of Anne Frank* had made my manuscript superfluous.

Frank read my manuscript and said he liked it. When the manuscript was rejected by publishers, he took those judgments at face value and said little about it. Occasionally, when Julie would ask me about whether I had boyfriends before I married Frank, I'd tell her about Walter and that he had been killed during the Holocaust. "You would have liked him," I told her.

I think the worst time for me was when Julie entered her teen years, beginning about 1978. She was so pretty, with her dark hair and eyes and bright smile, and she was popular with the boys. As she began doing the things that teenagers do, like playing rock music and going to parties, I began having dreams and flashbacks. I'd have nightmares about Mutti and Walter in concentration camps, trying to get out. I'd dream about myself at le Vernet, trying to reach them through the barbed wire.

Five years went by, bringing me to my current pathetic, drugged state. I can't tell you what happened. My body fell apart, limb by limb and organ by organ.

Skin problems like those I had at Seyre started acting up again. I had to be hospitalized for two weeks because a sore on my hip didn't heal properly and became infected. My kidneys began malfunctioning. I was having digestion problems. I began taking various pain relievers to dull the stomach pains. I was sure it all had something to do with my malnutrition during the war years. When I put on even a few pounds, I was certain I was becoming overweight, so I began taking diet pills to curb my appetite and improve my mood. And on and on it went, until I lost track of what pills I was supposed to take when. As in Seyre, when I indulged in red wine, I once again felt my connection to Papa — we were both drug addicts.

Before long, I stayed in bed entire days, sleeping on and off and moaning and crying for Mutti. In my drug-induced fog, I'd see Dela, Inge H., and Manfred.

Then I began to have blackouts in my kitchen. I was in and out of Weiss Memorial Hospital, this time as a patient. The doctors cautioned me I was taking too many different pills. I yelled at them, challenging them to cure my illnesses. I could no longer hold my job. My publisher was anxious for me to complete a third textbook about nursing, for good reason — my other texts were selling well, generating significant income. I wanted so badly to complete that book, but I kept stretching the deadlines until the publisher finally gave up.

I hate looking at that photo of Walter, Haskelevich, and me, and thinking about what might have been. I try to capture the feeling I had standing up to the German border commander. If I could simply go back to that night in January 1943 and wait for my execution. I was prepared to take my punishment then, without fear. I want to feel that way now. But I have no energy. There are no Germans to stand up to. Only myself. I am a much more troublesome enemy.

Epilogue

O N THE EVENING of June 29, 1983, Inge went to bed alone in her townhouse on Chicago's North Side. Her daughter, Julie, was staying with a friend. Her husband, Frank, was staying at a nearby apartment he maintained for his engineering consulting business. The next morning, Frank discovered Inge's body when he returned from the apartment. She had died from a drug overdose.

Afterword

THE STORY of Inge is really a story without an ending.

The last time I saw Inge was in May 1983, about a month before she died. I was living in the Boston area and was visiting Chicago on business. I stopped in at her small townhouse on Chicago's North Side and her husband, Frank, helped her down the stairs from the bedroom where she spent most of her time. He had advised me before I arrived she was weak and probably wouldn't be able to spend much time with me but definitely wanted me to stop in.

Even though he had prepared me, I was still shaken by what I saw. Inge was thin and, though only fifty-eight, almost frail. Her once-lustrous, light-brown hair was cut short and what remained hung limply, thin enough to reveal bald spots. I felt what I imagine Inge felt when she first saw her father in Brussels following his release from a German jail and expulsion from the country in 1939, nearly three years after he had been arrested — shocked by the disheveled appearance of an elder. I wanted to inquire about what had caused her deterioration but hesitated because I didn't want to upset her.

Inge was equally determined not to dwell on the negative, and though it was clearly an effort for her simply to speak, she inquired in much detail about my work and family. Only when I asked her if she was eating enough and taking care of herself did she become negative. "Nothing agrees with me. There's not much left to take care of," she said disparagingly, holding her arms up a bit. She added some comments about how the doctors continued to be of no help. Then she turned the conversation back to me, asking more about the details of my job as an editor at *The Harvard Business Review.*

As bad as Inge looked that day, and as upset as I was when I left her townhouse, it never occurred to me she was about to end her life. In retrospect, though, an accumulating number of signs showed things weren't right. I had grown up with my Aunt Inge and so, in many ways, knew her well. She had arrived in the United States a few months before I was born and enjoyed babysitting me almost as much as I loved having her as a babysitter. I clearly remember, when I was age four-and-a-half, her comforting presence when my mother went off to the hospital to give birth to my sister.

Visiting with her was always so much fun. Her dining room table was really a Ping-Pong table, and we would always play for a while before sitting down to dinner. On occasion I spent a weekend at her apartment and one time, when I was eight or nine, she and Frank took me to Chicago's huge amusement park, Riverview. (It's since been torn down.) I rode all the roller coasters and twisting rocket ships, mostly with Frank, and she would be waiting at the exit gates, laughing at my enthusiasm.

Even when she came to visit my parents' house, it was fun. She and Frank loved rich, European-style desserts, and they would bring a selection of pastries or a fancy cake from a French or Austrian bakery. The joke, when they arrived and my sister and I immediately sought out the white bakery box, was that they had really brought just "rolls." Of course, the box always contained delicious pastries. One time, though, they had the bakery fill a cake box with rolls, and Inge had a great time with my surprised disappointment, laughing as she pulled out the box with the real cake.

Beyond the fun and games, Inge was also a soul mate. During the trials and tribulations of high school, I would invariably turn to Inge for counsel. Where my mother might ratchet up my worries about a grade on an exam or whether I would get into the college of my choice, Inge would invariably offer encouragement. "You're smart. I know you'll do well," was her typical response. It was only on occasion, when my sister and I might argue about some minor possession or scheduling glitch, that Inge would offer a fleeting sense of her past: "I only wish I had such things to worry about when I was your age."

It wasn't until 1970, when I was in my mid-twenties, that I began noticing Inge's erratic behavior. I was married in December 1970 in New

York, an event I expected she would be certain to attend. When the time actually came, though, it turned out she had made arrangements to vacation in Hawaii. She was very apologetic, but I was hurt. We remained in close touch and continued to have much in common because of our careers. She had received a fellowship in the late 1960s to attend Northwestern University Medill School of Journalism and had earned a master's degree. It was a prelude to the writing component of her nursing career — she would write two widely accepted textbooks for obstetrical nursing students. I attended Columbia University Graduate School of Journalism in 1969 and became a newspaper reporter. When we spoke on the telephone or met in person, we compared notes about the trials and tribulations of meeting deadlines and dealing with editors.

My mother noticed, as time went on, Inge was becoming less reliable, more erratic in her behavior. In the late 1970s, her health deteriorated. She became ever thinner and had frequent hospitalizations, such as for a skin wound on her hip. When I saw her during visits to Chicago, she was obsessed with her health, going on about her kidney problems and the inability of the many doctors she visited to accurately diagnose the situation. She would bemoan her difficulties in trying to complete revisions of her first two books.

Yet she would also revert to the caring, sensitive aunt I grew up with. In 1977, when my wife, Jean, was expecting our first child, Inge telephoned frequently to inquire how things were going and to review with Jean her symptoms and questions. This was Inge's medical specialty, and she couldn't do enough to make Jean feel safe and secure in this unknown territory.

When Inge died in June 1983, a month after our last meeting, the living part of my relationship with her ended. But unknown to me, another kind of relationship was beginning. In a sense, I have had the good fortune of being reunited with her in the years since. Making the connection, however, came only after a long and arduous journey.

For years after Inge's death, I couldn't bear to enter her townhouse, where her daughter, Julie, continued to live. The memories of Inge were too fresh and her presence was too close. So I would usually meet Julie at a restaurant when I visited Chicago. Even so, I would break down in tears just talking about her.

Gradually, over the next ten years, I grew more at ease with Inge's departure. I still missed her, but the wound was less raw. By the early 1990s, I counted it an important accomplishment when I could meet Julie at the townhouse, have a pleasant visit, and leave, all without becoming teary.

One September evening in 1993, sitting in the same living room where I last met with Inge, Julie re-opened the wounds in quite a powerful, and positive, way when she presented me with the sixty-six-page manuscript that Inge had begun in 1959 about her wartime experiences. Julie had come across it while cleaning the basement. As I read the manuscript, I felt terrible because I knew so little about what Inge had endured. If I had known, perhaps I could have been more help to Inge during the last years of her struggle with drug abuse, physical illness, and the haunting memories of her teenage years.

But on another level, I was relieved, and even energized, to gain the opportunity to learn more about Inge. As much as we admired and loved one another, significant mystery surrounded her of which I wasn't fully conscious. Someone who has not grown up surrounded by Holocaust survivors, as I did, may find it strange that I learned so little about Inge's experience when she was alive. While today the Holocaust is openly discussed by most survivors, in my growing-up years such discussion was forbidden. Survivors didn't want to talk about it, and their children and nephews and nieces learned not to pry. I knew Inge had been in hiding in Europe during the Holocaust, but I knew none of the details.

With my new knowledge about how Inge spent the wartime years, I resolved to learn more about her experiences and fill in gaps in her manuscript about her time in Brussels and at la Hille and her relationship with Walter and other children — and most of all, about her feelings through all of it. But where to begin? I knew none of the people mentioned in her manuscript, and more than fifty years had passed since it had happened.

It turned out her husband, Frank, had one name and phone number from the past — Alix "Lixie" Grabkowicz, now Lixie Kowler, who lived in Lenox, Massachusetts, in the western part of the state, about 125 miles from my home. When I phoned her, she was about to leave with her husband, Max, on a trip to Austria. We agreed to meet at Boston's Logan Airport just before her departure. There, in a crowded airport cafeteria in October 1993, I was drawn further into the world of the Home Général Bernheim, Seyre, and Château la Hille. As Lixie described her experiences and recollections of Inge, it was as if I were being reintroduced to my aunt, meeting her as a confused and moody teenager. It was an experience I would be fortunate enough to duplicate many times, since it turned out, amazingly, that about ninety of the one hundred children at La Hille had survived and many remained in contact with one another from their adopted homes in the United States, Israel, France, Switzerland, and even Australia. Lixie was an active part of the network.

The following summer, I determined to follow Inge's path through Europe. I was also intent on making it a family affair, so I recruited my wife, Jean, our daughter, Laura, and our son, Jason. Laura was very intrigued, since she was fourteen, nearly the exact age Inge had been when she left home. Jason, seventeen, didn't want to be with his parents and was less enthusiastic, but was a good sport and came along.

Places not ordinarily of interest to tourists became terribly moving for me. One was the huge, yellow, wooden archives building in Darmstadt, where I discovered prison records of Inge's father, my grandfather, including his written request in late 1936 for sundries and the approval of everything except the razor for shaving. Another was the cavernous train station in Cologne, where Inge said her last good-bye to Mutti.

In Brussels, we searched in vain with a patient taxi driver for the Home Général Bernheim, but it had long since been replaced as part of a neighborhood rebuilding. And it was only appropriate that Jason, my son, should walk out in anger from a restaurant, much as Inge had done with Gustav Wurzweiler.

One of the Brussels highlights was a meeting with Arnold Frank, a brother of Alex Frank who, to my surprise, had hand-written recollections of the wartime years in France written by Alex's mother, Irene Frank, who had long since died. Jean and I spent hours that night feverishly photocopying dozens of those precious pages, with their descriptions of individual children, memories of the Swiss Red Cross Christmas celebrations, Elka's illnesses, how Irene acquired Walter Kamlet's piano, and the conflicts between Rösli and Alex, among much else.

From there we went to Paris, where I met Jacques Roth, the bookish teen who loved to translate literature, who had become an accomplished novelist, following on a long career in advertising. Over a beautiful lunch of French cheeses and smoked fish in his apartment, we cried as he recalled Inge's and Walter's devotion to one another.

In southern France, just southeast of Toulouse, we found the tiny village of Seyre and discovered the goat barn where the children lived for a year after escaping Brussels. It still smelled faintly of the barnyard and contained the faded wall paintings of Disney characters made by two of the children. The most moving part of our journey, though, was to visit Château la Hille which, from the outside, is as imposing and awe-inspiring as it was to the children in the early 1940s. It is owned by a French family who rents space out back for camping as well as a room in the château which once served as a classroom. During our three-day stay, we wandered the fields and hills where Inge and Walter walked and talked. From our room, we could just make out the peaks of the Pyrenees through which some of the children would attempt escape. Lying in bed at night, I was sure I heard movements from the famed "onion cellar" above us.

And then in Switzerland, Rösli Näf and Margrit Tännler, along with Anne Marie Piguet and one other former Swiss Red Cross staff member, Emi Ott, gathered in Bern to meet with me. Though they were now in their eighties and less mobile, they trekked from various parts of Switzerland to honor Inge's memory, which I represented. The restaurant where we met was noisy, and the women's memories had dimmed, but those factors didn't obscure the emotion of meeting with these true heroines, individuals who helped rescue Inge and other children. I would travel to Switzerland again the following winter to spend more time with Rösli, learning the details about her stunning decision to sit in at the le Vernet concentration camp and help get the children released. She revealed, as well, how personally crushed she had been by Switzerland's behavior following the failure of Inge's first escape attempt — to the extent she moved from Switzerland to Denmark following the war. She returned only in the early 1990s, having decided she wanted to die in the town where she was born.

Following my meeting with Rösli, I met again with Margrit, who had a special gift for me: Inge's forged "Irene Jerome" *carte d'identité,* which she had somehow obtained after the war.

The one other adult whom I met was Alex Frank, the children's supervisor in Seyre, and jointly with Rösli at la Hille. He was an ardent Socialist and had settled, after the war, in East Germany, much to the chagrin of many of the surviving children. They couldn't fathom how, after their long struggle for freedom, a member of their group would live in such a repressive society. But to Alex life was politics, and in his view, World War II was a fight against "the fascists," from which the Socialists emerged victorious. I actually met Alex three different times, always in the United States. He spent much of his last years traveling the world, visiting with la Hille survivors. He was as unsmiling and humorless in old age as he was as a young man, but always in his possession was a huge folder containing individual black-and-white head shots of each child under his care — "my children," as he referred to them, and which he welcomed the opportunity to pull out so he could identify each by name.

Both Rösli and Alex died in the late 1990s; I consider myself fortunate to have met and interviewed them.

In late 1995, I traveled to Israel, where a number of Inge's friends had settled, and was treated with openness and hospitality. I spent one night at the home of Frieda Steinberg Urman, who recalled details of Inge's state of mind in Brussels and how she told off Gustav Wurzweiler after he threw her out of his apartment. At a kibbutz on the northern border of Israel, within sight of the Golan Heights, I visited with Inge's close friend, Ruth Schütz Usrad. Still the cynical and pragmatic Zionist Inge described, Ruth recalled the taunting Inge endured and her attempted suicide at the children's home in Brussels; Ruth would eventually complete a book of her own, *Entrapped Adolescence*, published in Hebrew in Israel, which became an important resource for this book. Living at the same kibbutz was Peter Salz, one of the mathematically-oriented teens, who had one of the best collections of photos from la Hille that I have come across, and he was quite generous in allowing me to copy and use a number for this book.

In Haifa, I met with Lotte Nussbaum, the shy teenager who had challenged the first Swiss Red Cross Christmas celebration in Seyre. Like Inge, she had converted to Christianity after the war, but unlike Inge, she took her conversion so seriously that she decided to become a missionary and travel to Africa. She had never married and decided, in her later years, to settle in Israel, joining a tiny "Jews for Jesus" movement — not the most popular thing to do in Israel. She purposely lived in a poor housing development because she said she felt most comfortable around the downtrodden. She spoke in a very soft, gentle voice as she described her past. She died in 2000.

Also in Haifa, I met Ilse Brunell, who, though no longer a brunette, was as vivacious and gregarious as when she was a teen. She broke down in tears as she described her terrible assignment from Rösli to spy on the French police authorities after the le Vernet concentration camp episode and the enormous responsibility she had felt.

Ilse also had a shocking surprise awaiting me in Haifa: She had by chance, only a few months before my arrival, met Gisele Hochberger Gutman, the sister of Inge's close friend, Adele Hochberger. Dela was with Inge during the failed winter escape and was deported to Auschwitz. I was aware Dela had an older sister, but I never knew if she was alive, much less where to find her. There, in a small, run-down apartment in Haifa, I found myself on the other end of the interview process: Gisele wanted to know from me what information I had about the death of her younger sister. All she knew was that Dela had been caught at the Swiss-French border and deported to Auschwitz. I related to her the story around the third fence, and though she was quiet and wept during my tale, I sensed she was relieved to know the details of her sister's life.

The emotional experience of being myself a resource to Holocaust survivors was one I would repeat several years later, at a reunion of la Hille children in Toulouse. One of the surviving children had inadvertently stumbled on the young brother of Manfred Vos, who also was part of the group with Inge at the third fence. The brother, Henri, was living in Israel as Zvi Paz. Because Henri/Zvi was under ten during most of his time at la Hille, he remembered very little about his experiences and, like Dela's sister, knew only that his sibling had died trying to escape to Switzerland. He had come to the reunion with an entourage, including his wife, son, and infant grandson, in an effort to educate himself and them about his shrouded past. Once again, I was called on to relate key information. Zvi could only shake his head as I recounted the tale of how his older brother had been captured with Inge and the others and then beaten by the Nazis to extract information. It was as if he had somehow been made more whole by receiving the long-lost information about his brother.

Other such unexpected people appeared at random times during my research. One of the mysteries that I, and others, wondered about was what had become of Ruth Schütz's boyfriend, Werner Rindsberg. He had managed via relatives to leave France for the United States in late 1941. Ruth said she had last heard from him near the end of the war, and that he had joined the United States Army. After that he disappeared. In 1998, I received a call from another of the survivors, Hans Garfunkel, saying Werner Rindsberg had reappeared and was living in Chicago.

I immediately telephoned Werner and learned his intriguing story. He had wanted so badly to leave his past behind him that not long after he arrived in the United States, he changed his name (while keeping his initials) to the most American he could find: Walter Reed. While that wasn't so unusual among European immigrants, Werner/Walter had gone further. He had changed his entire identity. He married an American woman, Jeanne, had three sons with her, and fashioned a successful career in public relations. But while Jeanne knew about his past, to all his friends and business associates "Walter" was a native of Brooklyn who tragically lost his parents in an automobile accident.

He traveled frequently to Europe on business and on one of his trips decided to visit Château la Hille and the surrounding area. At the town hall of one of the villages near the château, he saw a name in a guest book that he recognized as that of another child from those years, and he got in touch. The word quickly spread that Werner/Walter was alive.

Not only did he renew his la Hille contacts, but Werner-Walter in a sense "came out of the closet." Now in his seventies, he disclosed his real past to friends and relatives in Chicago and became active in organizing reunions of la Hille survivors and searching out other survivors like Henri-Zvi, who had lost contact with the group.

Another of the mysteries — one I wasn't able to solve — was understanding the brilliant pianist, Walter Kamlet. He had continued as a musician after the war, and I was able to obtain his address in Bern. But alas, he never answered any of the several letters I wrote him trying to arrange meetings. On one trip to Switzerland, I actually went to his apartment, but he wasn't there, and once again, he didn't answer my note. I learned from la Hille survivors that he avoided contact with nearly all of them, with the exception of Edith Goldapper Rosenthal, the organizer of musical and theatrical performances at la Hille who would meet with him on her own trips to Switzerland. The mystery of Walter for me will have to remain just that, since he died in 2001.

In any event, Walter Reed has become a friend, as have a number of the la Hille survivors. One of the first children I met after Lixie was Edith Goldapper Rosenthal, who was often called "Omi" because of her adult ways. She wore thick glasses as a teen because her eyesight was poor, and today she is nearly blind, though she continues to remain active and enjoys classical concerts. She lives with her husband in the Tampa area of Florida, not far from my mother's home in Sarasota. Sometimes I see her on trips to visit my mother with whom she has also become friendly.

Then there was Hanni Schlimmer Schild, one of Inge's friends. During one of several visits I made to her home in Berkeley, California, she not only made another of her delicious hot lunches, but presented me with a handwritten notebook containing the words to a number of the songs the children had sung in Brussels, Seyre, and la Hille. She also put me in contact with Werner Epstein, one of the boys on an ill-fated escape attempt to

Spain. He was captured and sent to Auschwitz, and during a beautiful lunch at a Sausalito seafood restaurant overlooking San Francisco Bay, he told me his story of escaping roundups for the gas chambers by hiding in overflowing latrines. And then there was Inge Berlin, the articulate intellectual who at one time had a run-in with Walter Strauss. She didn't like to talk about those days, I think in part because she lost a brother, Egon, who was killed when he left la Hille and joined the French Underground. Yet she agreed to meet with me at her home in Rochester, New York, and dredge up those long-ago memories.

I still regularly see some of the survivors who settled in the Boston area. One is Manfred Manasse, the youngest of the la Hille children — the one who wet his bed and was cured by Jacques Roth and other older boys. Manfred, known as "Fred" to his family and friends, came to the United States near the end of the war, lived with various foster families, and eventually earned his Ph.D. in physics. He went on to teach and work with several large aerospace companies like Raytheon, helping design radar systems. He is as pugnacious and impetuous as Inge described him, always ready in his booming voice with a joke or comment, and referred to by close friends as "the Sherman Tank." But because he was so young while at la Hille, he remembers almost nothing of the experience.

And then there are Hans Garfunkel and Ilse Wulff Garfunkel, the only married couple that came out of la Hille. Ironically, they weren't very close friends while at la Hille, but when they met again after the war they discovered a chemistry that has kept them together since. Hans was the mathematician and went on to become a financial executive in New York. He is as contrarian and news-hungry now as he was at la Hille when he listened secretly to BBC broadcasts. Sometimes, when he experiences frustration getting his computer to send email or open word processing files, he calls upon me, "the expert," to make a house call. I am only too happy to have the opportunity to spend time with him, though I tease him about all the favors he will owe me as a result. Ilse, the skinny girl who became sick on the long train ride from Belgium to France and was kicked by Elka Frank, became a social worker and tended, among other people in a retirement home, to my mother-in-law after she was diagnosed with Alzheimer's Disease.

Finally, the story of my journey with Inge wouldn't be complete without describing the involvement of my mother, Lilo Joseph Gumpert. Though from Inge's viewpoint my mother disappointed Inge during her years on the run by failing to stay in regular contact, I realize now this was more the result of circumstances and events rather than any negligence on my mother's part. My mother was herself a teenager, living among various foster families and sometimes not getting enough to eat — hardly in a position to be fully absorbed in the challenges of her sister's life or a serious influence in getting Inge out of Europe. And like many in America, my mother didn't fully appreciate either the danger confronting Inge or the loneliness she was enduring.

Inge never fully shared with my mother the details of her experiences escaping the Nazis. So much of what Inge wrote in her manuscript, and what I learned in my research, were revelations to my mother. Yet despite the resentment Inge felt toward my mother and grandfather, my mother was totally committed to helping me unearth the full story of Inge's experiences. She discovered mounds of letters packed away in an attic that Inge wrote from Brussels in 1939 and 1940, providing insight into her real state of mind. She also went through letters from Mutti with her news from Darmstadt, which invariably brought tears to my mother's eyes. She translated from German to English endless letters, interviews, and remembrances, such as those from Irene Frank. She even got on the phone with me several times to help in conversations with la Hille survivors who didn't speak English.

I believe for my mother the experience represented a re-introduction to her younger sister. While she'll never get over the anguish of losing her sister at a young age, she at least understands and appreciates the source of the pain driving Inge to decide that living was too difficult; that understanding offers some comfort.

As might be expected in doing this kind of research, I encountered many kinds of "loose ends," beyond the mysteries involving the Hochberger and Vos siblings, Werner Rindsberg, and Walter Kamlet. One such loose end concerned the circumstances alluded to in the story wherein a handful of children were suddenly taken from la Hille and transported to the United States in the later summer and fall of 1941. That was a time when almost no one of any age was leaving Nazi Europe for the United States. How had that occurred, and how were the children selected? Those and other questions intrigued my daughter, Laura, enough that she decided to research the situation as her senior-year thesis at Haverford College in Philadelphia. She discovered that the American Friends Service Committee, a Quaker organization based in Philadelphia, played a key role in engineering the escape of the children with the help of American Jewish organizations and over the objections of key American bureaucrats. Why certain children were selected is still uncertain, though I suspect at least some had relatives in the United States who lobbied hard and with the right politicians and bureaucrats.

The most significant mystery remains how it was that Inge's Papa escaped from Germany and her Mutti remained trapped until she was deported and killed. The most logical explanation I have been able to piece together is that when Papa was expelled in July 1939, less than two months before the start of World War II, Mutti made a critical decision to remain behind for a few months to tie up loose ends with her own mother and her brother and sister. Once war broke out September 1, the rules for exiting changed for the worse and she was never quite able to coordinate the proper visa, exit, transport, or other arrangements because of the difficulties imposed by both the Nazis and the United States government. Still, as my mother observes, it is striking that Papa and his siblings, who had relatives in England and the United States, all managed to exit Germany, and Mutti and her siblings, who had no blood relatives in those countries, were blocked at every turn.

I have, in the end, reconciled myself to the fact there are nearly endless questions and only partial answers for a historical period that will never be fully understood. If adults can't understand, then what are children to do?

As painful as entering Inge's world turned out to be, and for all the sadness and tragedy it represented for her and many thousands of other children, it has provided a sense of closure and a reaffirmation in the strength of the human spirit under the most trying conditions. It also has given me an entire new "family" I have come to cherish.

DAVID E. GUMPERT